Anthropology Matters

ANTHROPOLOGY
MATTERS

second edition

Shirley A. Fedorak

UNIVERSITY OF TORONTO PRESS

Library and Archives Canada Cataloguing in Publication

Fedorak, Shirley
   Anthropology matters / Shirley A. Fedorak. — 2nd ed.

Includes bibliographical references and index.
ISBN 978-1-4426-0593-0

   1. Anthropology—Textbooks.   I. Title.

GN25.F43 2012   301   C2012-905875-0

We welcome comments and suggestions regarding any aspect of our publications—please feel free to contact us at news@utphighereducation.com or visit our Internet site at www.utppublishing.com.

North America
5201 Dufferin Street
North York, Ontario, Canada, M3H 5T8

2250 Military Road
Tonawanda, New York, USA, 14150

UK, Ireland, and continental Europe
NBN International
Estover Road, Plymouth, PL6 7PY, UK
ORDERS PHONE: 44 (0) 1752 202301
ORDERS FAX: 44 (0) 1752 202333
ORDERS E-MAIL:
enquiries@nbninternational.com

ORDERS PHONE: 1-800-565-9523
ORDERS FAX: 1-800-221-9985
ORDERS E-MAIL: utpbooks@utpress.utoronto.ca

The University of Toronto Press acknowledges the financial support for its publishing activities of the Government of Canada through the Canada Book Fund.

This book is printed on paper containing 100% post-consumer fibre.

Printed in Canada

To my students, who have asked these questions.

CONTENTS

THEMATIC GUIDE TO CONTENT

CULTURE CHANGE

CULTURAL IMPERIALISM

CULTURAL RELATIVISM

DIFFUSION

ENCULTURATION

ETHICS IN ANTHROPOLOGY

ETHNICITY

ETHNOCENTRISM, DISCRIMINATION, AND STRATIFICATION

ETHNOGRAPHIC FIELDWORK AND PARTICIPANT OBSERVATION

FAMILY AND KINSHIP

FEMINIST ANTHROPOLOGY AND GENDER

GLOBALIZATION

LANGUAGE AND COMMUNICATION

POPULAR CULTURE

SEXUALITY

AUTHOR PROFILE

Shirley A. Fedorak taught socio-cultural anthropology and archaeology at the University of Saskatchewan for sixteen years. In the 1990s she worked on several curriculum projects, including "People in Their World. A Study of First Nations Peoples on the Plains," sponsored by the Saskatoon Public School Board. She has also written and developed multimedia courses in anthropology and archaeology for the University of Saskatchewan Extension Division.

In addition to serving as lead author for the first, second, and third Canadian editions of William A. Haviland's *Cultural Anthropology* (2002, 2005, 2009), Shirley Fedorak has co-authored a Canadian supplement for archaeology and biological anthropology courses, *Canadian Perspectives on Archaeology and Biological Anthropology* (2002), and the first Canadian edition of William A. Haviland's *Human Evolution and Prehistory* (2005). Her most recent publications include *Windows on the World: Case Studies in Anthropology* (2006), *Anthropology Matters!* (2007), and *Pop Culture: The Culture of Everyday Life* (2009).

She taught social sciences at Cairo American College in Cairo, Egypt, and now lives in Lake Chapala, Mexico, where she continues to write.

Shirley Fedorak considers socio-cultural anthropology one of the most valuable forms of education in today's rapidly changing world: "Of all the disciplines we teach at university, socio-cultural anthropology is the one where students actually learn about what it means to be citizens of the world."

ACKNOWLEDGEMENTS

Over the years when students approached me with a concern, or searched for the answers to troubling questions, it became increasingly apparent to me that anthropology is more than an academic discipline. Therefore, I wish to extend my heartfelt thanks to my students, who have grappled with difficult questions and turned to anthropology for at least part of their answers. I also wish to thank my students at Cairo American College, who taught me a great deal about Egyptian culture, language, and people. Their refreshing perspectives on life have enriched my understanding of what it means to be a person in the twenty-first century, regardless of place of origin. I am especially grateful to Yasmin Shawky, Johnathan Shimabuku, and Sohyun Kim for their insights into what it means to be a Third Culture Kid. I would also like to thank the teachers at Cairo American College who have assisted me in various ways with the preparation of this book, with a special thank you to Beau Cain and Dr. Heba Farouk.

I am grateful to Anne Brackenbury, executive editor for University of Toronto Press, for recognizing the value of this text. Her enthusiasm and willingness to let me find the direction this book would take are appreciated, as is all the help that editorial assistant Ashley Rayner, project manager Judith Earnshaw, and copyeditor Martin Boyne have provided.

I would also like to acknowledge Dr. William A. Haviland, a man I consider my mentor even though we have never personally met. His books taught me what the world of anthropology could mean to me, my local community, and the global community.

And finally, I would like to thank my husband, Rob. Over the years he has played the roles of sounding board, editorial critic, bibliographer, librarian, subject specialist, and instructional designer during my writing projects. I wish to thank him for his encouragement and support, and for his careful scrutiny of the glossary in this edition.

TO THE INSTRUCTOR

Many instructors use anthropology courses to prepare students for their future roles in society. To that end, *Anthropology Matters* provides instructors and students with two avenues for considering anthropology's relevance: exploration of the research methods, perspectives, and application of anthropology to demonstrate how anthropologists acquire their knowledge; and analysis of contemporary and often controversial issues that influence people's lives and the way they view the world around them.

PEDAGOGICAL VALUE

Written primarily for first- or second-year university students, *Anthropology Matters* is designed to supplement introductory anthropology textbooks. *Anthropology Matters* makes anthropology more accessible to its audience by linking concepts commonly discussed in anthropology classes to contemporary issues and practices:

- participant observation and fieldwork;
- applied economic anthropology and consumer behaviour;
- applied linguistic anthropology and language revitalization;
- enculturation and global nomads;
- ethnicity and genocide;
- cultural diffusion and body image;
- cultural relativism and female circumcision;
- inequality and same-sex marriage;
- culture change and social media;
- ethnocentrism and human migration;
- cultural imperialism and international aid; and
- gender stratification and *purdah*.

Anthropology Matters addresses these timely and socially relevant topics from a global perspective to generate class discussions about the relevance of anthropology in understanding our modern world.

Anthropology Matters offers students the opportunity for cross-cultural comparative studies. For example, students will compare differing interpretations of human rights when examining the practice of *purdah* and female circumcision, or investigating the underlying reasons for ethnic and religious intolerance and the ensuing conflicts. Global variations in the ideal body image, the power of social media, the socio-economic impact of NGOs in developing countries, and the dynamics of same-sex marriage also lend themselves to a comparative approach.

Anthropology does not exist in isolation. Anthropologists rely on the knowledge and expertise of scholars from many disciplines (e.g., history, economics, sociology, linguistics, gender studies, law and politics, indigenous and international studies). This multidisciplinary perspective allows students to gain a broader understanding of the questions posed in *Anthropology Matters.* For an insider's view, each chapter offers personal narratives from people directly affected by an issue, or from anthropologists native to the group being studied. For example, Sierra Leone anthropologist Fuambai Ahmadu was circumcised as an adult; she is therefore able to offer both an anthropological and a participatory perspective. At times the insights of my students are presented in this work; they are not trained anthropologists, nor do they have much experience "out in the real world," but what they do possess is a sense of clarity not yet clouded with confusing and conflicting theory. Their candour is often refreshing and eye-opening.

Anthropology Matters complements the subjects covered in anthropology textbooks. Instructors may assign readings from *Anthropology Matters* that correspond to topics covered in class. Some of the topics, such as body image, were chosen because of their interest quotient for students. Other topics were chosen because of their current social or political significance, such as the debate concerning same-sex marriage, or the influence of social media on socio-economic and political revolutions currently taking place. Some topics, such as language revitalization, were chosen to encourage students to examine a subject seldom considered by young people.

Instructors may draw on a variety of instructional tools to expand students' comprehension. The Questions for Consideration and Classroom Activities in each chapter are designed to encourage critical thinking and group discussions, and will challenge students to apply the knowledge they have gained to compare, analyse, and interpret the material. The questions may also guide students in identifying the major themes and anthropological concepts found in each chapter. Classroom activities and online lesson plans for instructors, located at the end of the book and divided by chapter, will engage students in participatory activities relevant to the topics. Many of the chapters also include maps of the cultural groups studied. The Suggested Readings in each chapter offer students the opportunity to investigate the subject matter in greater detail and from several perspectives. Bolded terms throughout the text highlight key anthropological concepts that are then defined in the Glossary at the end of the text.

ORGANIZATION OF THE TEXT

Anthropology Matters is divided into two main sections: anthropological research and contemporary issues. Part One contains three chapters devoted to research methods, while Part Two contains nine chapters concerned with issues. A basic template is followed, including a list of key terms, an introduction, an investigation of anthropology's connection to the issue, a discussion of the issue, and a conclusion.

Part One, "How Does Anthropology Work?", investigates the relevance of anthropology as a discipline—how anthropologists acquire their understanding of human behaviour. We begin with a look at the challenges of anthropological fieldwork, followed by the anthropology of shopping. Finally, we will investigate language loss and the role of applied linguistic anthropologists in preserving endangered languages. These three chapters introduce students to the "doing" of anthropology, and in particular, applied anthropology, while also linking the world of anthropology to their everyday lives. Key concepts, such as ethnographic fieldwork, participant observation, applied anthropology, and cultural relativism are featured in this opening section of the book.

Chapter 1, "What Are the Challenges in Ethnographic Fieldwork?", explores the research methods of anthropology, including participant observation. The challenges faced by anthropologists when they are "in the field" are a major consideration. New to this edition are an expanded discussion of ethics in fieldwork and a brief look at the changing concepts of field and community. This chapter provides students with a basic understanding of anthropological research methods and their efficacy, as well as limitations associated with qualitative research.

Anthropology is the study of humankind, yet until recently anthropologists have focused on the exotic "other" and ignored their own and other industrial societies. In Chapter 2, "Of What Use Is Anthropology to the Business World? The Anthropology of Shopping," we consider the relevance of anthropology in the world of business. Our case study features "anthropology in action" as applied economic anthropologists study marketing and the sometimes humorous consumer behaviour in North American malls. The value of ethnographic research is demonstrated in an examination of how Indian grocery stores in San Francisco reconstruct Indian culture. Students will recognize the practical application of anthropology in an environment very familiar to them.

There are between 6,000 and 7,000 extant languages in the world today, many in imminent danger of extinction. Some will not be saved, but others, through the efforts of speech communities and dedicated applied linguistic anthropologists, may be revitalized or at least preserved. This is the topic of discussion in the new Chapter 3, "What

Roles Do Anthropologists and Speech Communities Play in Language Retention and Revitalization?" This chapter exposes students to the cultural meaning of language, the implications of language loss, and the ongoing efforts to preserve and revitalize endangered languages.

In Part Two, "Why Does Anthropology Matter?", socially relevant issues such as human migration, foreign aid, and social media are discussed from an anthropological perspective. This section challenges students to re-evaluate their media-shaped positions and helps reduce or eliminate ill-conceived stereotypes. Several key concepts, including cultural relativism, ethnocentrism, cultural diffusion, gender, and cultural imperialism, provide interrelated themes running through this section.

Chapter 4, "How Do Living, Studying, and Working in a Foreign Culture Affect People?", addresses the impact of living abroad for professionals (e.g., anthropologists, diplomats, and teachers) and students—often called global nomads. One consequence of families living abroad is Third Culture Kids (TCKs)—children who have lived much of their lives in foreign environments. Their lives and their outlook on life is a focus of this chapter. This discussion may prepare students to meet people who are "different" than they are—who speak a different language, or who look, believe, and behave differently.

Ethnic and religious intolerance is rampant the world over. In Chapter 5, "What Are the Underlying Reasons for Ethnic Conflict, and the Consequences of These Conflicts?", the economic, political, social, and religious reasons behind conflict are addressed through the ongoing conflict in Darfur. Ethnic conflict is not only a political issue; it creates human victims known as refugees, whose plight is examined from an anthropological perspective. This discussion reinforces the fact that cultural institutions are integrated, and that anthropologists cannot be informed about complex issues without understanding the interconnections with other systems of culture.

Chapter 6, "How Does Body Image Affect Self-Esteem, Well-Being, and Identity?", provides an opportunity to investigate the transnational flow of Western ideas—in this case, the ideal body—to the rest of the world. The discussion on eating disorders has been expanded, and new to this edition is an exploration of the concept of fatness as symbolic capital among the Tuareg of Nigeria, and body modification practices among queer and Modern Primitive subcultures. The value of cross-cultural comparisons when studying issues such as body image is reinforced in this chapter.

Chapter 7, "Is Female Circumcision a Violation of Human Rights or a Cherished Cultural Tradition?", comprises a discussion of the problems with maintaining a neutral, culturally relativistic stance while conducting research on contentious issues. The political, socio-economic, and historical factors that contribute to the persistence of female circumcision are explored. This discussion offers a forum for the voices of women who value this custom, as well as those who oppose it. With such a sensitive topic, viewing it through the lens of anthropology may assist students in developing a culturally relativistic perspective.

Chapter 8, "What Are the Socio-economic, Religious, and Political Implications of Same-sex Marriages and Changing Family Structure?", is an examination of same-sex marriage as the institution is viewed and defined cross-culturally. Three opposing schools of thought—social conservative, critical feminist/queer, and gay and lesbian assimilationalist—are featured in this chapter. This discussion may help students make some sense of the debate over same-sex marriage and provide evidence of how cultural values and practices are constantly changing.

Chapter 9, "What Is the Role of Social Media in Socio-political Revolution?", is a new chapter that addresses the power of social media in spearheading socio-economic and political protest. This topic is particularly timely given the Arab Spring in the Middle East and the Occupy Wall Street protests in North America; however, students should recognize that the use of social media continues to evolve.

The mass migration of people fleeing economic servitude, political instability, environmental degradation, or religious intolerance has increased dramatically in recent decades, causing conflict and dissension in host countries. In Chapter 10, "What Are the Socio-economic and Political Impacts of Human Migration?", human migration is situated within the context of globalization processes as we explore discrimination in France, the sex trade in Thailand, and human trafficking. This chapter offers students an opportunity to consider the inequities that immigrants face, and perhaps develop more empathy for the plight of immigrants.

Chapter 11, "What Benefits Do NGOs Provide Developing Countries, and How Can Their Presence Generate New Challenges?", provides an opportunity to critically assess the impact of NGOs, using Haiti as our case study. This chapter provides students with information on the nature of aid and the legitimacy of aid agencies outside the usual Western congratulatory tone.

Chapter 12, "Is the Practice of *Purdah* and Wearing *Hijab* Oppressive to Women or an Expression of Their Identity?", offers a cross-cultural comparison of differing, and often contradictory, perspectives on *purdah* and *hijab*. This chapter is designed to dispel some of the misconceptions that people in the West hold regarding the status of women in Muslim nations, while also addressing the volatile nature of gender stratification and oppression.

Obviously, the questions posed in *Anthropology Matters* will not be answered in any definitive way, but they are probed, analysed, and critiqued to the point where readers should possess a broader, more balanced sense of these issues. *Anthropology Matters* was written for anyone interested in the anthropological study of humankind and the issues that have meaning for people from many walks of life. This is not a theoretical discourse; rather, much like the field of anthropology itself, *Anthropology Matters* challenges readers to rise above their current level of understanding—to think outside and beyond the box.

INTRODUCTION

Key Terms: anthropology, applied anthropology, cross-cultural comparison, cultural diversity, cultural imperialism, cultural relativism, culture, ethical dilemma, ethnocentrism, ethnography, genocide, holistic approach, human rights, participant observation, rituals

---

What good is anthropology, anyway? This is a question I have been asked on several occasions—the first time when I was an undergraduate student struggling to absorb the basic concepts of anthropology. The person asking had little experience with academia or the world outside her community, and I had even less experience with answering such a complex question. Later, as an instructor, I asked my students a similar question: "Of what relevance is anthropology—to you, to your community, and to the global community?" The answer to this question is the subject of *Anthropology Matters*.

WHAT IS ANTHROPOLOGY?

Anthropology is the study of humankind. Anthropologists seek to explain human behaviour and understand the diverse ways people organize their lives. Although anthropologists have traditionally studied small-scale, non-Western cultures, today they are also interested in the lives of people in modern, industrialized societies. In support of this shift in focus, *Anthropology Matters* examines contemporary issues such as body image, same-sex marriage, human migration, and ethnic conflict.

Although anthropologists have gathered detailed information on many cultural groups, anthropology is far more than a receptacle for cultural knowledge. In the field of **applied anthropology**, the knowledge and methods of anthropologists are put to practical use to solve or alleviate societal problems that humans face. This may evoke images of anthropologists marching into a crisis situation and saving the day, yet more often it is the knowledge and insights that anthropologists possess that are of value when addressing the concerns of humankind. Anthropology is approached from an applied perspective in *Anthropology Matters*, although it is not the practice of anthropology itself, but rather the principles of anthropology and the way these principles may assist us in understanding people, that are stressed throughout the book.

THE RELEVANCE OF ANTHROPOLOGY

Anthropology, like most academic disciplines, is being challenged to justify its existence and its relevance in contemporary society. The underlying philosophies of anthropology, if applied to everyday life, can provide fascinating insights into human behaviour. If we view the world in the same way as anthropologists do, and if we deal with the issues and concerns of the world around us from an anthropological perspective, we may be surprised at the value of this discipline. Beyond the academic, theoretical, ethnographic, and even applied, anthropology speaks to the heart of humankind. Anthropologists ask questions such as "Who are we?" and "Why do we behave in the way we do?" As Philip Conrad Kottak (2000: 17) so succinctly states, anthropologists have "a lot to tell the public."

Eminent anthropologist Franz Boas encouraged his colleagues to recognize the uniqueness and validity of every cultural group. This is a laudable sentiment, one that anthropologists attempt to pass on to the general public. By increasing cultural awareness and the appreciation of **cultural diversity**, anthropology teaches us to recognize that regardless of "difference" we all share the same basic humanity. *Anthropology Matters* champions this stance, consistently promoting the value of other world views and other ways of living.

Students, the audience for the book, live in a world mired in conflict and inequalities. Through rapidly changing forms of media they are exposed to human problems and contentious issues at home and abroad that cause them great concern, and they know that in the very near future they will have to step into that world and make some sense of it. *Anthropology Matters* therefore addresses contemporary issues and global concerns, and exposes the false notions of gender, racial, and cultural superiority. To further demonstrate the relevance of the discipline, *Anthropology Matters* also features topics of special interest to students, such as the influence of social media, distorted body image, and facing challenges when living and travelling in a foreign environment.

One of the most important responsibilities for contemporary anthropologists is to make anthropological knowledge available to the public—sharing research knowledge makes it relevant, while hiding it away in an academic journal that few outside the profession will ever read lends itself to the question, is anthropology relevant?

METHODS OF ANTHROPOLOGY

Attempting to quantify human behaviour and to reduce this behaviour to a set of statistics is difficult and likely meaningless. Instead, anthropologists rely on qualitative research—**ethnography**, which involves long-term observation of, and participation in, the daily lives and activities of the people they are studying. This is known as **participant observation**, and its value cannot be overstated. Living in close proximity to the study group, learning their language, and participating in their daily lives allow anthropologists to develop a much deeper understanding of the range of human behaviour. The adage "See me as I do, not as I say" is remarkably accurate when studying human behaviour. For both anthropologists and the general public, trying to understand other people by listening, observing, and even participating goes a long way toward dispelling some of the stereotypes and intolerance we hold for other ways of living.

Participant observation has also become an integral research method in other fields that study human behaviour, rather than relying on surveys and questionnaires that at best provide superficial information. For example, students of educational psychology work in clinics to gain first-hand experience in counselling students who are dealing with death or divorce in the family, and economists use ethnographic research methods in the market and design industry. As the relevance of anthropological research methods becomes better known, other researchers from diverse fields of human study may also adopt some form of participant observation.

However, anthropologists face many **ethical dilemmas** in their practice. For example, how involved should they become in the community they are studying, and should they interject with suggestions for the "betterment" of the community? At what point does advice become interference? In the following chapters you will encounter many instances of this challenge, such as the ancient practice of *purdah*, which is the concealing of women in the home or beneath coverings. *Purdah* elicits strong and often negative reactions from people outside Muslim cultures. The ethical questions that anthropologists face are significant because they also reflect the struggles that occur between cultural groups in our own increasingly pluralistic societies.

APPROACHES IN ANTHROPOLOGY

Anthropologists approach their research from three interrelated perspectives: holism, cross-cultural comparison, and cultural relativism. Every culture is composed of integrated cultural systems (e.g., economic, social, political, and religious) that interact and influence each other; therefore, if one system is interfered with or destroyed, then the other systems of that culture will also be affected. This means that anthropologists must consider the influence of each of these systems on one another. For example, marriage practices in a cultural group are likely to be influenced or even controlled by religious beliefs; if that group's religious beliefs change, then probably so will its marriage customs. In light of this reality, anthropologists take a **holistic approach**—examining the culture as a whole, rather than as discrete parts.

Many of the issues discussed in *Anthropology Matters* use ethnographic information from a **cross-cultural comparison**. This means a custom or practice common to humans—for example, exchange—is compared from one culture to another, although we should never think of comparison as a means of determining the superiority of one culture's custom over another's. Rather, anthropologists gather data to make generalizations about human behaviour as a whole. For example, cross-cultural comparison of body image has shown that the concept of beauty is a universal concept influenced by cultural ideals.

Anthropology has always been "global" in that the groups studied have come from all over the world. Today, however, anthropologists themselves originate in many regions of the world, and they provide diverse voices and interpretations of culture. The quest to understand other people is a paramount goal of any anthropologist; consequently, the pluralism within the field adds a new dimension to the cross-cultural study of humankind.

The third perspective in anthropology, cultural relativism, is an approach so fundamental to anthropology, and so contentious because of conflicting ideals and human rights issues, that it will be discussed in some detail in the following section.

KEY CONCEPTS AND ISSUES IN ANTHROPOLOGY

In *Anthropology Matters* we will be exploring several contemporary issues from an anthropological perspective. This requires an understanding of key concepts in anthropology that will be addressed in the discussions, including the concepts of culture, cultural relativism, human rights, ethnocentrism, cultural imperialism, and genocide. **Culture** may be defined as "the shared ideals, values, and beliefs that people use to interpret, experience, and generate behaviour" (Haviland, Fedorak, & Lee 2009), or, in other words, "the whole way of life." All cultural groups determine the most effective way of making a living given their environmental circumstances. Social organization facilitates the formation of conjugal (marital) bonds, family units, and kinship networks. Cultural groups express their religious beliefs through **rituals** and traditions, develop systems for maintaining social order within and between societies, and communicate symbolically through dress and decoration, art, music, and language.

Anthropologists attempt to understand other cultures through their practices, values, and world view—what Overing (1985) calls the moral universe. In other words, anthropologists try to understand a cultural group based on how the people understand themselves and the world around them. This approach, known as **cultural relativism**, acknowledges that the way "others" see the world is as valid as the way we see the world. Thus, anthropologists do not set out to disprove anyone's beliefs or traditions, although they certainly form their own opinions. Rather, their goal is to understand the reasons behind these practices within the context of that culture. To do anything else would make anthropology irrelevant.

Cultural relativism is a fundamental principle in anthropology that has helped shape the discipline. However, cultural relativism is not without controversy, especially when it concerns customs that threaten the well-being of individuals, for example, female circumcision. Nor has a consensus ever been reached as to what cultural relativism truly means. Simply put, cultural relativism is the belief that all cultures are equally valid in their own right. This suggests, for some, that the beliefs and traditions of cultural groups must be accepted, regardless of whether they fit into our idea of acceptable behaviour. For others, the issue of human rights and equality supersedes cultural traditions: if a practice has the potential to harm, either physically or emotionally, then it should be stopped, regardless of its cultural value or historical context.

Yet **human rights** is a difficult concept to define—it is a vague, contradictory, and often misused term. On its most basic level, human rights refers to "reasonable demands for personal security and basic well-being" (Messer 1993: 222). Depending on the agency or organization, human rights may also include political and civil rights, socio-economic and cultural rights, development rights, and indigenous rights. However, what is or is not considered a human right differs from one nation to another: why is there opposition to same-sex couples who want the same right to marry as heterosexual couples? Why do Westerners consider male circumcision acceptable, while female circumcision is labelled a violation of human rights? The role of anthropologists in these debates is to serve as a conduit for voices that would otherwise go unheard. Although at times it is extremely difficult, anthropologists—and indeed all reflective people—must strike a balance between cultural relativism and human rights.

The concept of cultural relativism elicits fear in some people, including some anthropologists, because it calls into question, and even rejects, their own sense of right and wrong. Much of this fear can be traced to misunderstanding the basic tenets of cultural relativism. It is not that all ideas are true, but rather that all ideas deserve consideration. Cultural relativism is not about "anything goes"; it is about *respect*—respect for other ways of living, believing, and practising, and respect for the rights of all cultural groups to self-determination.

Cultural relativism serves to counter **ethnocentrism**, the belief that one's own culture and way of life are superior to all others. If we fail to recognize that there are other world views, and other ways of living, then there is a very real danger of **cultural imperialism**—promoting one nation's values, beliefs, and behaviour over all others. This is particularly prevalent in the West, where our economic, political, religious, and military power has been used to "blackmail" other nations into adopting Western values and giving up their traditional way of life.

Critics often focus on extreme behaviours of the past to point out the weaknesses in cultural relativism. Hitler's extermination of Jews during World War II is often cited as an example of cultural relativism taken too far. What they mean is that, for too long, leaders in other countries stood by and "allowed" Hitler to kill Jews, rather than interfere and take a stand against it. Even more significant to this discussion, extermination of a group of people is *not* a cultural tradition; it is a crime against humanity, as are all acts of **genocide**—and the failure to act in time is an example of apathy, not relativism. Thus, in any discussion of the merits or limitations of cultural relativism, the difference between a cultural tradition and deviant or criminal behaviour must be considered.

Anthropologists also recognize that as outsiders, we may never fully understand another culture and its practices; nor can anthropologists remain completely objective or value-free given the "cultural baggage" and social identities they carry with them into field research. In fact, it is extremely difficult to reach the degree of impartiality expected of anthropologists. This will become apparent as we examine complex issues such as female circumcision. Indeed, as Ginsburg (1991: 17) suggests, the practice of female circumcision presents one of the "strongest challenges to anthropology's central tenet of cultural relativism."

As should be evident by now, we will be discussing some rather complex issues in *Anthropology Matters*. It is not the goal of this text to solve these issues, but to investigate them from an anthropological perspective. Throughout *Anthropology Matters* we will consider the question "What good is anthropology, anyway?"

Part One

HOW DOES ANTHROPOLOGY WORK?

Anthropology has an exotic reputation—those unfamiliar with the discipline hold images of intrepid, bespectacled scientists trekking through the dense forest in search of a "lost" tribe, then single-mindedly studying them to gain some insight into "primitive" man. Although it is true that early anthropologists focused on exotic cultures hidden away in distant lands, today anthropologists are interested in all things human, including those things modern. They may study the reciprocity system of men on skid row (Hauch 1992), shopping habits in large suburban malls (Underhill 1999), the AIDS epidemic in Africa (Lee 2009), mock wedding traditions on the Canadian Prairies (Taft 2009), or social control at Disneyland (Shearing & Stenning 1987). These topics, and many more, are of interest to anthropologists as they attempt to comprehend and explain the human condition.

In this first section of *Anthropology Matters*, all three chapters illustrate the unique ways in which anthropologists study human behaviour, including their approach to fieldwork, the relevance of research methods when applied to the study of consumer behaviour, and their collaborative efforts in the struggle to save endangered languages. In Chapter 1, we will examine the nature of anthropological research, emphasizing, through examples and narrative, the methods, challenges, and ethics of "doing fieldwork."

Anthropology is not only an academic endeavour; anthropologists put their research methods and skills to practical use, as is the case with business anthropology. In Chapter 2, readers will be introduced to the anthropological exploration of shopping as an economic and social experience, and learn more about consumer behaviour and its many meanings. Quite simply, we will address the question "Why do people shop?"

In recent years, applied linguistic anthropologists have become proactive in the growing field of language preservation and revitalization, often working with speech communities to save endangered languages. This is the topic of Chapter 3.

Part One, then, demonstrates how anthropology works, and also sets the stage for Part Two, which examines contemporary issues on which anthropologists, through their ethnographic research, have developed unique perspectives.

Chapter 1

WHAT ARE THE CHALLENGES IN ETHNOGRAPHIC FIELDWORK?

Key Terms: applied anthropology, cultural relativism, culture shock, ethical dilemma, ethnographer, ethnography, fieldwork, gender, indigenous peoples, inequality, key informant, participant observation, qualitative research, quantitative research, rite of passage

---

INTRODUCTION

Fieldwork is a humbling experience. This statement holds true today as much as it did 50 years ago. Anthropologists are seldom fully prepared for what they encounter in the field, and the onslaught of new sights, sounds, and smells can be overwhelming. Despite romantic images of anthropological fieldwork, the work is tedious and fraught with frustrations, physical discomfort, and loneliness. Indeed, fieldwork is often called a **rite of passage**—the time when an anthropologist learns to adapt to a foreign environment, and in the process learns to face the personal and moral challenges of fieldwork.

Anthropologists owe their allegiance first and foremost to the people they are studying—without their trust, an anthropologist's research becomes difficult if not impossible. Most anthropologists develop an attachment to the people they are studying and feel personally responsible for their well-being. They take every possible measure to protect the privacy and dignity of their study group. Nonetheless, incidents of the privacy or safety of study groups being compromised have occurred, leading to a call for an anthropological code of ethics.

In this chapter the nature of ethnographic fieldwork, and in particular, participant observation, will be explored. In the field, anthropologists encounter numerous socio-emotional, research, and ethical challenges; of particular significance are the power relations inherent in ethnographic fieldwork and the ethical dilemmas that often arise. These issues will be addressed through the reflections of "seasoned" anthropologists who have spent considerable time in the field.

ANTHROPOLOGISTS AND FIELDWORK

The field anthropologist, also known as an **ethnographer**, is a stranger in a strange land. Unaware of the local customs and unable to predict behaviour, an ethnographer lives in constant fear of behaving inappropriately. This is what Annette Weiner (1987: 1) encountered early in her fieldwork with the Kiriwini Trobrianders of New Guinea: "Walking into a village at the beginning of fieldwork is entering a world without cultural guideposts." While learning the values and norms of the Kiriwina, Weiner also had to let go of her cultural assumptions about work, power, death, family, and friends. To be successful in the field, then, anthropologists must be flexible, adaptable, and creative.

"Fieldwork is best described as the ultimate learning experience, as you begin like a child and gradually absorb knowledge—and wisdom and insight if all goes well—which matures you in the eyes of your teachers and, ideally, wins you their approval ... the good things have heavily outweighed the bad." Anthropologist Robert Tonkinson (1991: 18)

Anthropologists specialize in **qualitative** (ethnographic) data collection and analysis, employing interviews, observing, and carrying on informal conversations; however, in some cases **quantitative research** is also necessary. When Jon D. Holtzman (2000: 11) studied Nuer immigrants in Minnesota, he administered quantitative surveys to compile a community profile that included demographics, such as "age, gender, tribal and clan affiliation, education and work experiences, and basic outlines of the Nuer refugee experience." Holtzman did not rely solely on his quantitative data; he also recorded life histories, conducted in-depth, structured interviews, and created detailed case studies.

Fieldwork is a journey of discovery for anthropologists, not only professionally, but also personally. According to James Clifford (1997: 91), "sojourning somewhere else, learning a language, putting oneself in odd situations and trying to figure them out can be a good way to learn something new, simultaneously about oneself and about the places one visits." The role of an ethnographer is to understand, as best he or she can, the symbols and traditions that hold meaning for members of a cultural group, and then to convey this understanding to others. For this reason, Alice Reich considers the people anthropologists study to be the real teachers (Kutsche 1998). Indeed, most anthropologists return from the field with a stronger sense of self, a new-found confidence in their abilities, and an expanded world view. Knauft (2005: 37) sums up his fieldwork experience in Papua New Guinea: "We came to see cultural anthropology as a kind of dialogue—a conversation between Gebusi meanings and our own understandings."

THE NATURE OF FIELDWORK

In anthropology, **fieldwork** involves an anthropologist moving into the study group and beginning the long process of collecting descriptive data on the group's daily activities. Fieldwork is essential to anthropology; indeed, Whitehead and Conaway (1986) suggest that anthropology is shaped by fieldwork, and that anthropologists are shaped by field experiences. As such, fieldwork defines anthropology and gives it a distinct identity.

Participant observation is the research method of fieldwork. Participant observation involves living with a cultural group for an extended period of time, observing their daily activities, taking detailed fieldnotes, conducting personal interviews, and participating in their lives as much as possible. This is where the humbling experience begins. Indeed, Reich calls participant observation "a time honoured tradition of making a fool of oneself for a point" (Kutsche 1998: 5).

To ease the transition into a community, ethnographers attempt to develop a rapport with members of the study group—in particular, **key informants**, who are experts in the social complexities of their culture. Participant observation enables an ethnographer to collect richly descriptive data that describes "behaviors, intentions, situations, and events as understood by one's informants" (DeMunck & Sobo 1998: 43). In essence, ethnographers use all five of their senses to generate a "written photograph" (Erlandson et al. 1993) that reflects how people really live. Participant observation also provides ethnographers with a better understanding of what is really happening and why people behave the way they do, by relying primarily on personal interactions. Margaret Mead recognized the value of this research method in the 1920s; she was one of the first anthropologists to apply a scientific, participant-observation model to her study of adolescent Samoan girls. Mead participated in the living culture and recorded their daily cultural activities, learning what held meaning and what was important to them (Kawulich 2005).

> "I continue to believe that anthropology is the quintessential liberal arts discipline because it is about meaningful human life, not as a set of answers, but as a series of engaged conversations." Anthropologist Alice Reich, quoted in Kutsche (1998: 4)

Although participant observation can set in motion moral and ethical dilemmas, as you will see later in this chapter, it is still a valued research method today. When Robert Anderson (2005: 3) studied the ghosts of Iceland, he joined séance groups to observe and record conversations between the living and dead, and he regularly attended lectures at spirit schools and spirit-society coffee klatches. These informal participatory activities enabled him to grasp their day-to-day behaviours and beliefs. In this way anthropologists observe, first-hand, how activities are carried out as opposed to relying only on descriptions supplied by informants during interviews.

Ethnographic research is dynamic, and efforts to modernize the discipline are ongoing—as society evolves, so too will ethnographic research methods. One major change is that anthropologists have moved away from exotic small-scale cultures and turned their attention to modern, complex institutions such as the World Bank, corporate and industry headquarters, NGOs in the field, and even the neighbourhood grocery store. The concept of "the field" is also changing. Isolated, culturally distinct groups of people are becoming rare today; most cultural systems have become pluralistic due to transnational flows of people and the ensuing political, economic, and social influences of these migrations. Anthropologists have reconceptualized the "field" to mean a political location, rather than a locality. Ethnographic fieldwork has become multi-sited, as anthropologists study the flow of people, wealth, and ideas back and forth across social networks (Wittel 2000).

The Internet is now a driving force in social interaction, acquisition of information, economic activity, political discourse, and popular culture. Indeed, Laura Miller (1995) calls the Internet a rich soup of world cultures. Consequently, ethnographers have turned their attention to the study of computer-mediated communication and cultural aggregates known as virtual communities (Fedorak 2009). These communities are built on relationships and shared activities—a social rather than a physical space. Like site ethnography, virtual ethnography requires immersion in the culture. Correll (1995), for example, studied lesbian members of a virtual café by becoming part of the community. She gained the trust of the members as she participated in the daily activities in the café and was able to acquire valuable information on the formation and maintenance of special-interest virtual communities. Therefore, although ethnographic fieldwork is changing as society changes, participant observation remains the underlying research method.

Ethnographers have studied virtually every cultural group in existence, and the knowledge they have garnered is academically valuable, but is that enough? This is where **applied anthropology** comes into play. The quest for relevance often turns to this branch of the discipline, where the knowledge hidden in anthropological research is put to practical use. The opportunities for anthropologists to contribute to the real world are many, not the least of which is development, discussed in Chapter 11. One area of increasing influence is business anthropology, discussed in the next chapter, where applied economic anthropologists specialize in studying organizational change, consumer behaviour, and product design. For example, Susan Squires (2002) investigated whether consumers would use hand lotion at the office. She discovered the products had to be in containers that fit with an office rather than a home environment.

The culmination of months, even years, in the field is an **ethnography**—a detailed descriptive account of the daily lives of a cultural group. The ethnography is written when the anthropologist returns home, compiled from copious field notes. At all times, anthropologists work to ensure the validity and objectivity of their information and their interpretations. As study groups have increasingly demanded that their voices be heard, anthropologists have become recorders as well as interpreters of cultural data. Narratives from the people themselves offer another level of information and understanding.

CHALLENGES IN FIELDWORK

Participant observation, by its very nature, lends itself to numerous challenges and researcher quandaries. In this section, we will explore the **ethical dilemmas** and the problems that ethnographers encounter in the field through the experiences of several anthropologists.

The ethical dilemmas Jun Li (2008) experienced while conducting a female gambling study reflect many of the research and personal issues that ethnographers encounter. Li set out to examine "how women come to gamble and develop gambling problems" in Ontario (100). Although she employed two data-collection methods—participant observation and in-depth interviewing—participant observation is the focus of this discussion since it is here, as an embedded participant observer, that Li experienced most of her problems.

Li was conducting what is known as "sensitive" research, which means "the study of secretive, stigmatized, or deviant human activity and behaviour involving vulnerable research subjects" (102). Her subjects, female gamblers, tend to be wary of the public's perception of them, and for this reason participant observation works well since it does not interfere with the subjects' lives or interrupt their activities, but still allows the ethnographer to gather "honest data" that tells the story of what people really do (101). According to Alder and Alder (1987, quoted in Li 2008), if the activities are secretive, then the researcher must participate in the activities to understand the subculture from an insider's perspective. Li took the bus to casinos along with other gamblers, wrote up her fieldnotes in isolation to avoid suspicion, and obtained a "players card" that identified her as a beginning player. Thus, Li immersed herself in the gambling subculture to represent the female gamblers' perspective, and to see, feel, and experience the world through their eyes.

Although participant observation can be covert or overt, Li chose to conduct covert observations, given the sensitivity of the activity, the unwillingness of people to talk about their gambling, and the likelihood that more detailed data about the lives of these women could be collected. Li believed that disclosing her identity would cause gamblers either to flee or to behave differently. However, covert participant observation is deceptive in nature, opening up questions regarding the ethics of this type of research (see Chapter 2 for more discussion of deceptive research).

The problems began early in the fieldwork. First, since Li was a "pretend" gambler and using budgeted research money ($20 per day) to gamble, she never felt like a full participant and never "went native," since she did not share the same values or experience the same emotional highs and lows as the other gamblers (103). She did grasp the fact that female gamblers were complex, and different both from any participants in earlier quantitative studies and from common stereotypes, and that their gambling had to be contextualized within their socio-economic and personal circumstances. But from an ethical standpoint, Li felt awkward and uneasy as a secret researcher and psychologically unprepared for her emotional response to the deceptive nature of the research. On three separate occasions, seasoned gamblers tried to inform her about the dangers of gambling, making Li feel so guilty that she finally confessed her real identity and research plans to ease their worries (105). Part of her guilt stemmed from the sense that she was infringing on the subjects' right to privacy. In response to her inner turmoil, Li decided to "come clean" and changed her ethnographic research to overt participant observation. However, she found that the gamblers were now unwilling to participate in the research.

Li's disclosure "changed the social relationships and silenced voices" (107). She became an outsider, which made her feel even more awkward. In a third attempt to gather valid data, Li shifted to a covert peripheral research role: she still participated in gambling, but limited personal contacts, simply recording her observations and the conversations she overheard. Thus, she avoided the earlier personal moral dilemmas, and this compromise allowed her to participate as an insider and observe as an outsider.

In summary, Li experienced a quandary when the people she wanted to study were protective of her, making her feel guilty about her subterfuge and eventually leading to her confession. Learning the truth eased the women's worries, but it also silenced their voices. As a result, Li continues to believe that participant observation is the best method for collecting data on sensitive topics, but she feels that researchers need to be psychologically prepared for the dilemmas and to carefully consider the sensitivity of the topic and protect the well-being of their vulnerable study group.

"A woman gambler explained her reticence: 'You know why I don't want to come to your study? I would feel guilty if I come to your interviews because I know I would lie to you. I don't want to talk because I don't want my private life going public. Believe me—the gamblers who come to you will lie to you. You won't get the truth.'" Li (2008: 106)

As you have seen with Li's study, ethnographers deal with constant uncertainty, both personal and professional. When Robert Tonkinson arrived in the Gibson Desert in Western Australia to study the Mardu Aborigines, he was plagued with self-doubt and constantly second-guessed his behaviour. When offered some chewing tobacco, Tonkinson worried, "Will refusal offend? Is this what our teachers meant when they said rapport must be established at all costs?" (Tonkinson 1991: 16). This is an example of the insecurity that can come from not fully understanding the behaviour patterns of a group of people.

When an anthropologist moves into a community for a long-term research project, bombardment with new stimuli will likely result in **culture shock**, especially if the culture is very different. Culture shock is a stress-related syndrome that causes feelings of confusion, hostility, disorientation, and depression (Nolan 1990). When William C. Young headed into the field to study the Rashaayda Bedouin of Sudan in 1978, he found himself in a vastly different world from the one he left behind in the United States (Young 1996). Instead of cars, he rode a camel, and instead of cities with tall buildings, shops, restaurants, and freeways, he lived in a goat-hair tent in the middle of a vast desert. At first, Young felt awkward living in a close-knit and highly structured society, but gradually he became friends with his Rashaayda hosts and grew comfortable with his new lifestyle. He learned the language, wore traditional clothing, and learned to think and live like a Rashiidi. Before leaving the United States, Young had converted to Islam, hoping this would make him more acceptable to the Rashaayda and help him understand their world view—a drastic step, and not one many anthropologists would undergo. Overcoming culture shock is a long process filled with setbacks, but if the anthropologist is fortunate enough to develop friendships within the community, the sense of isolation and disorientation can quickly disappear.

Anthropologists struggle to find a balance in their fieldwork. They must remain neutral and objective, report what they learn, and maintain a culturally relativistic perspective by not passing judgment or interfering in the lives of the study group. Yet, Knauft (2005) wonders, at what point do we draw a line between appreciation of cultural diversity and critiquing some of the cultural practices and beliefs that are obviously harmful? Although Knauft saw the richness and vibrancy of the Gebusi culture, he also saw the underside—the male dominance and subjugation of women, and the accusations of sorcery that often ended in the murder of an innocent person.

Gender is one of the determining factors in field experiences. Many ethnographers come from societies where gender equality is a strived-for goal, but this may not be the case in the field, and when confronted with situations where gender **inequality** is obvious, ethnographers are placed in a moral quandary. Bruce Knauft (2005) found himself unsure of how to deal with his own sense of morality and justice in the face of Gebusi patriarchy, where the women were excluded from spirit séances and other festive activities, their productive work (e.g., gardening, cooking) was not openly appreciated, and wife beating was fairly common. Knauft had to reconcile his sense of gender rights and roles with those of the community he was living in—an example of **cultural relativism** at work. If Knauft had interfered, his fieldwork might have ended right there, yet the desire to step in and help in such cases is almost overwhelming. Cassell and Jacobs (2006: 1) caution, though, that to interfere with the behaviour of people in a fieldwork situation will more likely lead to confrontations than to any moral "improvement."

FIGURE 1.1 DR. BRUCE KNAUFT IN THE MIDST OF ARMED GEBUSI MEN

"The Gebusi became not only human to us but also, despite their tragic violence, wonderful people. ... Vibrant and friendly, they turned life's cruellest ironies into their best jokes, and its biggest tensions into their most elaborate fantasies. Their humor, spirituality, deep togetherness ... made them, for the most part, great fun to be with. ... To lump them together as simply 'Gebusi' is as bland as it would be to describe David Letterman, Michael Jordan ... and Hillary Rodham Clinton as simply 'American.'"
Anthropologist Bruce Knauft (2005: 3-4)

Ethnographers also have to deal with research limitations due to gender. Male anthropologists have difficulty crossing gender barriers and discussing "women's issues" with the women, either because the women are unwilling or the men will not allow it. So, too, are female ethnographers often relegated to the women's side of society and refused entry into the man's world. Knauft's wife, Eileen, found herself barred from male activities in the village even though she was an outsider—her gender, not her nationality, established her place (Knauft 2005). For Li (2008), her gender was paramount to the success of her study: she had to be a female to participate in women's gambling activities; a male anthropologist would not have gained entrance. However, Li's ethnicity (Chinese) may have hindered her access to the many Chinese gamblers because gambling is a culturally unacceptable behaviour in Chinese culture and the gamblers would have been embarrassed for a young Chinese woman to witness their behaviour.

One of the valuable lessons of fieldwork is experiencing, even for a short time, what it feels like to be a minority person. Most ethnographers have come from Western societies where people of European descent are the "mainstream" and enjoy the highest position in society. To become the object of curiosity, the "odd" one, or the "other" is an eye-opening experience that can fundamentally change the way we view ourselves and others.

ETHICS IN ANTHROPOLOGY

Although we have dealt with ethical issues and dilemmas throughout this chapter, a brief historical overview of the evolution of ethical guidelines in anthropology may contextualize the ongoing concern for ethics in anthropology. During World War II, American anthropologists were recruited by the military to gather intelligence on insurgency and counterinsurgency activities (Hill 2006). Criticism of this activity was swift; many anthropologists viewed this type of work as a threat to the integrity of the discipline and a risk to anthropology's reputation. They feared that this subterfuge would end field opportunities, or that ethnographic data gathered might be used to harm **indigenous peoples**. Since then, anthropologists have shied away from secret or clandestine research, which is one reason why deceptive ethnographic research is not viewed positively by many anthropologists.

The American Anthropological Association has developed a code of ethics that urges anthropologists to "respect the rights of others, fulfill obligations, avoid harm, and augment benefits to those we interact with as anthropologists" (Cassell & Jacobs 2006: 1). This code of ethics is taken very seriously by most anthropologists. Unfortunately, the issue seems to have come full circle: anthropologists in the twenty-first century are being recruited by the United States security sector for the "war on terror," raising fears that anthropological information will be used to intervene in developing countries, such as Iran or Iraq.

The ethnographer has several ethical responsibilities: to bring the research project before an ethics board of the funding agency (e.g., a university); to inform the study group of the purpose of study; to receive the group's permission to conduct the study; and to share the research findings with the community (Marshall & Batten 2004). In recent years, there has been a major shift in ethnographic fieldwork: study groups have become partners, working in collaboration with the anthropologists—their voices are heard as much as those of the anthropologists (Plemmons & Albro 2011).

I close this discussion of ethnographic challenges and ethical dilemmas with a description of a situation that may seem humorous now but created a serious ethical dilemma at the time. Knauft (2005) found himself facing a quandary concerning sexuality while living with the Gebusi of Papua New Guinea. The issue of human sexuality is always a delicate subject; indeed, anthropologists have been negligent in elaborating

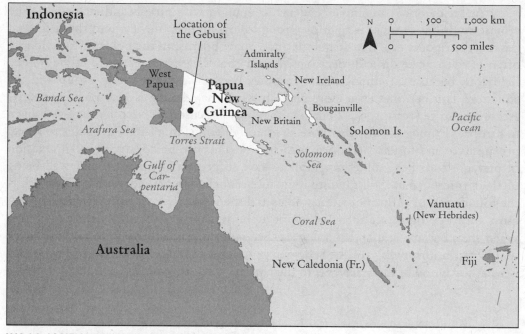

MAP 1.1 LOCATION OF GEBUSI IN PAPUA NEW GUINEA

on the sexual practices in various cultures, partly because it is such a sensitive subject. Knauft hoped to rectify this ethnographic negligence with his research among the Gebusi. He knew that Gebusi men took part in homosexual acts during spirit séances and other festivities, but he did not know the extent of the practice. One night at a spirit séance, when Bruce Knauft's wife Eileen was away from the village, a Gebusi man propositioned him. Knauft was caught off guard: if he refused, would he lose the trust of the Gebusi men and their willingness to include him in male activities? Would they be angry and insulted? Yet participant observation only goes so far. Knauft handled the situation remarkably well, telling the man that although some men in his culture did have sex with other men, this was not his custom. Fortunately, the Gebusi man understood, since the same held true for his people.

CONCLUSION

Ethnographic fieldwork is a unique research tool for learning about people and their behaviour. As mentioned in the introduction to this text, the efficacy of this research method has not gone unnoticed in other disciplines, including psychology, sociology, and education. These disciplines and others have "borrowed" participant observation and qualitative research and incorporated this type of research into their studies.

Yet fieldwork is a complex endeavour, fraught with pitfalls and challenges. The ethical questions of what is right or wrong follow anthropologists into the field, and despite the rigours of ethics standards and review boards, in the field anthropologists often have to make difficult decisions. Moral choices are a constant in ethnographic fieldwork because an ethnographer becomes very close to the study group and the situation. This becomes even more obvious when the research is of a sensitive nature. According to Li (2008: 109), "doing ethnography in sensitive research is like walking a tightrope." Ethnography is therefore an ethical dilemma in itself—the goal is to reveal private lives and to tell the informants' stories. This can be construed as an invasion of privacy, and above all, ethnographers have to protect the privacy and well-being of their study group. Still, despite its inherent challenges, ethnographic fieldwork is the foundation of anthropological studies and the source of rich cultural data. Indeed, most anthropologists see their fieldwork, upon reflection, as a rite of passage, a time when they became real anthropologists. So important is fieldwork to anthropology that British anthropologist C.G. Seligman proclaimed, "Field research in anthropology is what the blood of the martyrs is to the church" (Lewis 1976: 27).

QUESTIONS FOR CONSIDERATION AND CLASSROOM ACTIVITIES

1. If an anthropologist moved into your community (be it your hometown, university dorm, etc.), how would you respond to this person's continuing presence in your life? What types of questions would you be willing to answer, and what aspects of your life would you consider too private to share with a stranger? Would the gender or age of the anthropologist make any difference to what you would share?

2. Li considered deceptive participant observation to have infringed on the subjects' privacy. Do you agree or disagree? Explain your answer. Despite her ethical dilemma, Li feels that participant observation is the best research method to use. In your opinion, does "the end justify the means"?

3. Choose a setting where you can observe activities for a period of 30 minutes (e.g., a restaurant, football game, etc.). Record everything you notice, using all of your senses, on one side of the paper; on the other, write your thoughts, feelings, and ideas about what is happening. This exercise helps you learn to write detailed notes while also observing.

4. In groups of four, choose a site and activity to observe and participate in (e.g., grocery store, movie theatre) for at least two hours. During this activity, do *not* take notes. After the activity ends, record your recollections in as much detail as possible. Group members should then compare their fieldnotes to see what they missed, what they remembered, and what they remembered differently. You will learn that through participation you are able to better interpret what happened.

You may also discover that participant observation improves your memory of the activity.

SUGGESTED READINGS

DeVitta, P.R. (Ed.). (1992). *The naked anthropologist. Tales from around the world.* Belmont, CA: Wadsworth Publishing.

DeVitta has put together a collection of stories that recount sometimes embarrassing, sometimes startling, experiences of anthropologists in the field. Readers should gain an understanding of the challenges faced by anthropologists as they deal with their insecurities, ignorance, isolation, missteps, and happenstance.

Van Maanen, J. (2011). *Tales of the field: On writing ethnography* (2nd ed.). Chicago: University of Chicago Press.

A humorous and accessible book that provides an introduction to fieldwork, and examines objectivity, truth, voice, and so on. This second edition brings readers up to date with the changes that are taking place in ethnographic fieldwork.

Chapter 2

OF WHAT USE IS ANTHROPOLOGY TO THE BUSINESS WORLD? THE ANTHROPOLOGY OF SHOPPING

Key Terms: applied economic anthropology, business/corporate anthropology, class, commercial anthropology, consumer behaviour, corporate ethnography, economic anthropology, ethics, gendered behaviour, participant observation, retail/consumer anthropology

INTRODUCTION

Economic life is composed of "the activities through which people produce, circulate and consume things, the ways that people and societies secure their subsistence or provision themselves" (Carrier 2005: 3), and includes material objects, labour services, and knowledge. Anthropology can be a window into this economic life. The core concept in anthropology is culture, and since a great deal of **consumer behaviour** is culturally determined, anthropology is well positioned to understand the cultural phenomenon of shopping. Indeed, applied economic anthropology is one area where most anthropologists agree that anthropology is relevant.

As you learned in Chapter 1, anthropologists use ethnographic fieldwork to explore human behaviour and patterns of living, and although there are several approaches to the study of business and consumer behaviour, ethnographic research has proven to be one of the most effective. Ethnography's qualitative methods and observational practices enable anthropologists to truly understand consumers and their behaviour.

Applied economic anthropology has several specialized subfields. **Retail or consumer anthropology**, which is the study of shoppers, is a good example of contemporary anthropological research. Consumer ethnographers attempt to study the lived experiences of consumers to understand their wants and needs, taking into consideration values, beliefs, gender, age, and ethnicity. Recently, what Suchman (2003) calls **business or corporate anthropology** has been used to refer to anthropologists working in private industry, applying anthropological concepts, theories, and methods to business-related issues. Jordan (2010) divides business anthropology into the following areas: organizational anthropology, the study of complex organization culture; marketing and consumer behaviour; and design anthropology. **Commercial anthropology** is another term common in the discipline, referring to anthropologists hired as consultants for private firms. All of these specializations are applied, and obviously there is a great deal of overlap, since the terms seem to be used interchangeably.

Since most consumers spend a great deal of time shopping, shopping must hold some meaning beyond acquiring goods. We will investigate the economic and social meaning of shopping through the research of anthropologist Paco Underhill, who has been applying his anthropological skills and knowledge to the study of shopping and shopping malls for more than 20 years. More specifically we will address questions such as these: Why do people shop? What enhances the shopping experience? How does gender affect product placement and organization of retail space?

Retailers and producers constantly search for ways to encourage consumers to purchase their goods and services. We will explore the role(s) of applied economic anthropologists in a business environment as consumer anthropologists apply ethnographic research to understand consumer behaviour and assist corporations in successfully marketing their wares. Although the focus in this chapter is applied consumer anthropology and business anthropology, we will also consider academic ethnographic research. To demonstrate the value of ethnographic research in economic anthropology, we will explore Purnima Mankekar's cultural analysis of the construction, by Indian grocery stores in the San Francisco Bay area, of Indian culture for the Indian diaspora.

ANTHROPOLOGISTS AND THE BUSINESS WORLD

Not all anthropologists work in academia; in fact, more anthropologists are now employed in international development, government, education, health, and environmental issues than are teaching in university settings. Indeed, many anthropology students will apply cultural analysis in museum settings, journalism, government, and private corporations (Ehn and Löfgren 2009). One area where anthropologists have made great strides is in the field of **economic anthropology**, which can be defined as "the study of economic institutions and behaviour done in anthropological places and in ethnographic style" (Plattner 1989a: 1). Economic anthropologists are interested in all things economic—from the social significance of the Ju/'hoansi *hxaro* exchange system to the gendered division of labour among Yanomami horticulturalists, from the annual migrations of Basseri pastoralists in search of new pasture lands to the productive strategies of Mayan peasant farmers. Obviously, the field of economic anthropology is broad in scope, and in recent years economic anthropologists have expanded their interests to industry, technology, commerce, and marketing (Suchman 2003).

In the 1990s, business anthropology developed into a significant specialization within applied economic anthropology. Indeed, Jordan (2010: 20) calls it a "growth industry." Business anthropologists aspire to understand "the cultural meanings of consumer behaviour." Corporate leaders and business people were beginning to recognize the value of understanding their consumers, and taking note of the methods and expertise of anthropologists. Corporations hired anthropologists to conduct **corporate ethnography** to facilitate labour and community relations, resource and economic development, product design, and employee training (Kedia 2008: 19). These anthropologists became engaged in marketing and public relations to analyse consumer trends and behaviour, community changes, and workplace organization (Ehn & Löfgren 2009). Indeed, Suchman (2003) suggests that anthropology itself has become a consumable commodity.

How has anthropology become relevant to the business world? One obvious application is the anthropologist's access to consumers as they conduct their everyday shopping. Using ethnographic methods, anthropologists explore the social context of shopping, which may assist businesses in predicting product success and in understanding trends, attitudes, and other factors that may influence consumer purchases. Indeed, anthropological research and cultural analysis turn a seemingly mundane activity like shopping into an exotic and mysterious experience.

"Factory floors, corporate offices and 'middle class' homes, assumed to be so transparently familiar as to not warrant anthropological attention, are turned into sites as mysterious as the colonies once were by the mere fact of the anthropologist's presence." Suchman (2003: 3)

Unfortunately, anthropologists who work within organizations and corporations are sometimes viewed with suspicion, especially by academics who question whether anthropologists should "be involved in gathering data that will be used to target a particular group with consumer goods" (Herselman 2008: 45). Applied cultural research is considered shallow, ethically compromised, and not "real" research by some (Ehn and Löfgren 2009: 31), creating heated debate regarding the commercialization of anthropology. Corporate agendas embedded in applied consumer ethnography do not seem compatible with academic theorizing; thus, a significant divide remains between academic research and corporate ethnography, which hampers communication and the flow of knowledge between the two camps. Ehn and Löfgren (2009: 33) exhort academic anthropologists and commercial anthropologists to open dialogue to avoid "unproductive polarization"—pure vs. impure research, deep vs. shallow studies, slow vs. fast ethnography, and the academic ivory-tower syndrome vs. the real world.

Questions of **ethics** in consumer anthropology have been raised both inside and outside the discipline. Similar to general concerns for applied anthropology, among the concerns in business anthropology are that corporate employers might use anthropological information against the workers, or that a market study might result in manipulation of consumers (Jordan 2010). Before agreeing to a study, Jordan carefully examines the motives of her potential employer, and if there is any evidence that the individuals being studied could be harmed, she refuses the contract.

The use of deception in market research, such as hidden cameras in a store, has garnered extensive debate among anthropologists and other researchers, with little agreement (Herselman 2008). To deal with ethical implications, a code of ethics[1] for consultants and academics has been established (Ehn & Löfgren 2009), but very little direction has been given to anthropologists involved in consumer research (Smith, Klein, & Kimmell 2002).

Sunderland and Denny (2007) also warn of the proliferation of consumer ethnographic research that lacks cultural analysis and is therefore not scientifically valid. Ethnography has become a buzzword used by market researchers with very little understanding of what it means or how to go about conducting rigorous ethnography—instead they do what Handwerker (2002) calls "quick and dirty ethnography." Despite the reservations of some anthropologists, the demand for business anthropologists to conduct ethnographic research in marketing and advertising has increased dramatically.

Applied economic anthropologists work in many areas of business, employing anthropological methods and a holistic perspective to understand the issues that have an impact on commerce. Business anthropologists have influenced market research by pointing out that, to be successful, marketers must understand people—what they do and how they live. For example, Steve Barnett, who holds a PhD in anthropology, is senior vice president of market strategy at ICM Breakpoint (GBN Global Business Network 2005). He has pioneered the use of anthropological research methods to analyse consumer behaviour. Barnett has also studied long-term global and cultural trends in patterns of consumption.

Business anthropologists tackle many kinds of problems, such as how to improve work processes by observing how people work or how to design products that better serve the needs of employees. For example, Lucy Suchman's observations of the complexity of copy machines led to Xerox designing the green copy button that everyone recognizes (Jordan 2010). Anthropologists doing design ethnography may also reveal discrepancies between the intended use of a product and the way consumers actually use the product (Wasson 2000).

Business has gone global, and with this increasing globalization economic anthropologists have turned their attention to multinational corporations, in particular how corporate cultures differ from one nation to another (Jordan 2010). Jordan studied a tertiary-care hospital in Riyadh, Saudi Arabia, to learn how individuals from 64 nationalities interacted in the working environment. She found that the two dominant cultures at the hospital, American and Saudi, had a tense relationship even after 30 years of working in the same hospital.

Retail anthropology merges anthropological interests with those of marketers and the corporate world. Applied retail anthropologists work as consultants and researchers for merchants, restaurateurs, marketers, and bankers, investigating the interaction between people and merchandise, and the way people react to the organization of public spaces. For example, why do teenagers choose to congregate at a mall? Who

---

[1] This code of ethics is a work in progress, with not everyone agreeing on every principle.

does most of the shopping, and why? Why have retailers chosen to supply shoppers with entertainment?

Retail anthropologists conduct their research in much the same way as other ethnographers—through observations of people's lives as they are lived in their natural environment, in other words, through **participant observation**, living in (or extensively visiting) the community they are studying and becoming involved in the daily activities of the people to understand their point of view (Plattner 1989b). Participant observation is a constructive way of understanding what consumers need and want—this is particularly helpful today, as consumers are far more sophisticated, demanding, and indifferent to the products being offered. By observing consumers in a shopping environment, anthropologists offer the corporate world a more accurate and detailed assessment of consumer products.

Marketing results in the flow of goods and services from the producer (or retailer) to the consumer. Anthropological consultation has encouraged retailers and corporate leaders to take cultural phenomena into consideration when planning their marketing strategies, and to acknowledge that consumers' perceptions, attitudes, beliefs, and values influence their behaviour. In other words, anthropologists try to understand how social organization, including gender and class or socio-economic status, affects consumer behaviour (Herselman 2008). Daniel Miller (1998: 9) cautions against anthropologists becoming too involved in analyzing consumable products lest "we find ourselves contributing to, rather than refiguring, dominant forms of commodity fetishism." Rather, Miller suggests that anthropologists remain true to their anthropological goals—in this case, attempting to understand consumer behaviour. To this end, Miller (2001) examined the meaning of the shopping experience and how this experience informs us about social relationships and consumer culture in North London. For example, how does taking children on shopping expeditions affect the parent–child relationship? What social relationships are formed when teenagers gather to shop, visit, and enjoy the entertainment? Miller discovered that shopping created and maintained social relationships between family members and other kin, as well as pets.

> "Ethnographic study can be a useful and complementary tool, giving us what the individual may be unable to or unwilling to vocalize to other researchers.... If you can observe the subject or consumer in action, you gain a better understanding of possible ways to enrich the consumer's experience, and also better understand the responses obtained from interviews and surveys." Ajay Kohli, professor of marketing at the Emory's Goizueta Business School (NAPA 2005)

THE NATURE OF SHOPPING AND CONSUMER BEHAVIOUR

Imagine a marketplace where shoppers casually stroll past an array of shops filled with all manner of merchandise. A group of young people, dressed in sloppy clothes, stand in the centre of the market, joking and teasing each other. Nearby, serious-looking musicians play a catchy melody and a troupe of young entertainers dance in time to the music. A juggler ambles by, his face twisted in concentration as he tosses four colourful balls into the air. Children follow him, laughing in delight each time he drops a ball. A clock chimes, signalling the noon hour, and delicious smells waft through the air from a nearby food stall, making shoppers' mouths water. Then an angry shriek fills the air as a harried-looking mother drags her two tired and crying children to the nearest exit—the shopping day is over for them.

The above scenario may sound like a traditional souk or bazaar in an exotic locale such as Cairo, Egypt, but in fact it describes a typical day in one of the many suburban malls located across North America. The mall is not a new concept; it is merely the most recent manifestation of a place for people to congregate and participate in commerce, trade, and socializing. Indeed, malls are the marketplaces of wealthy industrialized societies (Plattner 1989b). Since the 1950s, this phenomenon has diffused to all corners of the world, and today's malls have become a mainstay of urban life. Anthropologist Paco Underhill (2004: 4) calls them the "dominant arena of American shopping" and "an economic force the likes of which the world has never known."

"If you really want to observe entire middle-class multi-generational American families, you have to go to the mall."
Anthropologist Paco Underhill (2004: 9)

The anthropological study of shopping may seem, at first glance, a frivolous choice for research, but in reality it can inform us about economic life in state societies. Indeed, John Seely Brown, former director of Xerox PARC, suggests that "anthropologists let you view behaviour through a new set of eyeglasses" (Deutsch 1991). Consumers flock to shopping malls and, through their spending, significantly influence the economy. Shopping malls showcase the people of a community in their natural state: how people dress in their everyday lives; the food they eat when they think no one is watching; and how they interact with their parents and children, friends and spouses in a public space.

Underhill (2004) and his associates visit shopping malls, armed with video equipment, maps, and customer-profile sheets, to make detailed observations of consumer behaviour. Underhill often relies on key informants to help him understand shoppers; he even spent an afternoon shopping with three teenaged girls in an American suburban mall. By doing so, he gained insight into the shopping habits of young women. Underhill discovered that choice of clothing styles among teenagers signals group (tribal) affiliations, such as punks, preps, skaters, and skas. This trend continues into adulthood, when individuals, especially women, signal their **class**, ideology, and lifestyle by the type of clothing they wear. By giving voice to these young women, Underhill expanded his analysis of the meaning of the shopping experience.

The organization of public space follows a similar pattern in most malls and plays a significant role in the overall consumer experience and ensuing behaviour. Some of the larger malls have vast amusement parks with swimming pools and waterslides, rock climbing walls, ice rinks, aquatic displays, rides resembling a smaller version of Disneyland, video arcades, and so on. These "sideshows" are designed to make the shopping experience more enjoyable, especially for children, which in turn may

FIGURE 2.1 SHOPPING MALLS HAVE BECOME CENTRES OF FAMILY ENTERTAINMENT, AS THIS "FANTASYLAND" AT THE WEST EDMONTON MALL DEMONSTRATES

encourage shoppers to stay longer and shop more. Malls become one-stop entertainment facilities, and as Underhill (2004) notes, non-retail components give a mall its character and reputation.

The consumer experience is central to any shopping mall; if the consumer is unhappy, frustrated, inconvenienced, or unable to easily locate appropriate merchandise, then the shopping experience becomes negative, which translates into limited economic growth for the retailers. Underhill coined the phrase "butt-brush theory," which holds that if a woman's bottom is touched, brushed, or jostled while she is examining merchandise, she will likely leave the store (Gladwell 1996). The lesson from this knowledge is that women's products requiring close examination should never be situated in narrow aisles.

Organization of public space in malls reflects **gendered behaviour**—male "hunters" spend very little time in the mall if they are lost, while female "gatherers" exhibit more patience and may even ask for help in locating a store (Underhill 2004). Shopping habits based on gender influence product placement, displays, and general set-up in a store. Underhill discovered that putting a women's shoe department and cosmetics department side by side makes perfect sense, since a woman waiting for the clerk to bring shoes in her size will occupy her time looking over the cosmetics. This placement recognizes that for women, waiting and boredom take the fun out of power shopping.

With the exception of computer components or tools, men do not like shopping, nor do they like malls. Underhill (2004) called the men's underwear section in a department store the "dead zone" because until recently men did not buy underwear. Their wives or girlfriends bought them underwear, but only at Christmas or perhaps on their birthdays. Yet the dearth of male shoppers in malls is becoming a thing of the past. Men are remaining single longer, and they are learning to shop. When they marry, they are expected to continue performing at least some of the shopping duties because their wives are also working (Underhill 1999). Most interesting, a new gender-based trend has emerged: men now buy their own underwear, leading to a re-evaluation of product placement in stores. Those merchants that recognize the potential in this untapped market will reap economic rewards.

THE SOCIAL ROLE OF SHOPPING MALLS

Malls, like traditional marketplaces, are places to meet friends, hear the latest gossip and news, find a date or even a spouse, and enjoy the local entertainment. They are also gathering places for charitable organizations, school groups, artists, and the elderly. Mall walking for senior citizens began soon after the first enclosed malls opened and has been gaining popularity ever since, especially in cold climates (Underhill 2004).

Teenaged girls love malls for all sorts of reasons, most of which have something to do with socialization. They like Internet cafés to hang out with friends; they enjoy movie theatres for the same reason. Videogames, bowling, miniature golf, and rock climbing draw teenagers to the mall, as do amusement parks. Surprisingly, even though teenaged girls spend an enormous amount of time in malls, they have the lowest conversion rate—of the percentage of people who buy something, they are the lowest of all demographic groups visiting malls (Underhill 2004). Nonetheless, teenaged girls represent a powerhouse of spending and shopping, and are future adult consumers of material goods.

Adult women also like the social aspects of the mall, but social opportunities are secondary to purchasing goods and services. Indeed, women have always been the targeted consumers. Women have historically shopped to provide for their households while men earned wages. Today, as wage earners, they have more disposable income for making purchases and more independence to make these purchases on their own. However, none of this explains why women *like* to shop more than men, unless we want to return to the "woman the gatherer" hypothesis.

Miller (2001) found that shopping and purchasing is determined to an extent by the consumers' ethnic, political, and ethical identity. For example, consumers may refuse to purchase products known to be manufactured in so-called sweatshops. Taste or choice in purchases may also be determined by various identities, such as class, age, gender, and ethnicity, although Miller found that choices are often influenced by familial relationships: for example, the choices parents made in the past may influence the choices their children will make.

Stratification of shoppers is readily evident in malls. Mall "rats" and mall "junkies" are two identifiable microcultures. Mall junkies are always at the mall; these young people do not shop so much as "hang out." Mall rats, who are usually teenagers, visit the mall quite often and are more likely to purchase merchandise or participate in some of the activities while there. Consequently, store owners are constantly challenged to renew merchandise for these shoppers (Underhill 2004).

There is little doubt that mall operators like to encourage certain types of customers (e.g., middle-class families, professionals, teenagers with credit cards), and discourage others, (e.g., gang members, vagrants, or the poor). Malls are filled with people of similar class, drawn together in a community of shoppers. Yet even this seeming homogeneity is an illusion; a cross-section of diverse ethnic groups, age categories, and socioeconomic status is evident in most large malls, perhaps more so than in neighbourhood shopping centres that cater to distinct classes of similar age and economic situations.

Aesthetics send messages regarding the expected clientele. Malls with marble flooring, glass and chrome elevators, bright lights, and soothing music, and stores such as Versace, Victoria's Secret, and Saks are catering to the middle and upper classes, while malls with Wal-Mart and Dollar Stores are frequented by people looking for lower-cost merchandise. In Shanghai, China, modern shopping malls are beautiful, enticing buildings. These malls are for the rich, and they stand in sharp contrast to small stalls in local markets where many locals and tourists search for low-cost merchandise.

However, according to Underhill (2004) the mall era is in decline—it is no longer the defining concept of retail activity. Amazon.com, eBay, and other Internet shopping sites have had an impact on mall shopping. Online shopping will likely continue as consumer demand increases, expanding into smaller establishments with worldwide customers. Still, online shopping does little to satisfy the social aspects of shopping. Mall owners can counter this decline by considering further anthropological research into the meaning of shopping and the ways they can ensure that shoppers will find the shopping-mall experience worthwhile.

TRANSNATIONAL CONFIGURATION AND SHOPPING

According to Sunderland and Denny (2007), consumer ethnography has grown in the past 20 years to the point where companies hire ethnographers to incorporate ethnographic data into their qualitative consumer research. Sunderland and Denny see consumer ethnography as a way to take the ordinary and make it extraordinary by using cultural analysis. The value of ethnography is thus not in its methods (e.g., participant observation) but in the cultural approach and analysis of consumer behaviour.

Purnima Mankekar (2002) undertook a study of objects on display and social spaces created in Indian grocery stores in the San Francisco Bay area as part of an ethnographic study of transnationality. Mankekar used a cultural approach and analysis in order to understand the production and consumption of commodities that facilitate the construction of Indian culture in this community.

Mankekar concluded that these grocery stores play a pivotal role in the transnational circulation of commodities between India and the diaspora. Through a combination of ambiance, products on display, images, and discourse, an "India" familiar to the consumers has been constructed. Indian immigrants visit these stores to purchase products familiar to them, but the stores are also social spaces and sites of Indian cultural production. The stores cater to Indians from diverse classes, ethnic backgrounds, and regions of origin in India. Shoppers consume the products and atmosphere of these stores, though not without contested emotions that range from nostalgia to ambivalence to antagonism. Therefore, these stores are complex social spaces or sites of public culture that are reflected through the objects and products sold in the stores and consumed by the customers.

> According to one shopper, "Oh, people don't just come here to buy groceries. They come for the whole package. They come for India shopping."
> Mankekar (2002: 80)

Daniel Miller (1995b: 277) points out that "consumption is a use of goods and services in which the object or activity becomes simultaneously a practice in the world and a form in which we construct our understandings of ourselves in the world." The Indian grocery stores, then, are markers of ethnicity and Indian culture. The stores allow Indian communities to represent themselves to the larger community, providing space for Indians to gather and create social networks. The products in the grocery stores "create the images by which we understand who we have been, who we are, and who we might or should be in the future" (Miller 1995a: 35). In other words, the stores provide discourse on home, family, community, nation, and gender identity. The Indian grocery stores are sites of Indian cultural production outside of India and have become a crucial node in the transnational circulation and consumption of commodities and discussion about India (Mankekar 2002: 92).

CONCLUSION

Anthropologists are often asked, "Of what use is anthropology in the business world?" Applied economic anthropology and its subfields of corporate/business and retail/consumer anthropology are growing fields of research in the commercial world. Anthropology's value lies in the first-hand information generated through ethnographic research methods, including participant observation at the community level, and the cultural analysis of this data. These ethnographers have a great deal to offer businesses, corporations, and retailers as they endeavour to understand consumers better.

To demonstrate the importance of consumer experience in economic life, shopping is portrayed as an important and meaningful human activity. Regardless of how people choose to perform this activity, the impact on the ever-evolving consumer culture and the economic well-being of societies should not be discounted. Applied retail anthropology has a significant role to play in improving the quality of shopping experiences, and the economic viability of commercial districts. Although on the surface malls appear fairly straightforward, further examination through the eyes of an applied retail anthropologist such as Paco Underhill suggests that malls are complex socio-economic systems that perform many roles in contemporary society and, despite their waning popularity, will continue to do so for years to come.

Some economic anthropologists are also conducting ethnographic research into the needs of ethnic populations within the context of economic life. Indian grocery stores, as an example, are social places where Indian identity is on display and consumed by shoppers, even as it is contested in some ways. This research has long term implications for the development of commercial enterprises that serve immigrant populations.

The goal of anthropology is to understand humans, in all their variation. From an applied perspective, this information is then used to solve or mitigate problems. Applied economic anthropologists use critical thinking to question long-held assumptions in the business world, by describing and analysing real-time, observed behaviour. Convincing corporations and businesses that anthropology has anything to offer has been a long road, but in recent decades the efficacy of anthropology has become more apparent and the field looks to expand in the future.

QUESTIONS FOR CONSIDERATION AND CLASSROOM ACTIVITIES

1. When you enter a shopping mall, what factors influence your shopping patterns? Do you head to the shops with the best bargains, the nicest displays, the most selection, or are you selectively searching for a particular store to buy an already identified product? Do you like shopping in malls or prefer small, independent stores?

2. Does the availability of other entertainment besides shopping entice you to certain malls? What factors create a positive shopping experience for you, and what factors create a negative experience? Do you use the mall as a social outlet? Why or why not?

3. Analyse your patronage of shopping malls. How have your patterns of shopping behaviour changed as you've grown older? Do you visit malls to the same extent as when you were younger or have you changed your preferences? Identify the reasons for your changing shopping patterns.

4. Develop a retail anthropology research project. Choose a store in a mall and describe the layout and use of floor space. Observe customers entering and leaving the store; describe their shopping behaviour. Is the store well organized

and the merchandise easily accessible? Are the window displays appealing or distracting? Analyse the success (or failure) of this mall in meeting the expectations and needs of its consumers.

SUGGESTED READINGS

Miller, D., & Woodward, S. (2012). *Blue jeans. The art of the ordinary.* **Berkeley and Los Angeles, CA: University of California Press.**

Daniel Miller presents a cultural analysis of the meaning of ordinary, using ethnography to ask why people wear blue jeans.

Sunderland, P.L., & Denny, R.M. (2007). *Doing anthropology in consumer research.* **Walnut Creek, CA: Left Coast Press. www.lcoastpress.com/book_get_file. php?id=116&type=excerpt**

This easy-to-read book brings to light the new order of anthropology— consumer ethnography. Sunderland and Denny offer a mix of theory and applied practice while examining consumer environments. The case studies range from coffee in Bangkok and boredom in New Zealand to computing in the United States. Of particular value is the blurring of lines between applied and academic anthropology, showing how this artificial divide is no longer acceptable.

Underhill, P. (2004). *Call of the mall.* **New York: Simon & Schuster.**

Underhill provides an entertaining and enlightening discussion of the significance of mall shopping, with a minimum of academic jargon. He also provides many examples to highlight his points about use of public space and consumer behaviour.

Chapter 3

WHAT ROLES DO ANTHROPOLOGISTS AND SPEECH COMMUNITIES PLAY IN LANGUAGE RETENTION AND REVITALIZATION?

Key Terms: applied linguistic anthropology, endangered languages, heritage languages, language, language isolates, language loss, language nests, language retention and revitalization, language shift, linguicism, linguistic anthropology, linguistic diversity, linguistic homogenization, linguistics, norms, speech community

INTRODUCTION

If we were to choose one characteristic that separates humans from other animals, it would be complex language. **Language** is communicating with sounds or gestures that are organized in meaningful ways, according to a set of rules. We transmit information and share our lived experiences with others through language. Language, then, provides a medium for expressing our ideas and concerns, beliefs and values, and is vital to our cultural integrity and identity. In other words, language is an essential cultural marker, one that defines who we are, where we come from, and how we view the world around us.

The study of language is important to anthropologists since language transmits culture from one person to another and from one generation to the next. The modern scientific study of language is known as **linguistics**. **Linguistic anthropologists** explore the way humans use language to create, practise, and transmit culture, and the way members of a **speech community** use language to form social relationships.

However, **linguistic diversity** is threatened the world over. Of the 6,000–7,000 languages still surviving in the early years of the twenty-first century, at least half of them are considered endangered. Ostler (2001) estimates that a language is lost every two weeks. Indeed, some linguists predict that by the end of the twenty-first century 90 per cent of human languages may be lost (Krauss 1992: 7.). Languages disappear because of population loss and language shift. The loss of languages and their vocabularies is a form of cultural impoverishment; communities are

"Linguistic diversity is one of the most important parts of our human heritage." Linguistic anthropologist K. David Harrison, quoted in Munro (2012: n.p.)

deprived of their historical connections, cultural and environmental knowledge, and human experience. Speech communities lose their unique identity, artistic expression, and the world view attached to their language.

The loss of linguistic diversity is of great concern to linguists. In this chapter we will examine this global phenomenon from a linguistic and anthropological perspective, focusing on **language retention and revitalization. Applied linguistic anthropologists**, in collaboration with other linguists and funding bodies, such as *National Geographic*, have launched programs to save or at least record and preserve many endangered languages. Questions addressed in this chapter include the following: What do we lose when a language disappears? What processes cause languages to fade and disappear? What are linguists doing to mitigate language loss? We will investigate why some language revitalization projects are more successful than others by examining the Maori, Irish Gaelic, Hebrew, and Basque revitalization projects.

ANTHROPOLOGISTS AND LANGUAGE REVITALIZATION

Linguistic anthropologists are committed to helping communities revitalize their languages. Indeed, linguistic anthropologists such as Anvita Abbi have been involved in numerous preservation and revitalization programs. Abbi served as investigator/director of a major documentation project called *Vanishing Voices of the Great Andamanese*. The Great Andamanese people of the Andaman Islands in the Indian Ocean speak a language that no one else in the world speaks, a language that may be one of the few surviving Paleolithic languages (VOGA n.d.).

"Take [language] away from the culture, and you take away its greetings, its curses, its praises, its laws, its literature, its songs, its riddles, its proverbs, its cures, its wisdom, its prayers ... . You are losing all those things that essentially are the way of life, the way of thought, the way of valuing, and the human reality." Fishman (1996: 81)

As recently as the early eighteenth century, the Great Andamanese spoke 10 dialects, but then the people adopted a corrupted form of Hindi that gradually replaced Great Andamanese. Today, Great Andamanese is an **endangered language** with only seven speakers remaining, and even they tend to use a mixed language in everyday conversation. In attempts to restore the language, Abbi and her colleagues compiled a 5,000-word trilingual dictionary with translations in English and Hindi, a comprehensive grammar, and extensive video and audio recordings of narratives, songs, etc. Research during this documentation project confirmed that Great Andamanese is the fifth language family of India (Abbi 2009).[1] Abbi and her team also collected oral histories, photos of local habitats, and sociolinguistic sketches representing local beliefs and knowledge of the biodiversity of the islands. These preservation activities are important according to linguistic anthropologist K. David Harrison since

---

1 Genetic studies have confirmed this hypothesis. Besides the four recognized original language families of India—Indo-Aryan, Dravidian, Tibeto-Burman, and Austro-Asiatic—all other Indian languages were classified as "Other" until this discovery.

losing a language causes an erosion of cultural knowledge about local plant and animal life: "information about local ecosystems is so intricately woven into these languages that it cannot be replaced simply through translation" (Swarthmore News 2012: n.p.). Harrison reiterates the concerns of many linguistic anthropologists that abandoning indigenous or **heritage languages** initiates a massive loss of knowledge and culture. To that end, Harrison has documented little-known Turkic languages, including Tuvan, Monchak Tsenggel Tuva, Tofa, Ös, and Tuha in central Siberia and western Mongolia (Munro 2012).

Although globalization processes are often blamed for language loss, in some cases communities and language activists, including linguistic anthropologists, are using web-based technology to save endangered languages. Bud Lane III is one of the last surviving speakers of Siletz-Dee-ni, an indigenous language in a small community in Oregon (Munro 2012). Siletz-Dee-ni began to decline in the mid-1850s when several cultural groups, speaking different languages and dialects, were placed on the same reservation. To communicate, they began speaking a Chinook jargon that displaced Siletz-Dee-ni. Fortunately, this language has been immortalized on a "talking dictionary" using Lane's own voice. This talking dictionary now contains 14,000 words and, with the language on the Internet, young people in the community are beginning to learn the language once again—they even text in Siletz-Dee-ni. Other communities with endangered languages are also embracing social media—YouTube, text messaging, and websites—as a vehicle for saving their languages. For example, Microsoft programs have been translated into Inuktitut for the Inuit.

> "Endangered language communities are adopting digital technology to aid their survival and to make their voices heard around the world. This is a positive effect of globalization." K. David Harrison, quoted in Gray (2012)

National Geographic and linguistic anthropologists Harrison and Anderson have launched the *Enduring Voices* project, which to date has created eight talking dictionaries with 32,000 word entries and more than 24,000 audio recordings from native speakers. One of the best-documented languages is Tuvan, spoken in Siberia and Mongolia, with over 7,000 dictionary entries, 3,000 audio files, and 49 images. Even the Matukar Panau community in Papua New Guinea, which has approximately 600 speakers, knew about the Internet and requested that their language be put on the Web, despite not having electricity in their community. Harrison and his team helped them create a talking dictionary (Messieh 2012). Harrison believes that going global with a language sends a powerful message of pride throughout the speech community, and provides heritage languages with increased status and prestige in the global linguistic community. Speakers, especially the young, learn that their heritage language is as good as any other language, including English (Munro 2012).

THE NATURE OF LANGUAGE LOSS AND REVITALIZATION

In the fifteenth century, there were approximately 15,000 extant languages, but wars and ethnic conflicts, genocide, government bans on languages, and colonial expansion and assimilation agendas destroyed half of these languages in the next five centuries (Sampat 2002). **Language loss** continues today at an alarming rate: of the 250 indigenous languages spoken in Australia, 90 per cent are nearing extinction; many South American languages disappeared following the Spanish conquest; in Africa, 200 languages are endangered; and more than half of the indigenous languages in Asia have fewer than 10,000 speakers (Sampat 2002). In Europe, language loss is very much a reality. Colonialist policies caused Manx, once spoken on the Isle of Man, to become

"Our language has been ripped from the world, stripped of shape, smell, color and form, cleansed of the grit and graffiti, the rumpus and commotion that make up real life." Goenawan Mohamad, founding editor of the Jakarta-based *Tempo* newsmagazine, quoted in Goswami (2003: n.p.)

extinct in 1974, when its last speaker died. However, the language's demise was overstated, and today Manx is undergoing a revival, partly because the language was well recorded. On a less positive note, Ubykh, a language spoken in the Caucasus region that had the highest number of consonants ever recorded, disappeared when Turkish farmer Tefvik Esenç died in 1992 (Haspelmath 1993). One of the Celtic languages, Cornish, began its decline at the end of the nineteenth century. Several attempts to renew the language failed until 1995 when a new version of United Cornish was developed, and an English-Cornish dictionary was created in 2000 (Binion & Shook 2007).

In Asia, globalization has posed a challenge to many languages (Goswami 2003). According to Dr. Rujaya Abhakorn, historian at Chiang Mai University in Thailand, people in Southeast Asia consider English their path to economic success. The region possesses the greatest linguistic diversity on that side of the world; however, many languages have become extinct. The Tibeto-Burman language Pyu, spoken in Myanmar, is one example, as is Rangkas, a Western Himalayan language that survived into the twentieth century before dying out (van Driem 2007). Linguists speculate that it is English, the dominant language of economy and the Internet, that represents the greatest threat to other languages.

The process of language loss and shift in Asia is particularly prevalent among **language isolates**, which are "languages that have not been demonstrated to belong to any other major language family or linguistic phylum" (van Driem 2007: 305). Great Andamanese, reviewed earlier, is an example of a language isolate, as is the Vedda language in Sri Lanka. Ryklof van Goens recorded this language in 1675, after which most Veddas became assimilated into Tamil- and Sinhalese-speaking populations, through intermarriage, government acculturation policies, and linguistic shift. Whether this language is completely extinct is unknown.

In North America and South America the situation is dire for indigenous languages. Only two of the 20 native Alaskan languages, Central Alaskan Yupik and Siberian Yupik, are still taught to children, meaning all of the others will disappear when the adult speakers die. Fifty of 300 Central American languages and 110 of 400 South American languages are considered moribund, or no longer sustainable (Krauss n.d.). Efforts to revitalize these languages are ongoing, but with differing degrees of success. Indigenous peoples in Canada are divided into three groups: First Nations, Inuit, and Métis. First Nations peoples speak languages that belong to 10 different families. Linguists estimate that somewhere between 300 and 500 First Nations languages were spoken before Europeans arrived in North America. Two hundred of these languages remain, although First Nations children learn only 34 of them as first languages (Krauss 1998). Indigenous languages in Canada are fragile, the only exceptions being Cree and Ojibwa in the Algonquian language family and Inuktitut in the Aleut-Eskimo language family. Even these vibrant languages are in decline as youth increasingly turn to English.

Since language is so important to cultural and personal identity, the indigenous peoples of Canada worry that the nineteenth-century colonialist government assimilation policies may become a reality in the twenty-first century (Haviland, Fedorak, & Lee 2009). Revitalizing indigenous languages in Canada is difficult because many linguistic enclaves are surrounded by English- or French-speaking people. Nonetheless, indigenous language curricula, educational programs, a national policy on indigenous languages, and a recent renewal of passion for heritage languages among some youth offer hope.

"When I was in school, we were beaten for speaking our language. They wanted to make us ashamed ... I have 17- and 18-year-old kids coming to me crying because the elders of their tribes won't teach them their own language." Marie Smith Jones, a full-blooded Alaskan Eyak, quoted in Raymond (1998: n.p.)

As mentioned earlier, when a language disappears, so does a great deal of cultural knowledge. In central Siberia, Ket is an endangered language with less than 200 speakers in the upper Yenisei Valley. Ket has one of the most complex grammars ever documented by linguists, and the language "is filled with living links to their ancestors, their past, and their traditions" (Solash 2010: n.p.). A Russian-only linguistic policy during the Soviet era led to the demise of this unique language. The impact of losing Ket is incalculable, including for sciences like anthropology; early studies suggest that Ket may be related to Navajo. If this theory proves accurate, then Ket substantiates the theory of prehistoric migration from Asia to North America, and extends the prevailing estimates of the scale of these human migrations.

A dominant language is unlikely to become extinct, regardless of the number of speakers; however, it can happen. For example, Icelandic has 250,000 speakers and although not considered in imminent danger, even this language is threatened by the increasing use of English. On the other hand, Breton, formerly with a million speakers but now with approximately half that number (Ethnologue 2012), is struggling to survive following decades of suppression by the French government (Krauss n.d.). Navajo, an indigenous language of the southwestern United States, was thriving in the 1960s with 200,000 speakers, but began to decline when the United States Bureau of Indian Affairs imposed English as the first language (Krauss n.d.). Even the primary languages

---

FIGURE 3.1 SCALE FOR THREATENED LANGUAGES[a]

Stage One: Spoken within national government and in higher education.

Stage Two: Spoken at the local government level, and used by media in the community.

Stage Three: Spoken in business arenas and by employees in less specialized work areas.

Stage Four: Language of instruction in elementary schools.

Stage Five: Language still spoken in the community.

Stage Six: Spoken between generations, e.g., grandparents and grandchildren.

Stage Seven: Adults of second generation speak the language; their children do not.

Stage Eight: Only a few elders speak the language.

---

a Based on an adaptation of Fishman's scale.

---

of the world are not safe from decline. According to Černý (2010), German and Italian could be reduced by 10 per cent in the next 50 years, and Russian will also lose speakers because of the recent independence of former Soviet republics. However, Spanish and Portuguese will continue to grow as their populations grow in Europe and Latin America. Although France's population has peaked, French is still prestigious and the country remains an economic, cultural, and military powerhouse; its strength outside France, though, for example in Canada and former French colonies, is open to question. As for English, no language rules forever.

> "You deal with it by speaking English, and that way you don't have to face the hurt of the loss ... you hide behind the language of the dominant society for a while."
> A Cree informant quoted in Kouritzen (1999: 66–67)

Anthropologist Joshua Fishman (1991: 88–91) identified eight stages through which a language passes on its way to extinction (see Figure 3.1). Language activists, with the assistance of linguists, have developed strategies to protect and promote languages in all of these stages.

As suggested by Figure 3.1, reasons for language loss are complex, but various internal and external factors reduce language use until it disappears. At the most basic level, if fewer and fewer young people are learning their heritage language each generation, it becomes moribund and then dies. In fact, a measure of the health of a heritage language is whether the children are being taught their language at home. The second internal issue is the notion foisted on members of speech communities, especially children in school, that their language is inferior. They are shamed into speaking the dominant language and coerced into rejecting their own language. Language activists often draw attention to the social inequalities and human rights abuses at the root of this treatment. Therefore, internal socio-political factors, such as seeking social acceptance and inclusion, conforming to

norms of mainstream society, and the necessity of communicating with peers may lead to rejection of a heritage language and a shift to the dominant language.

External factors also contribute to language loss. Earthquakes, floods, and other natural disasters can destroy a small speech community, as can drought and other environmental disasters that force people to move away, likely into an area with a different, often more dominant, language (Černý 2010). For example, in Kuala Lumpur, Malaysia, migration patterns made the Sindhis a linguistic minority and resulted in their having to learn English (Khemlani-David 1991).

Mass media, heavily loaded with English, presents an ideal picture of English-speaking life that spurs indigenous peoples, especially the youth, to abandon their way of life and their heritage languages (Ostler 2001). This immersion in English media plays a powerful role in weakening heritage languages. As discussed later, linguists often encourage the development of local media, such as television programming, to help heritage languages gain visibility and prestige.

Language suppression is one of the ways in which states overpower minority cultures. An historical example is the Nazi German attempt to destroy the Slovene culture by demanding the surrender of all Slovene books, even prayer books (Lemkin 1944: 244, quoted in Jacobs 2005: 425). In the United States, powerful political and social processes promote English to the detriment of other languages: "To be American, one must speak English" (Fillmore 2000: 207). Speaking English represents social acceptance, loyalty to the American ideal, and economic opportunity. This creates an unbalanced contact situation where one group dominates politically, militarily, economically, or religiously (Yamamoto, Brenzinger, & Villalón 2008). In Canada, in the early twentieth century, First Nations children were forcefully removed from their homes and families and enrolled in residential schools by the colonial government. At these schools indigenous languages were forbidden, and children who spoke their heritage language were physically punished. In the mid-twentieth century the government changed its assimilationist policies, and by the 1970s, First Nations children could attend band-operated schools with instruction in their traditional indigenous language. Not only states but also religious institutions can foster cultural and linguistic genocide (Jacobs 2005: 426). For example, missionaries set out to eliminate the Koorie languages of Australia in order to more easily convert them to Christianity. If the Koories spoke their language they were beaten and not given any food as punishment. Destroying the Koorie languages meant that their liturgy, initiation, and ceremony also suffered (Fesl 1993: 83, quoted in Jacobs 2005: 426). Indeed, this process is not only historical; for example, more recently missionaries have contacted the Huaorani indigenous people in Ecuador, to send their children to school in Spanish (Ostler 2001).

People choose to speak one language over another based on social, economic, and political factors; this causes **language shift**, which means that speakers are turning away from their heritage language and adopting another language, either by force or voluntarily (Nettle & Romaine 2000). Giving up a heritage language will eventually lead to its extinction. Class, status, ethnicity, and outside influences, such as media

MAP 3.1 GAELTACHT REGION OF IRELAND

and education, affect language and influence language shifts. For example, in Mexico, Spanish is most closely identified with literacy and academics (Francis & Nieto Andrade 1996: 167) and ultimately higher class. In a colonization situation, the smaller culture invariably must accommodate the dominant culture, and this is when language shift will most likely take place.

Irish Gaelic, also known as Erse, is an Indo-European language with an ancient history that has suffered drastic decline due to language shift. The shift began in the seventeenth century when Ireland was conquered by British forces (Laukaitis 2010) and English became the language of power. Irish Gaelic continued its decline during the Great Famine (1845–52), when poor economic conditions forced many to migrate to English-speaking countries in search of work. This led parents to encourage their children to learn English in the hopes of future employment. Irish soon became stigmatized as the language of the poor. The Gaelic League was formed in 1893 to address the persistent decline of Irish Gaelic. The League began promoting Gaelic in the context of national unity. However, by 1901 only 14 per cent of the population could still speak Irish Gaelic (McMahon 2008).

The goal of the Gaelic League was to de-Anglicize Ireland (Laukaitis 2010), and the political underpinnings of this campaign demonized England and uplifted Ireland to create a nationalistic consciousness. As the twentieth century progressed, nationalism grew, and the Legion was able to establish Irish in schools. Unfortunately, their efforts were doomed because of the status and prestige English had acquired. Parents, leaders, and the Catholic priests all approved of and promoted English. Without the community's support Irish Gaelic could not flourish. Today, less than 10 per cent of Irish are fluent in Gaelic (GaelicMatters.com 2011); however, immersion courses are being established that may improve the position of Irish Gaelic in the future.

LANGUAGE PRESERVATION AND REVITALIZATION

Ostler (2001) estimates that a language is lost every two weeks. To be "safe," a language needs state support and a large number of speakers, as well as children learning the language at home. Linguistic anthropologist Akira Yamamoto (1998) identified nine factors that can help save a language, including the need for speakers to possess a strong sense of ethnic identity, bilingual educational programs in the schools, and environments where speaking a heritage language is encouraged by teachers, parents, and community leaders (Ottenheimer 2009). In this environment, the dominant culture must support linguistic diversity or any attempts to rejuvenate and protect a language are doomed. UNESCO has played a vital role in mobilizing worldwide efforts and attention to save endangered languages (Gallegos, Murray, & Evans 2010). In 2001 the organization adopted the Universal Declaration of Cultural Diversity, calling on a participatory and collaborative approach to the documentation, maintenance, and revitalization of languages.

When the Māori language, te reo Māori, was in danger of extinction more than 30 years ago, elders and other community members developed immersion programs called *Te Kohanga reo*, which means language nests. **Language nests** are immersion programs that teach very young children their heritage languages. Elders are teamed with young people to form these nests (Reyhner 1999). Language nests have become role models for indigenous language revitalization programs around the world. These community-based

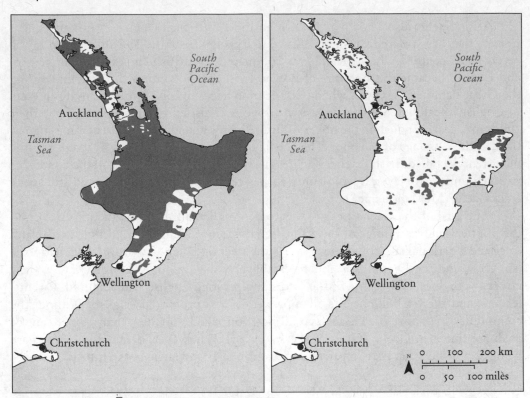

MAP 3.2A AND 3.2B MĀORI TERRITORY IN 1860 AND 2000

immersion education programs were key to the te reo Māori language's survival. Today, te reo Māori is in stage one of Fishman's eight-stage classification system, with 150,000 speakers (Gallegos, Murray, & Evans 2010). However, this was not always the case.

By the mid-1800s, in order to acculturate the Māori people, the colonialist government established English as the dominant language in New Zealand and the language that would be used in British schools. Te reo Māori was banned in schools as early as 1905. The Māori accepted this move, seeing English as a means to economic opportunity. Urbanization in World War II also eroded the Māori culture and furthered the decline of the Māori language. Consequently, by the 1980s te reo Māori was on the brink of diglossia, with English having become the privileged language (Gallegos, Murray, & Evans 2010). Māori people, especially the youth, had grown ashamed of their language, believing it was lower class and uncouth. By 1985, only 12 per cent of the Māori could speak te reo Māori.

In 1985, the Māori Language Board of Wellington filed a Treaty claim asking for te reo Māori to be declared an official language of Aotearoa, New Zealand. Their request was granted in 1986, and the Māori Language Act of 1987 established a Māori Language Commission to develop language policies and to assist in the revitalization

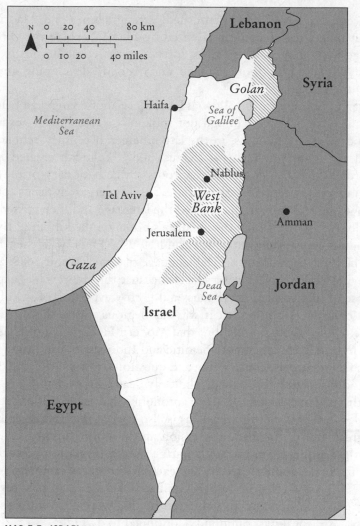

MAP 3.3 ISRAEL

of the language (Gallegos, Murray, & Evans 2010). The 1987 Act placed te reo Māori on an even par with English, which went a long way toward increasing the status of the language. The Māori people established hundreds of nursery schools, kindergartens, and day-care language nests with their own curriculum and teaching consistent with Māori values. All subjects in the school are taught in te reo Māori, and the schools maintain close ties with families and community. Today, the New Zealand government funds the language schools at the elementary and secondary levels.

Although the immersion programs have been a resounding success and the Māori children are thriving, all those involved recognize that in order for te reo Māori to flourish, the entire family and community must remain involved. To that end, Māori television programs have been established, strengthening the Māori voice.[2] The language-nest model has since been adopted by Hawaii, where they created Pünana Leo (language nest) immersion schools. First Nations communities in Canada have followed suit, with the Blackfoot, Arapaho, and Mohawk developing similar programs (Out of the Jungle 2006).

An amazing success story follows Hebrew, a Semitic language belonging to the Afro-Asiatic language family. Though not spoken for 1,500 years,[3] except in liturgical rituals and scholarly pursuits, in the late nineteenth century scholar Eliezer Ben Yehudah led the revival of Hebrew (Krauss n.d.). Yehudah created 4,000 modern Hebrew words based on ancient Hebrew roots and a dictionary of the language, beginning with carpentry terms for the parents and kindergarten terms for the children (Fishman 1996: 89). A few teachers learned the language and then passed it on to their students, who lived with them in the children's home on the kibbutz.[4] By 1916, 40 per cent of the adults and 75 per cent of the children used Hebrew as their first language, and in 1921 Hebrew became the official language of Israel (Nahir 1988: 289).

This revitalization project was a success because the Hebrew language gave Jewish people a sense of unified identity (Krauss n.d.). However, the revival of Hebrew was not without controversy; some felt it was sacrilegious to use the sacred language in everyday life, while others pointed out that Modern Hebrew is not Classical Hebrew but rather a hybrid language of both Semitic and Indo-European origin (Zuckermann & Walsh 2011). Despite the controversy and questions of true origin, Modern Hebrew remains the only successfully revived "clinically dead" language.

As with the Israelis, struggles for autonomy and international recognition are often struggles for linguistic survival. This is also true of the Basque people, who have endured a great deal of linguistic repression and political suppression. Euskera, the language of the Basques, is an ancient language isolate, thousands of years old, though it was used only in the domestic sphere and excluded from government, administration, and religion (López-Goñi 2003). Despite calls for reviving Euskera throughout the nineteenth and twentieth centuries, the Basque-speaking community continued to dwindle.

"Every people has a right to their own language, to preserve it as a cultural resource and to transmit it to their children." Nettle and Romaine (2000: 14)

During the rule of Franco (1892–1975), Euskera was labelled vulgar, barbaric, uncouth, and animalistic, which shamed the Basque people. Only Castilian Spanish was allowed outside the home—Basque names could not even be placed on tombstones (López-Goñi 2003). This is a classic case of linguistic discrimination or **linguicism**—forbidding the use of a language and/or the intentional destruction of a language (Jacobs 2005: 424). In a backlash to this repression, the Basque people united around their language and it became a symbol of Basque identity (Krauss n.d.).

---

2 There are other precedents for this action. Egyptian Arabic is understood by Arabic-speaking people in other countries because movies and television programs are produced in Egypt, using Egyptian Arabic.

3 The number of years since Hebrew was last spoken varies widely, depending on the source.

4 In the Israeli kibbutzim, children do not live with their parents, but rather in an age-grade dormitory with caregivers/teachers.

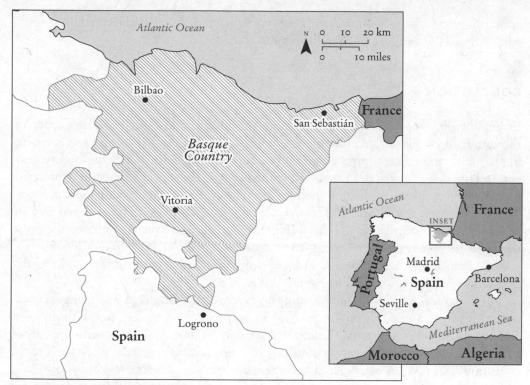

MAP 3.4 BASQUE-SPEAKING TERRITORIES

Euskera provided the people with a platform from which to demand their rights to a cultural and linguistic identity (López-Goñi 2003: 671) as well as ideological and political freedom.

The role of education in language survival should not be underestimated. The Basque people wanted to reinstate Euskera as a living language with national status. *Ikastolas*, which are community-based schools, played a key role in revitalizing Euskera. Under Franco, Basque was outlawed and the schools disappeared, only to be revived in the 1960s. These semi-clandestine schools became a haven for Basque people, creating a cultural space that supported their language (Fishman 1996: 89). Parents enrolled their children in *ikastolas* because of the identity they gained through the Basque language and because they did not want their children to endure the Franco-era schooling they had endured (López-Goñi 2003).

"To choose to use a language is an act of identity or belonging to a particular community. We believe the choice to be who one wishes to be is a human right." Nettle & Romaine (2000: 174)

Today, *ikastolas* are mixed infant schools set up in local villages. In some of these schools children are taught in Basque, while in others they are taught Basque itself. *Ikastolas* became a symbol of Basque nationality and a social microcosm. The schools are run by parents, with assistance from young people, community members, and teachers. Thus, participation of community members in the education of their children helped revive Euskera.

CONCLUSION

Fishman (1996: 82) calls language the mind, the soul, and the spirit of the people. Yet thousands of languages are in imminent danger of extinction. Protecting and revitalizing heritage languages requires community effort—parents, teachers, community leaders, and linguists all need to be involved in the process. Parents are extremely important in supporting and strengthening their children's heritage language skills in the home. This reinforcement will help children retain their language even as they learn English at school, and after they leave school (Fillmore 2000). The prestige of a language also needs to be enhanced by teaching it in schools or using it in public spaces such as government offices and churches. These actions all increase the visibility and prestige of a language (Yamamoto, Brenzinger, & Villalón 2008: 61).

The responsibilities of documenting and recording a language, and using technology to disperse it (e.g., through television programs and websites), lies with linguists and linguistic anthropologists (Krauss n.d.). Globalization and homogenizing forces, including English-only education policies, are a serious challenge to linguists and to the communities in which endangered languages are spoken. The revitalization of Gaelic was not a success because the community felt English would be of more benefit for their children, whereas Euskera, te reo Māori, and Hebrew revitalization projects were successful because they symbolized national identity.

Language loss and the ensuing **linguistic homogenization** are part of a global process, fuelled by increased economic transactions, communications, and transportation systems rooted in dominant world languages, at the sacrifice of heritage languages and linguistic diversity. This is a loss for us all. The human species needs linguistic diversity as much as biological diversity, because languages express identity, are repositories of history, and preserve millions of years of accumulated knowledge.

QUESTIONS FOR CONSIDERATION AND CLASSROOM ACTIVITIES

1. Do you speak a heritage language? In your opinion, how important is speaking a mother tongue? Explain your answer.
2. "Speak English!" seems to have become a crusade for some Canadians. How would you feel if people in your adoptive country treated you with disrespect because you had not learned their language yet? What impact would their insistence that you give up your native language and speak only their language have on your sense of well-being and identity?

3. There has been some controversy regarding language revitalization projects. Critics suggest that if there was only one world language, there would be more unity and communication between nations, and commerce would flow more freely. What would we lose and what would we gain if we had one world language? Create a PowerPoint presentation highlighting the pros and cons.
4. Trace the history of a dominant language. Now trace the history of an isolate. How are they different; how are they the same?

SUGGESTED READINGS

Crystal, D. (2000). *Language death.* Cambridge: Cambridge University Press. http://dx.doi.org/10.1017/CBO9781139106856

David Crystal addresses the fundamental question, "Why is language death so important?" in a readable, concise analysis. He presents the crisis of endangered languages but also reviews the projects and programs being developed to preserve and revitalize endangered languages. One of the highlights of this book is the "personal" examination of languages that are dying and what this means to the communities.

Harrison, K.D. (2008). *When languages die: The extinction of the world's languages and the erosion of human knowledge.* Oxford: Oxford University Press.

K. David Harrison addresses what humans lose when a language is lost from a global perspective. Of particular relevance is the cultural and environmental knowledge that we lose. This book is enjoyable to read because of the anecdotes and portraits of the last remaining speakers of some of these languages. Up to date, it is a fascinating read.

Part Two

WHY DOES ANTHROPOLOGY MATTER?

Anthropology is a descriptive, explanatory, and issue-based discipline, allowing anthropologists to view culture from a fairly broad scope. In this section, we will examine several important issues that affect people and their cultural systems, as well as the roles anthropologists play in analysing and understanding these issues.

The nine chapters in Part Two focus on three general topics: the political nature of humans in ethnic conflict and NGOs; equality issues in *purdah*, female circumcision, and same-sex marriage; and transnational flow through social media, living abroad, body image, and human migration. Each of these chapters offers an in-depth examination of the issue from a holistic, cross-cultural, and multidisciplinary perspective. Cultural relativism and its antithesis, cultural imperialism, run through these discussions.

A growing demographic known as global nomads is the subject of Chapter 4, which deals with the effects of living and working in a foreign culture. This discussion is relevant to the millions of people who live, work, or study in a foreign environment. Third Culture Kids who attend international schools and interact with other children from myriad backgrounds are a major focus in this discussion. Culture is integrated; thus internal and external political organization can have a dramatic impact upon other components of a culture. This becomes evident in Chapter 5, as we investigate the implications of the ongoing conflict in Darfur, and the plight of Darfurian refugees.

In the next two chapters, humans as social beings are examined from several perspectives. First, our desire to project a certain image to gain status and security is investigated in Chapter 6. We will explore differing perceptions of beauty, the spreading of these perceptions to other parts of the world, and the political, cultural, and economic factors at work in modifying our bodies. In Chapter 7, the ancient custom of altering female genitalia in order for women to become more desirable and marriageable, and thereby gain a higher position within society, is examined. Western opposition to this practice and the obvious cultural imperialism at work is considered in some detail.

In Chapter 8, the interrelatedness of social norms, religious tenets, economic realities, and political manipulation regarding the contentious issue of same-sex marriage are addressed using three schools of thought. In Chapter 9, the influence of social media on our perceptions of the world around us, and its power to rouse people to political activism, is addressed using the Egyptian revolution as our case study. In Chapter 10, the political nature of human interaction and the impact that politics can have on the social, economic, and political dynamics of a cultural group are emphasized as we examine discrimination against immigrants in France, the sex trade in Thailand, and human trafficking.

The recurring themes of cultural imperialism and inequality arise once again in the final two chapters. In Chapter 11, we engage in a critical assessment of the true value and nature of NGOs. Chapter 12 explores the concept of oppression of women. The influence of religious beliefs on our lifestyle and behaviour is considered from a cross-cultural perspective.

These chapters reveal the work of anthropologists and provide a comprehensive discussion of each issue. As you will see, the relevance of anthropology becomes particularly evident when trying to comprehend such difficult subject matter, although in several instances, such as the study of social media, it is obvious that anthropologists must shift focus to become relevant to the discourse. Part Two is designed to show readers how anthropology matters—or could matter—in today's world, and how anthropology's role in understanding, mitigating, and sustaining cultural diversity will only increase in the coming years.

Chapter 4

HOW DO LIVING, STUDYING, AND WORKING IN A FOREIGN CULTURE AFFECT PEOPLE?

Key Terms: biculturalism, cosmopolitanism, cultural identity, culture, culture-bound, culture change, culture shock, enculturation, ethnoscapes, expatriates/expats, globalization, global nomads, reverse culture shock, rite of passage, sojourners, subculture, Third Culture Kids (TCKs), transcultural, transcultural literacy, transnational, transnational flow

---

INTRODUCTION

Nolan (1990: 2) defines **culture** as "a pattern of meaning, a way of defining the world" that enables humans to prosper. Each of us has a sense of the way things ought to be—this sense is deeply ingrained, and learned from birth through the process of **enculturation**. Our ideals, values, and beliefs generate acceptable behaviour in our cultural environment, but when we move to another cultural milieu, we leave behind our familiar world and enter one that operates under a different set of rules and expectations. In this new environment, we are no longer able to predict the behaviour of other people, and we no longer feel secure until we "learn" the new culture. This conceptualization of culture corresponds well with global nomads, since "culture" takes on new meanings for people living in a foreign country who do not own "roots" or a defined homeland. **Global nomads** are people who leave their passport or natal country and move to another country for economic, political, or experiential reasons. For global nomads, then, "home" may be fluid, constantly changing and existing in multiple places, and the concept of "culture" may become deterritorialized (King 1991).

These movements of people—what Appadurai (1991) calls **ethnoscapes**—have created a diaspora of dispersed persons in virtually every country in the world. In 2010, approximately 200 million people lived abroad (Just Landed 2009),[1] some as permanent residents, others as temporary **sojourners**. Global nomads are mainly missionaries, military personnel, professional or business people (e.g., oil executives, educators, and

---

1 Only estimates are available since most countries do not keep records on people who have moved out of a country. In 2009, 2.8 million Canadians lived abroad (CBC News 2009).

diplomats), and students in study-abroad[2] programs, who may live in several countries in their lifetime.

The experiences of global nomads, also known as **expatriates** (expats), often differ, depending on the reason why they moved to a foreign country, their economic circumstances, the countries they originate from, the countries they move to, and the length of time they live abroad. One of the most interesting phenomena to arise from global nomadism is **Third Culture Kids (TCKs)**, who are children or young people who have lived in one or more cultures outside their home country. These children have been largely invisible until recently; however, understanding the world through the eyes of a TCK is meaningful since most TCKs return to their passport country for university and have a great deal of international knowledge and skills to offer their community.

In this chapter we will explore the experience of global nomads when living in a foreign environment. Our focus will be on adult sojourners, students in study-abroad programs, and TCKs. We will examine the impact on their identity and world view from spending their formative years in a foreign environment, as well as their experiences with repatriating to their home country. Since anthropology is based on qualitative research, personal narratives from Adult Third Culture Kids (ATCKs) and TCKs are found throughout this chapter. In keeping with the multidisciplinary nature of anthropology, we will draw upon the expertise and insights of psychologists, theologians, educators, and sociologists as we explore twenty-first-century global nomads.

ANTHROPOLOGISTS AND LIVING ABROAD

Anthropologists have always been interested in cultural adaptation and **culture change**, and, most recently, globalization processes. **Globalization** refers to "social, economic, cultural, and demographic processes that take place within nations but also transcend them" (Basch, Glick Schiller, & Szanton-Blanc 1994). The migration of people from one country to another is a product of globalization, and anthropologists are uniquely qualified to explore this flow of people and cultural knowledge and, ultimately, the creation of **transcultural** and **transnational** identities (Kearney 1995). However, until recently the anthropological investigation of transnational processes has focused on immigrants moving from developing countries to developed countries. Global nomads who move from developed states to other countries have been largely ignored.

One reason for anthropology's neglect of global nomads and expatriate life may be the discipline's traditional emphasis on studying the exotic "Other" who live in isolated, distant localities and who practise traditional customs and rituals, rather than contemporary social and cultural trends in modern societies. In 1994, the American Anthropological Association predicted that anthropology would begin to place greater emphasis on the contemporary world and global change, become more interdisciplinary,

---

2 Retirees living in other countries are not discussed here. See Chapter 10 for a discussion of economic or political immigrants and refugees.

and begin to investigate comparative global perspectives, global interdependence, and internationalization (Kearney 1995). To some extent this is happening, although investigation of the *people* involved in processes of globalization, in this case global nomads, is still limited.

Nevertheless, several anthropologists have studied the everyday lives of adult expats living in a foreign country. For example, Anne-Meike Fechter (2007) conducted an ethnographic study of the relationship between expats and the local people living in Jakarta, Indonesia, that provided valuable insights, producing the first book-length ethnography on expats' experiences in her work *Transnational Lives*. During her fieldwork in Indonesia, Fechter determined that boundaries were far more important to expats, especially expat wives, than previously realized. These boundaries were erected to separate their orderly lives and the chaotic world around them—their houses versus the streets, Western food at home versus street vendors' fare, and, the expat "bubble" communities versus the city surrounding them. Fechter argues that the study of elite migration contradicts current transnationalism that emphasizes "global flows" and immersion in new cultural milieux.

Although much has been made of the melding of two or more cultures to create a third culture, like Fechter, others are not convinced that foreigners immerse themselves in their host culture or lose any of their "home" identity. Graduate student Nancy Thigpen (2010) investigated how expat teachers in Shanghai, China, construct boundaries around housing and social clubs, to separate themselves from the locals, both physically and socially. Thigpen determined that there is little interaction between expats and local people in their non-work lives. Work lives, then, may be the most significant avenue of interaction, as I noted while working at an international school in Egypt. At my school, social activities were organized to include both local and expat employees of the school, overtly encouraging interaction. Boundaries seemed most obvious between the support staff, who were all Egyptian, and the faculty, who were both Egyptian and foreign. In the work environment, Egyptian and foreign teachers interacted daily, sharing, supporting, collaborating, and socializing. Close friendships developed between many expat and local faculty. Students in this international school also interacted with each other regardless of ethnicity during the school day, especially in class; however, during breaks they tended to associate with their group or clique, which were often based on country of origin or ethnicity.

Anthropologist/sociologist Dr. Ruth Hill Useem conducted a pioneering study of Americans living and working in India in 1957 (Useem 1993). These Americans were foreign-service officers, business people, missionaries, aid workers, educators, and media reps. Useem found that despite the heterogeneity of American expats, they had enough commonalities to form a distinct **subculture** or third culture, different from their home culture or the host culture. During this research, Useem first applied the term Third Culture Kids to refer to children who accompany their parents abroad. Although Useem was referring to American TCKs, a growing body of evidence suggests that young people of other nationalities share the same characteristics and face the same dilemmas.

In the 1990s, a research project on TCKs, to which Useem was also a contributor, sought to uncover the positive contributions that TCKs make to their home communities, workplace, and society in general (Useem 1993). This study focused on adult TCKs living in the United States. Some of the questions asked in this study included the following: What happens to TCKs when they grow up? What skills, world views, and opinions do they bring from a third-culture childhood? How are they affected by having spent some or all of their child/teen years abroad? More recently, sociologists David C. Pollock and Ruth van Reken's pivotal book, *Third Culture Kids: The experience of growing up among worlds* (2009) has become a major source of information on TCKs. Indeed, many TCKs and Adult Third Culture Kids (ATCKs) consider this book a crucial resource as they attempt to understand their feelings and experiences, some even calling it their "bible." The study of TCKs is of paramount importance given that they are "uniquely suited for life in today's increasingly global society" (Bowman 2012: 1).

> "I have a continuing love affair with Third Culture Kids (TCKs). They are all my children because they carry my name. They are the most interesting people because their rich inner lives belie their often bland, dull, and sometimes wary, presentation of themselves to others." Useem (1993: 2)

THE NATURE OF LIVING ABROAD

Living abroad is a worldwide trend that is increasing at a phenomenal rate. Technological innovations in transportation and communication have accelerated the **transnational flow** of people and ideas (Rao & Walton 2004). Adult global nomads, because of their cross-cultural experiences, tend to understand issues from multiple perspectives and recognize that people of diverse backgrounds have different values and beliefs (Langford 1998). Global nomads, then, have a greater appreciation for cultural diversity. Even those expats who attempt to hide in an "expat bubble" are affected by the culture of the host country. Conversely, global nomads have difficulty developing a "local" view, preferring an international perspective. As a result, they may never fully reintegrate into their home country and may become impatient with the **culture-bound** attitudes of their peers.

Researchers have identified numerous benefits from global nomadism. The most commonly reported advantage of living abroad is an expanded world view that develops from living in another cultural milieu and associating with people from the host culture as well as other foreign sojourners. Global nomads learn to be flexible, appreciative of difference, and more open-minded. They also learn to adapt and compromise, and they acquire cultural knowledge and skills that are different from what they previously possessed. Yet living abroad also brings challenges: frequent moves cause difficulties adjusting to a new cultural environment, culture shock, and sadness at losing friends and the lifestyle once enjoyed. Global nomadism also affects kinship and family structure in the home country through long separations from loved ones.

From a gendered perspective, Useem (1993) found that women living in a foreign country are more concerned about interpersonal relations and experience more difficulty leaving friends and re-entering their home country than males. They feel more stress about moving and are torn between a mobile, exciting international life and sedentary stability in their home community. Psychologist Cheryl Smith investigated lifestyle adjustment among expat spouses in China. She found that these spouses had a difficult time adjusting to living in a foreign environment. Alcoholism, depression, anxiety disorders, and marital problems were common (Farrar 2009). Nonetheless, these women believed that international experiences enhanced their social relations and community involvement.

Ward, Bochner, and Furnham (2001: 51) identify culture learning as the "process whereby sojourners acquire culturally relevant social knowledge and skills in order to survive and thrive in their new society." Although it would be naive to suggest that people who move to a new country completely assume a new **cultural identity**, over time global nomads may take on many of the characteristics of an adopted culture. Ultimately, global nomads may develop multiple identities—their expat identity, their home culture identity, and their professional identity. A form of **biculturalism** develops, where they identify with and become a part of two cultures. At times, this comes about through developing a rapport with members of the host community, at other times simply from repeated exposure to the host culture. One example is clothing. Although I have always been fairly easy-going about what people wear, after five years in Egypt, where even women who choose not to wear a *gallabiayya*[3] and *hijab*[4] dress conservatively, on my return to North America I was shocked at the scanty, unflattering clothing that many women wear.

"Study abroad is often a voyage inward rather than outward, a recognition of limits, rather than an expansion of borders." Calderwood (2011: n.p.)

Culture shock, discussed in Chapter 1, is very much a reality for people living in a foreign environment. Expats learn various coping strategies to deal with culture shock, one of the most common responses being the creation of the private spaces or boundaries studied by Fechter (2008). Forming close-knit communities, most likely at the private internationals schools their children attend, is also a common coping strategy. Here, members of the community support each other and assist in familiarizing new expats with the community and creating social networks that alleviate loneliness and depression. Despite these efforts most expats, including anthropologists, suffer bouts of culture shock. Once foreigners learn the social norms and behaviours of their new culture, they accomplish a degree of cultural transition, becoming more comfortable in their new surroundings and less prone to culture shock. For adults this adjustment does not change their values system, sense of identity, or alter their close relationships with friends and family "back home." Children, on the

---

3 Full-length, loose garment.
4 Head covering/scarf.

other hand, have yet to firmly establish their sense of identity, personal or cultural, which has important implications for who they become in the future.

When global nomads return to their home culture, they may experience **reverse culture shock**,[5] which is defined as the "temporal psychological difficulties returnees experience in the initial stage of the adjustment process at home after having lived abroad for some time" (Uehara 1983: 420). Setting aside everything they have learned and readjusting to a home culture can be challenging, as you will see in the discussion on TCKs below.

STUDY-ABROAD PROGRAMS

Like ethnographic research, study-abroad programs are a **rite of passage**, where participants separate from their home culture and identity and make the transition into a new identity in their host country; they then reintegrate into their home culture upon return, with new values and insights. Students in a study-abroad program must learn to cope with a new culture and environment. As they make this transition, they develop an awareness and acceptance of cultural differences. This rite of passage should also enable students to see their home culture more objectively (Miller 1993).

Study-abroad programs grew dramatically in the last half of the twentieth century. The Open Doors Report on International Educational Exchange reports that 260,327 American students studied abroad in the year 2008–09 (Miller 2010). As Bond (2009: 8–9) describes it, "Study abroad is understood to include participation in any internationally based program or experience including exchange, clinical placement, field study, internship, co-op placement, practicum or voluntary service/work placement, which is offered by a post-secondary institution…." These students experience culture shock, loneliness, and uncertainty as they attempt to learn the cultural mores of their host country. When they return home they often suffer severe reverse culture shock; indeed, some of my Canadian students gave up and left Canada again, unable to readjust to "Canadian life." The longer an individual lives in another country, the harder the re-entry process becomes (Christofi & Thompson 2007).

> "When I landed at Dulles International Airport I found myself reacting negatively to much of what I saw. It struck me as a terrible waste of money to have an expensive machine polishing the floor at the airport; what was the point of having a gleaming floor? I was disgusted by the many ads for alcoholic beverages and their photos of people in immodest, revealing clothing." Young (1996: 136)

THIRD CULTURE KIDS (TCKs)

The term Third Culture Kids (TCKs) was first coined by anthropologist Dr. Ruth Hill Useem in the 1960s (Ridout 2010). Since then, academic and professional research has expanded our understanding of TCKs and, by extrapolation, Adult Third Culture Kids

---

5 Nolan (1990) calls this phase the re-entry crisis.

Graduation June, 2007

FIGURE 4.1 A GRADUATING CLASS FROM CAIRO AMERICAN COLLEGE AT THE PYRAMIDS. THE MAJORITY OF THE STUDENTS AT THIS SCHOOL ARE THIRD CULTURE KIDS

(ATCKs). A TCK is "a person who has spent a significant part of his or her development years outside the parents' culture. The TCK frequently builds relationships to all of the cultures, while not having full ownership in any. Although elements from each culture may be assimilated into the TCK's life experience, the sense of belonging is in relationship to similar backgrounds" (Pollock & van Reken 2001: 19, quoted in Ridout 2010: 4–5). TCKs may be Korean children growing up in Cairo, Egypt; Canadian children living in Rio de Janeiro, Brazil; or American children in Moscow, Russia. Regardless of where they live or where they come from, these youths blend elements from all the cultures they experience to create a third culture that influences their values, beliefs, and world view (Pollock & van Reken 2001). Indeed, their life experiences create a unique sense of identity that can have a dramatic impact on their lives and the lives of those around them when they return "home."

> "The Third Culture Kid is always 'standing in the doorway,' on a threshold between two or more cultures in which s/he never has 'full ownership.'"
> Ridout (2010: 5)

"Growing up as a TCK has been a gift and has significantly shaped my life and work. As I interact with world leaders one day and with those living in refugee camps the next, I continually draw upon my experience of living among different cultures. I am delighted to see the lessons learned from the traditional TCK experience live on in this new edition of 'Third Culture Kids.'" Scott Gration, Maj. Gen. USAF (RET), President Obama's Special Envoy to Sudan, quoted in Amazon.com reviews of Pollock and van Reken (2001)

TCKs share many common characteristics, to the extent that Pollock and van Reken (2009) have identified TCKs as a distinct subculture. TCKs tend to possess strong self-esteem, advanced social skills, and adaptability, moving from one country to another with seeming ease. Generally speaking, they feel comfortable with foreigners or "cultural otherness," are fluent in several foreign languages, and are aware, from an insider's perspective, of other cultures. This is known as **transcultural literacy**, a phenomenon that Heyward (2002: 10) defines as "the understandings, competencies, attitudes, language proficiencies, participation and identities necessary for successful cross-cultural engagement." Those possessing transcultural literacy can "read" a new culture and quickly learn and adapt to new symbols of everyday life.

TCKs enjoy significant benefits from growing up in a foreign culture, in particular, cross-cultural experiences that enrich their lives and create a multidimensional world view (Gould 2002). As a result, TCKs tend to view themselves as global citizens rather than identifying with members of their own ethnic group or even home country. The degree to which this holds true varies, depending on whether their parents insist that they attend weekend language schools, whether they associate with other students of their ethnicity, visit their home country often, and maintain close family ties.

"When I first came to Egypt, ten years ago, I faced some challenges dealing with local students. In a Canadian school, where mostly Egyptian students attend, I was mocked for my appearance. In addition, Egypt was the first foreign country that I have lived, so it was extremely difficult to communicate with other people in the school. As I got exposed to various other students from different countries, when I moved to CAC, I became more familiar with the different cultures and ideas. I realized that when I visited my home country, Korea, after several years I could not look at things the way I looked at them before I came to Egypt. It was somewhat uncomfortable to interact the way I used to, before I was exposed to the variety of cultures." Sohyun Kim, an international student at Cairo American College

Nevertheless, even TCKs in this type of situation may express reservations about returning to their home country permanently. When TCKs become adults, they tend to raise their children to appreciate the cultural diversity with which they are familiar, rather than stressing a national or ethnic identity (Cottrell & Useem 1993b).

In the Useem study (1993), Anne Baker Cottrell found that international experience made TCKs more understanding and aware of other people and cultures than most Americans are. TCKs tend to seek international occupations, hold a strong desire to visit and live abroad, and like to meet foreigners. Because of their experiences, they tend to be adaptable and relate easily to cultural diversity. They also possess more cross-cultural knowledge and skills, but this is also a challenge since most felt they did not have ample opportunities in America to use such knowledge and skill sets.

The experiences of TCKs differ, based on whether they are military kids, missionary kids, or their parents work in an embassy or oil company. Children of missionary parents, called Missionary Kids (MKs), are a subset of Third Culture Kids. These children may differ from other TCKs in not living in as affluent circumstances. They may not be posted in thriving urban areas, and they may not attend private international schools. In fact, many MKs spend their childhood away from their home country and away from their parents, living at boarding schools. Keuss and Willett (2009) call MKs "the sacredly mobile" in that they are not united by experiences, but by the lack of a definable home.

TCKs exhibit a strong **cosmopolitanism**, which means being comfortable in more than one cultural setting and owning multiple perspectives on serious issues, such as human rights (Vertovec & Cohen 2002). Thus, TCKs may provide a bridge between generations and become mediators between cultures. They are also more interested in international news and aware of what is happening, especially in countries where they have lived. TCKs of all types desire to associate with peers who have an understanding of the world, are comfortable with cultural diversity, and are able to embrace change. Their sense of home comes from relationships, not location. Indeed, many TCKs do not have a strong sense of home or feel that their host country is more home than their passport country.

Useem (1993) found that most TCKs tend to be high achievers, earning university degrees at a much higher rate than those in their home population. Their choice of program is often influenced by their international experience, choosing disciplines such as anthropology, international relations, and foreign languages, and choosing careers in international teaching, international relations, and international business.

Although TCKs enjoy intrinsic benefits in the form of enriched cultural experiences from living abroad, as well as extrinsic benefits such as receiving a superior education and offers from the most prestigious universities because of the quality of their education, they also face substantial challenges because this experience happens in their formative years. According to Hill (1986: 332), "psychological adjustment [can] be stressful and the individual [is] at risk from naiveté, inadequate acculturation to

"My MKness has completely shaped my life, my calling, my career, my major, my dreams, my identity, my taste in women, my nomadic behavior, my humor, my compassion, who my friends are, and so much more." An MK, quoted in Keuss and Millet (2009: 14)

"Spending time with people who are Third Culture Kids is always fun. My friends who are Third Culture Kids would often tell me of stories in places that sound amazing. We would hear about what the schools were like, and how different the culture was compared to the culture [in Egypt]. Conversations with my friends were always so interesting because they always had the most unique view on what we were talking about. Each person would always have unique sayings that they had picked up from other cultures that they would often use on a daily basis. As much as I love knowing people who come from such a diverse background, it's sad knowing that one of my friends may end up leaving at the end of the year because of the company that their parents work for. Social networking has made it a lot easier nowadays to keep in touch with my friends who have traveled across the globe." Yasmin Shawky, an Egyptian student at an international school

Western values, and competitive materialism." Many TCKs report rootlessness, feeling alienated from their peers in their home country, and an inability to make commitments (Useem 1993). Even TCKs who are still overseas may feel this way, becoming restless after several years in the same country and wanting to "move on" to new experiences. This rootlessness can affect their university education and careers: TCKs tend to change colleges and programs several times, or often leave college for a period to travel, which puts them out of synch with other students their age.

College-age TCKs think much differently and have different values, norms, and beliefs from their peers, which sets them apart. Nevertheless, TCKs are a hidden resource—they are cross-culturally savvy and can add diversity and an international world view to discussions through their participation in educational programs, as well as when they enter the professional world. However, returning sojourners tend to compare their home country with their host country, and often the comparison is not favourable for the home country. Thus, TCKs may feel like strangers in their own country (Bowman 2012). They also feel out of touch on a personal level: they stand out because they have not caught up on local pop culture, such as movie stars, sports, and jokes. TCKs tend to be dismayed by their peers' lack of worldliness, the racist perspective of some, and the lack of interest in the outside world of others (Kebshull & Pozo-Humphries n.d.). Consequently, they may reject their home culture and their parochial peers. Cottrell and Useem (1993a: n.p.), for instance, found that only one in ten participants in their study felt "completely attuned to everyday life in the U.S." Rather, TCKs tend to feel more comfortable with foreigners, exchange students, and non–English-speaking minorities because "they've been there."

"I love and enjoy being a third culture kid. I have lived in such countries as the United States, Japan, Thailand, Malaysia, and Egypt. I have been exposed to so many exotic cultures and it has changed my life in ways of how I looked at the world. Living in Egypt, I had the chance to live in history with the demonstrations going on. When I was a kid, I kept on wishing that I would move to the States, but now that I look back at my life, I don't want to trade any other life than the life I had. I did miss my friends every time I moved, and it was always hard to make new friends again, but over the countless times I have moved, I think I got used to it. It became part of my life. And I believe now that it is easier to make new friends.

I am also a Christian and I don't believe there was any trouble in keeping my faith in Egypt, with almost everyone being a Muslim. With all the Muslims surrounding me, and hearing the mosque calls every day, it has made me stronger in my faith and made me more assertive to my beliefs.

I did not struggle that much coming back to the States because my family and I went back to my father's home in Hawaii every year. So there wasn't that much of a culture shock. But it's always funny when people ask me where I'm from and so I say, Cairo, Egypt. Then they will say something like, 'Oh then do you know how to speak hieroglyphics?' or something like, 'Do you live in the pyramids?'" Johnathan Shimabuku, an international student formerly at Cairo American College

Pollock and van Reken (2009) identify what they call a "cycle of mobility" that refers to the experiences of TCKs. This cycle of mobility and separation has five stages: 1) involvement: the TCK belongs to a community and feels secure; 2) leaving: the TCK learns s/he is going to leave, and begins loosening interpersonal ties, emotionally separating from friends, and anticipates grief but tries to deny being sad; 3) transition: moving and all that entails, arriving in a new community, and feeling a sense of instability; 4) entering the new community: beginning the process of adapting, overcoming feelings of instability and insecurity, culture shock; and 5) reinvolvement: becoming a member of the new community. This cycle may occur several times in a TCK's pre-adult life and may prevent a TCK from developing close relationships for fear of the grief that accompanies separation. TCKs may view relationships as only short-term, even when they return to their home country, and they continue to suffer unresolved grief and sadness over those they left behind. On a more positive note, the Internet and social media allow TCKs (as well as other global nomads) to maintain relationships with family and friends back "home," as well as those they leave behind when moving from one country to another. This instant communication helps alleviate some of the grief and sense of loss from moving.

> "Although looking like an insider, an MK [or TCK] feels completely on the outside as he or she is lost in the slang or idioms, has acquired different tastes in food, struggles to maintain foreign customs, and is unfamiliar with the pop culture."
> Klemens and Bikos (2009)

TCKs may suffer reverse culture shock when they return to their home country. Pollock and van Reken (2009) call this "re-entry stress." According to Useem (1993), many never adjust, only adapt. Bikos et al. (2009) found that MKs returning to North America were surprised by the excess or conspicuous consumption of North American culture and marvelled at the size of cars and homes. Unlike other TCKs, MKs also had to deal with the label of "missionary kid" and the stereotypes and assumptions attached to that label.

TCKs from military families tend to have the fewest problems re-entering the United States because of highly Americanized bases overseas and because they tend to spend shorter periods of time (five or fewer years) abroad. They also appear to be the least critical of the United States (e.g., its foreign policy and military ventures), and least interested in international involvement (Useem 1993). TCKs whose parents are international educators, executives, or embassy personnel are the most eager to live abroad again, and have the strongest desire to maintain an international dimension in their lives.

CONCLUSION

Living abroad is a rewarding personal experience, tapping into an individual's resourcefulness, adaptability, and sense of self. Those who undertake a foreign posting, of whatever sort, gain an enhanced cross-cultural perspective, multidimensional world view, and ability to adapt to changing situations. They also face numerous challenges, ranging from culture shock to always having to say goodbye. When expats are repatriated to their home country they may have difficulty adjusting to excessive consumerism, provincial attitudes, community homogeneity, and a lower standard of living, while also grieving for the friends and lifestyle they left behind.

Culture shock is a common experience among people who spend an extended time in foreign environments. However, once they learn the customs, beliefs, and patterns of behaviour in their new culture, this sense of insecurity recedes. Cultural immersion suggests losing oneself in another cultural environment, but this is unrealistic; even after enculturation, a foreigner remains part of the "Other." Comparing culture shock to a rite of passage seems apt: it is a period of personal growth and learning and reflects on our ability to adapt and accept new and unfamiliar ways of living.

Third Culture Kids experience similar difficulties as sojourners but on a greater scale because of living outside their home country during their formative years. The most profound of the challenges is their lack of connection with their home country and their peers. They feel inadequate and cannot relate to the local pop culture, and they continue to value international interests more than local ones. Third Culture Kids struggle with identity and confused loyalties; they are not of one culture or of another, nor do they necessarily want to be: they are international, rather than local—they are the "Other." Third Culture Kids are always "standing in the doorway." On the other hand, TCKs are poised to take on a future role as cultural bridges and cultural brokers for their generation.

Considering the ever-expanding globalization processes, the need for further research into global nomadism and its implications for individuals, sponsoring agencies, host countries, and home countries is paramount. Interestingly, when expats are repatriated they may also be an "other" in the "home" country. Nonetheless, the benefits of living abroad far outweigh the challenges. People who have lived overseas, even if only for a few years, will never see the world or their country of origin in the same way again.

QUESTIONS FOR CONSIDERATION AND CLASSROOM ACTIVITIES

1. If you moved to another country temporarily, would you try to hold on to your cultural practices and values or would you adopt (assimilate into) your new country's culture? Do you think it is possible to completely give up a natal culture and immerse oneself in a new culture? Why or why not?

2. Imagine yourself in a strange place, with no friends or family, unable to speak the language, unfamiliar foods in the stores … you get the picture. How would you cope with this new life? Draft action plan for dealing with culture shock in your adopted country, including coping strategies that you would employ.

3. Investigate biculturalism. What advantages can you identify from having a bicultural perspective? What disadvantages?

4. Conduct an ethnographic interview with someone who has moved to your school from a different country. What problems did they encounter when they first arrived? How did they solve these problems? What elements of their culture are they maintaining, and what (if any) elements of their host country are they adopting?

5. Locate a TCK in your community and conduct an ethnographic interview. Organize your questions around challenges of living in a new country, benefits of an international lifestyle, and attitudes when they return home.

SUGGESTED READINGS

DeVitta, P.R. (Ed.). (1992). *The naked anthropologist: Tales from around the world.* Belmont, CA: Wadsworth Publishing.

DeVitta has put together a collection of stories that recount sometimes embarrassing, sometimes startling, experiences of anthropologists in the field. Readers should gain an understanding of the challenges faced by anthropologists as they deal with their insecurities, ignorance, isolation, and happenstance in fieldwork.

Pollock, D.C., & van Reken, R.E. (2009). *Third culture kids: The experience of growing up among worlds.* London: Nicholas Brealey & Intercultural Press.

This easy-to-read book explores the world of children who have grown up in cultures other than their passport country. The challenges they have faced and the amazing benefits of an international upbringing illustrate the realities of contemporary global nomads. A must-read book for anyone who has lived overseas or is contemplating a move abroad.

Chapter 5

WHAT ARE THE UNDERLYING REASONS FOR ETHNIC CONFLICT, AND THE CONSEQUENCES OF THESE CONFLICTS?

Key Terms: anthropology of genocide, anthropology of suffering, discrimination, emergency anthropology, emic approach, ethnic boundary markers, ethnic conflict, ethnic groups, ethnic identity, ethnicity, ethnic stratification, exploitation, genocide/ethnic cleansing, holistic approach, inequality, nation, nationality, race, refugees

---

INTRODUCTION

The above question is difficult to answer, given the many reasons behind ethnic conflict. Those of us who have not had first-hand experience in a conflict situation cannot understand what it means to harbour memories of wrongdoings passed down through generations, to be driven from our homes or lands, or to deal with daily **discrimination** and **exploitation** based on ethnicity or religion. These age-old resentments and a history of conflict and persecution can define a people and influence their perceptions of the world around them. Indeed, Davis (1992) suggests that war is embedded in the social experience of many societies, including the United States, where war, loss, and suffering have become integral parts of the culture.

This question is also misleading because it suggests that conflict is due to ethnic differences, when in fact power struggles over territory, resources, and political dominance are far more likely to cause conflict. Authoritarian states attempting to eliminate or destabilize ethnic groups[1] in order to access resources and territory is a contributing factor in many twentieth-century conflicts. However, to suggest that historical grievances, ethnicity, and religion do not play a part in these conflicts is also an oversimplification of the situation.

Hatred of a group of people because of their ethnicity or "otherness" has often resulted in persecution and conflict. The most notorious example of this is Hitler's extermination of Jews, Roma, Slavs, and homosexuals during World War II. More

---

1 The term ethnic group is used to avoid misleading terms such as race.

recently, the massacre of the minority Tutsi by Hutu extremists in Rwanda horrified the world, and violent clashes in India's northeastern states left thousands dead and many more displaced. In North America, indigenous peoples have a long history of conflict with the Europeans who dispossessed them of their land, and in the United States in particular, African Americans have experienced generations of discrimination and exploitation. Although all of these examples are predicated on economic and political factors, there is also a powerful element of social, religious, and ethnic prejudice.

One of the consequences of ethnic conflict is displaced persons, also known as **refugees**. Refugees are people who have been forced to flee their homes to escape persecution during conflicts. Anthropologists define refugees as "people who have undergone a violent 'rite' of separation" (Harrell-Bond & Voutira 1992: 6). Many refugees remain in a transient state that dramatically affects their legal, psychological, economic, and social status. Refugees and their adaptation to changing social and political conditions are addressed in this chapter. The conditions that lead to ethnic conflict will be explored through the ongoing genocidal conflict in Darfur, western Sudan. In this chapter, ethnic conflict is considered from an anthropological perspective; however, historical, economic, religious, and political insights contribute much to this discussion.

ANTHROPOLOGISTS AND ETHNIC CONFLICT

Anthropologists have played a pivotal role in documenting the traditions and customs of many of the world's ethnic groups, even as they have served as advocates for the rights of these groups. They have also studied violence, conflict, and warfare among pre-state societies; however, the study of ethnic conflict in state societies is somewhat lacking (Hinton 2002).

The reasons for anthropology's neglect of ethnic conflict in state societies are manifold. To study such a complex issue requires a multidisciplinary approach, one that researchers may not wish to undertake, despite the lip service paid to its value (Harrell-Bond & Voutira 1992, cited in Baker 1983). In addition, the study of ethnic conflict sits outside the parameters of "comfortable" anthropology, where anthropologists study well-established cultural systems in small-scale cultures. Displaced persons, one of the consequences of ethnic conflict, are often perceived (erroneously) to live outside of these cultural systems; they do not fit into a neat model of social change that "makes sense" (Bringa 1995). Conflict, displacement, and suffering have all been considered temporary aberrations in an otherwise stable community, making these situations less enticing as research projects. Indeed, Davis (1992) criticizes anthropologists for expending too much effort on studying orderly, harmonized social organizations, and neglecting disruption and despair—what he calls **emergency anthropology**. Davis believes that academic and applied anthropology should unite in the study of suffering, especially in the case of advocacy and policy development, while O'Neill (2004) suggests that understanding and mitigating genocide, the most extreme form of ethnic conflict, may be an important twenty-first-century challenge for anthropologists.

Theoretical bias may also play a role in this negligence: there is a tendency to downplay violence and unhappiness because anthropologists want to promote the stability and efficacy of non-Western cultures (Harrell-Bond & Voutira 1992, cited in Colson 1989). To study victims of systematic violence, such as mass rape, dislocation, and extermination, has been outside the experience and training of most anthropologists.

In recent years, the **anthropology of genocide** (Hinton 2002) and the **anthropology of suffering** (Davis 1992) have addressed some of the issues attached to ethnic conflict. Hinton (2002) argues that anthropology is uniquely positioned to determine why genocide occurs (a theoretical stance) and to develop policies for preventing future genocides (an applied stance). One area where anthropologists have a great deal to contribute is in the study of refugees (Harrell-Bond & Voutira 1992). This is relevant research since an estimated 135 million people were uprooted in the twentieth century (*Jerusalem Post* 2003).

Anthropologists have also investigated humanitarian aid and intervention, going so far as to work for aid agencies. Harrell-Bond (1986), for example, found that despite the goodwill and largesse attached to providing aid, refugees are often treated as villains and the aid workers as figures of authority, meaning the refugees have little power or control over their own welfare (Harrell-Bond & Voutira 1992). Aid workers also tend to homogenize refugees, giving little consideration to differing values, norms, and social organization among ethnic groups.

"My anthropological training had not prepared me to deal with the very rapid and total disintegration of the [Bosnian] community I was studying." Anthropologist Tone Bringa (1995: xviii)

Anthropology brings its own unique perspective and methodology to the study of ethnicity and ethnic conflict. First, anthropologists consider ethnic conflict from a **holistic approach** or perspective by employing a historical, economic, social, political, and religious perspective. Anthropologists also place the concept of culture in the forefront of their study of ethnic conflict. And finally, anthropologists listen to people and ask questions regarding the meaning of their ethnicity and the reasons behind the conflict. This **emic approach** has become increasingly important as ethnic groups have grown more insistent that their voices be heard and their histories recounted.

Do anthropologists have the solutions to ethnic conflict? No, but what they do have is the ability to understand the conflicts from a broad, holistic perspective using anthropological methods and research. As anthropologists become increasingly involved in the study of ethnic conflict, their roles will expand and they will become mediators between ethnic groups, and between refugees and authoritarian institutions.

THE NATURE OF ETHNICITY AND ETHNIC CONFLICT

To begin our discussion of ethnic conflict we will explore several relevant concepts. **Ethnicity** refers to a sense of identity based on cultural traits that have been passed down for generations and that possess meaning for a group of people (Fenton 2003). **Ethnic groups**, such as the Plains Cree of Canada or the Albanians of Montenegro, share a common identity, history, and territory of origin. Members of an ethnic group speak the same language, observe the same customs (e.g., dress, diet), and hold relatively the same beliefs and values. An ethnic group shares a memory of its cultural past and a sense of continuity from the past to the present. Its members see themselves as distinct and separate from other groups. For example, Indian immigrants to North America affiliate with other Indians based on their state of origin (e.g., Kerala), rather than on India as an entire country, and the Roma (Gypsies of Europe), who until recently were nomadic, do not claim a homeland but possess an ethnic identity based on their lifestyle (De Vos 1995). Today, there are approximately 5,000 ethnic groups in the world (Eller 1999), many of whom are seeking recognition as distinct nations.

Although sharing a sense of group identity based on ethnicity has a long history, the concept of **ethnic identity** is relatively new and the product of modern politics, involving state building, colonization, and globalization (Crawford 1998). Ethnic identity is determined by **ethnic boundary markers**, which are socially constructed in that they vary from one group to another and can be quite elusive (De Vos 1995). They are also fluid, changing in importance and purpose over time (Miyares & Airries 2007: 7).

Religion is one marker that may provide ethnic identity. Although the Serbs, Croats, and Bosniaks consider themselves distinct ethnic groups, they speak the same language and have lived similar lives. It is religion that separates these three ethnic groups: the Croats are Roman Catholic, the Serbs, Orthodox Christian, and the Bosniaks, Muslim. Despite the importance of ethnic boundary markers based on religion, followers of the same religion do not necessarily constitute a distinct ethnic group. Many people the world over follow Islam; for example, the Samals of the Philippines, the Moors of Sri Lanka, and the Pashtun of Afghanistan are all Muslims but come from diverse ethnic backgrounds. Still, if a group of people self-defines as an ethnic group, then they are an ethnic group, regardless of what categories outsiders may assign.

Language is another powerful marker of ethnic identity. For the Acadians of maritime Canada, for example, language is an integral component of their ethnic identity, although they separate their culture from that of other French-speaking Canadians. Despite its importance as an ethnic identity marker, language is often the first marker to disappear among immigrants, usually by the third generation (Miyares & Airries 2007: 8). Physical appearance, such as the distinctive features of Han Chinese, may also serve as an ethnic boundary marker. Distinctive clothing and food, such as Sikh turbans (dastar) and Hamitic Bedouin *jalabiyya*,[2] or Ukrainian perogies and Mexican tacos, are other symbols that make ethnic groups recognizable to outsiders. New ethnic groups may also arise; for example, Mexican, Peruvian, Chilean, and Guatemalan ethnic groups evolved out of the Spanish who immigrated to North and South America and mated with indigenous peoples already there.

---

2 A long hooded robe.

Quite similar to the concept of ethnicity and ethnic groups is the idea of nation or nationhood. A **nation** is a community "of people who see themselves as 'one people' on the basis of common ancestry, history, society, institutions, ideology, language, territory, and often religion" (Haviland, Fedorak, & Lee 2009: 306). Eller (1999: 144) believes that a nation must fulfill certain requirements in order to be called a nation: "a common culture, a consciousness of shared identity, and political organization toward a national goal." As an example, the people of Taiwan have owned a sense of national identity different from mainland China for more than a century (Dreyer 2003). Indeed, most of the population identifies as Taiwanese rather than Chinese. Various factors have contributed to this emerging identity: occupations by the Spanish, Portuguese, and Dutch; Japanese colonization; close proximity to Polynesian cultures; American influence during World War II; isolation from mainland China; and a brutal policy of assimilation by Chinese ruler Chiang Kai-shek between 1948 and 1975. Today, the Taiwanese want an independent nation.

Nationality is similar to ethnicity; however, nationality can encompass several ethnic groups that are politically unified (De Vos 1995). For example, Canada is a nation, and the citizens of Canada usually identify their nationality as Canadian, yet each person also possesses an ethnic identity, for example, Chinese, Ukrainian, or German. In other forms of nationhood, the Kurds of Iran consider themselves a nation though they do not possess autonomy.

Race is a difficult term to define, partly because it is based on erroneous facts. Usually race refers to a group of people who have been categorized based on biological and behavioural traits. However, people cannot be definitively categorized into specific racial groups based on rigorous scientific data. According to Boas (1932, quoted in Eller 1999: 57) there is as much physical variation within races as between races, there are no clear-cut geographic or biological lines between races, and there are no correlations between races and cultural or mental characteristics. Thus, a Northern European may be genetically more similar to a San from southern Africa than someone from southern Europe. The only clear biological difference between populations is blood type, but blood types do not correspond to so-called racial categories. This means the concept of race is culturally constructed according to economic, political, and social agendas, rather than any biological reality.

Ethnic stratification, which is often the precursor to ethnic conflict, means placing groups of people in a hierarchy of superior versus inferior, based on ethnicity, race, religion, historical origins, occupation, wealth, etc. Ethnic stratification limits a target group's access to reasonable wealth, power, and prestige—three important components of the well-being of an ethnic group. In a stratified society, people are ranked relative to other ethnic groups and face varying degrees of **inequality** and discrimination. In Canada, numerous ethnic groups have been viewed as inferior and undesirable—although the group(s) pinpointed as inferior change from one period to another. For example, when Ukrainians began immigrating to Canada at the end of the nineteenth century, Canadians of French and English descent were less than enthusiastic. An article appeared in the *Winnipeg Telegram* on May 13, 1901, expressing this aversion:

That there are few people who will affirm that Slavonic immigrants are desirable settlers, or that they are welcomed by the white people of Western Canada.... Those whose ignorance is impenetrable, whose customs are repulsive, whose civilization is primitive, and whose character and morals are justly condemned, are surely not the class of immigrants which the country's paid immigration agents should seek to attract. Better by far to keep our land for the children, children's children, of Canadians than to fill up the country with the scum of Europe. (Cheney 2000)

Therefore, discrimination, exploitation, and inequality breed resentment and hostile relationships between ethnic groups which, given the right circumstances and incentives, can lead to ethnic conflict.

ETHNIC CONFLICT

Ter-Gabrielian (1999: 1) defines **ethnic conflict** as "a conflict between two or more ethnic groups, one of which possesses the actual state power." Much of the ethnic conflict today can be traced to European colonialism in the nineteenth century, when political boundaries were created with little consideration for ethnicity or historic homelands. When European colonial powers granted independence to these colonies in the twentieth century, dominant ethnic groups quickly seized power to the detriment of other ethnic groups. This is what happened in Rwanda: the Belgians took control of the country in 1912 and began favouring the Tutsi with education and employment, while excluding the supposedly lower-class and impoverished Hutus. When the Belgians left Rwanda, Hutu extremists seized power and, spurred on by the media and political manoeuvres by local and national leaders, massacred a million Tutsis (Bowen 1996).

Evidence of ethnic conflict and its ramifications are everywhere: the Irish Republican Army versus the British government; the Serbs' ethnic cleansing of Bosniaks; Palestinian and Israeli conflict; Kurdish separatist movements in Iraq and Turkey; and ethno-nationalist conflicts on the periphery of Russia. Although by no means a comprehensive list, the prevalence of ethnic conflicts worldwide is a sobering reality—what Brubaker (2004: 88) calls the "new world disorder."

Most modern states are pluralistic, which means that more than one ethnic group exists within its borders. The pluralism in Western states is fairly obvious, but even in smaller states ethnic diversity is pronounced. For example, 120 ethnic groups coexist in Tanzania, many of whom are experiencing an ethnic resurgence (Omari 1987). Although some pluralistic states, such as Switzerland and Belgium, have managed to maintain relative peace and harmony, pluralism often results in discord that can spill over into ethnic conflict. Yet this conflict is not entirely *ethnic* in nature even though it is often blamed on ethnicity; rather, it is more likely due to economic, religious, or political factors (often all three), such as claims to territory and resources—what Ter-Gabrielian (1999) terms "conflict of secession," in which one or more ethnic groups wish to separate from the home state and create a new state with more autonomy and freedom. This form of ethnic conflict often escalates into open warfare, as in the case of the Tamil and Sudanese of Sri Lanka. An ethnic group may also seek political power or dominance over other ethnic groups within the state—what Ter-Gabrielian (1999) terms "conflict of replacement." In such a situation, one ethnic group wants to replace another at the centre of power. In this case, genocide is a very real possibility. The genocide in Rwanda is a good example of replacement conflict.

Genocide—or as became popular in twentieth-century media, **ethnic cleansing**— is the deliberate extermination of an ethnic group. Historic examples of genocide are numerous: in 1915, 1.8 million Armenians were murdered in the Ottoman Empire and the Caucasus; in the Soviet Union, Chechens, Tatars, and others were exterminated after World War II because of alleged collaboration with the Nazis; and, in 1971, up to three million Bengalis were killed by the Pakistani army, resulting in the secession of Bangladesh (Ter-Gabrielian 1999). Genocide almost always has an economic or political motivation. For instance, the Serbian extermination of Bosniaks and Croats in the former Yugoslavia in the 1990s was based on political motivation, although the reasons for this ugly page in Eastern European history are complex. Anthropologist Tone Bringa (1995: 3) discounts both the "age-old hatred" model of ethnic conflict and the "peaceful co-existence" approach. In the village where she lived, neither model fitted: "there was both co-existence and conflict, tolerance and prejudice, suspicion and friendship."

Bringa found that what hurt the most was neighbour turning on neighbour. The person next door became "a depersonalized alien, a member of the enemy ranks" (Bringa 1995: xvi). When the conflict was over, some Muslims returned to their villages, but the wounds from inter-communal violence take a long time to heal, and people remained socially distant. Out of Bringa's fieldwork came a book, *Being Muslim the Bosnian Way* (1995), which recounts the story of a community and its people before war destroyed their lives. Bringa's work preserves a way of life that has been all but lost because of ethnic conflict and genocide.

GENOCIDE IN DARFUR

On September 9, 2004, United States Secretary of State Colin Powell described the Sudanese government's policies toward the indigenous African people of Darfur as genocide—a term not used by the United States since the Holocaust of World War II (Welling 2007). As of 2010, this government-supported ethnic cleansing in Darfur had resulted in an estimated 300,000 deaths and 2.7 million displaced persons (UN News Centre 2010). The American Anthropological Association (2004: n.p.) issued a strongly worded statement regarding the conflict: "the violence is systematic, sustained and grossly disproportionate to quelling the military threat posed by Darfur's rebel groups.... Mass summary executions, the burning of entire villages, destruction of food stocks and livestock, and poisoning of wells, speak of an effort to destroy the entire basis of life of the targeted populations." This genocide has far-reaching political and humanitarian consequences, and the effects of this endemic violence and instability will be felt for generations to come.

To succinctly address the multidimensional socio-cultural, economic, political, and religious factors contributing to the Darfur conflict is as challenging as finding feasible solutions to the crisis. Anthropologists have conducted numerous analyses of the crisis, and stress the importance of understanding the conflict within a historical and ecological context.

Darfur is an environmentally fragile region in western Sudan, bordering Chad, Libya, and the Central African Republic. Seven million people belonging to Arab Muslim and non-Arab African ethnic groups inhabit Darfur (World Savvy Monitor 2008). Although Sudan is a heterogeneous society, with myriad languages, ethnicities, and tribal affiliations, many indigenous languages are dying out because of the government's attempt to homogenize and "Arabize" the country.

"We concluded—I concluded—that genocide has been committed in Darfur and that the government of Sudan and the *Janjaweed*[3] bear responsibility—and genocide may still be occurring." Secretary of State Powell giving testimony before the Senate Foreign Relations Committee, quoted in Mayroz (2008: 367)

Yet, despite the tendency to separate the Sudanese into Arabs and indigenous ethnic groups, anthropologists point out that all of the conflicting groups are indigenous.

The largest indigenous non-Arab African ethnic group is the Fur, who live in central Darfur, followed by the Zaghawa in the north and the Masalit in the west of Darfur, though more than 40 other ethnic groups also live in the region (Mulaj 2008). This cultural diversity is due to an influx of people from neighbouring countries during the nineteenth century (Adam 2008) and Arab migrations in the seventh and eighth centuries.

In Darfur, most Africans are sedentary farmers, while most Arabs are nomadic pastoralists, and until recently relations between the groups were peaceful. Indeed, in a remarkable system of reciprocity, farmers provided pastoralists with agricultural products, pastoralists provided farmers with animal products. Intermarriage and sharing of languages ensued—some African groups, such as the Berti, speak Arabic, and some Arabs speak Fur (Adam 2008). However, three decades of drought and desertification have increased competition between the farmers and herders for scarce water and grazing lands (Wadlow 2005). This is not an unusual situation; anthropologists have noted this volatility between other pastoral and agricultural groups (Parkington 1984). Yet anthropologists warn that suggesting that the conflict is between pastoralists and farmers is misleading, and it diverts attention from the underlying ecological and resource shortage problems. The tribal system for mediating disputes broke down over increasing competition for scarce resources (World Savvy Monitor). This tension was exacerbated by the government of Sudan. Battles between African farmers and Arab pastoralists broke out in 1987–89,

---

3 The *janjaweed* are bandits, criminals, demobilized Sudanese soldiers, young men from Arab tribes, tribal leaders, and fighters from Chad and Libya.

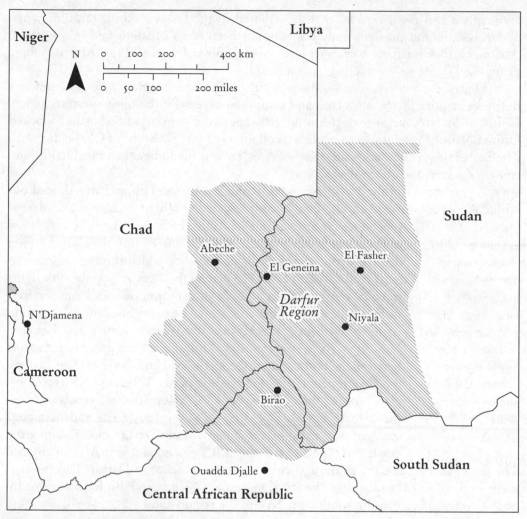

MAP 5.1 CONFLICT ZONES IN DARFUR

killing almost 3,000 people (Power 2004). Following the displacement of African farmers, few crops were grown or harvested, leading to food shortages.

During World War I, the British annexed Darfur, which had previously been an independent sultanate, to Sudan without considering whether the political borders would separate ethnic groups and tribes (Welling 2007). Sudan was dominated by the northern Arab ruling elite, which sought to economically and politically marginalize Darfur, a policy that increased following Sudan's independence in 1956. The people of Darfur received "less education, less development assistance, and fewer government posts" (Wadlow 2005: 2). This strategy began during colonialization, when administrators played different ethnic groups, tribes, and elites against each other in a pattern of favouritism and racist policies that contributed to the historic ethnic tension. When Sudan became independent, only the elite northern Arab Muslims and the southern Africans and Christians were involved in the political process; the African ethnic groups in Darfur were excluded (Adam 2008).

One of the main reasons for the genocide in Darfur is the Sudanese government's desire to acquire the region's land and resources, especially the oil in western Sudan. China, as Sudan's major investor in oil, has repeatedly supported Sudan and blocked United Nations resolutions to protect its oil interests (World without Genocide 2011). The Sudanese government's solution was to clear out the indigenous inhabitants, and free up the land and oil for development.

As early as 1977 the Sudan National Islamic Front and Umma Party singled out ethnic Africans, in particular the Fur, Kordofanis, and southern Sudanese, and stereo-typed them as inferior to elite Arabs. Following the 1985 overthrow of President Jaafar Numeiri, military moved into the Darfur region and the deputy minister of defence began distributing weapons to local Arabs (Adam 2008). To defend the African population's rights to equal representation and fair distribution of goods and services, including health care and education, the secular Sudanese Liberation Army/Movement (SLA/M) and the Islamist Justice and Equality Movement (JEM) were created. During the 2000 peace negotiations between the north and south, the SLA/M and the JEM tried to draw the government's attention to their needs. When the Khartoum re-gime ignored their "Black Book" of grievances, the rebels attacked the military base at El Fasher (Wadlow 2005). The Sudanese gov-ernment responded by arming militias in Darfur and recruiting the *janjaweed* ("devils on horseback") to raid and loot African villages.

"First, there is a reign of terror in this area; second, there is a scorched-earth policy; third, there is repeated war crimes and crimes against humanity; and fourth, this is taking place before our eyes." Bertrand Ramcharan, acting United Nations High Commissioner on Human Rights, quoted in Wadlow (2005)

The *janjaweed* became the prime agents of genocidal violence in Darfur. This govern-ment strategy set off widespread "destruction, sexual violence, and displacement that by 2008 affected more than four million people in the region and over 1,195 villages were destroyed" (US Department of State 2007, quoted in Apsel 2009: 241).

A great deal of propaganda was released by Sudan state media, especially under the rule of Omar al-Bashir, suggesting that the Fur were rebellious and must be militar-ily controlled for the stability and unity of the state (Apsel 2009), thus justifying the *janjaweed* campaign of murder and destruction which began in October 2002 (Burr & Collins 2006: 292). The government gave these bandits arms, uniforms, and equipment, and then bombed villages to lead the *janjaweed* to the preferred targets. The *janja-weed* were not paid for their efforts;[4] instead, they looted homes, crops, and livestock, captured slaves, and raped women and girls for payment. They burned crops, filled wells with sand, and displaced thousands of people, who subsequently fled to safer

---

4 There is some debate on this issue: Mulaj (2008) suggests that the Sudanese government pays them stipends that are double what soldiers receive.

FIGURE 5.1 A DARFUR CAMP

regions, fulfilling the government's mandate. The *janjaweed* destroyed villages under the pretext that the inhabitants supported the Sudan Liberation Army or the Justice and Equality Movement.

Religion also played a role in the Darfur conflict (Adam 2008). The military and government elite attempted to impose an Islamic state ideology on all citizens to stamp out cultural pluralism, heterogeneity, and traditional family and societal structure (Apsel 2009). The non-Arab Muslims of Darfur were relegated to the category of "Other," and identified by Islamists in the government as a hindrance to former Libyan leader Moammar Ghadafi's vision of a pure Arab state (Adam 2008). Ethnic riverine Sudanese were appointed to "impose fundamental Islam on the syncretic Muslims of Darfur, who retain some animistic beliefs, and make them all acceptable Arabs" (Markakis 1998: n.p.). Fuelled by Islamic zeal and the concept of *Alhizam Al'Arabi* (the Arab Belt), and fully armed, the Arabs targeted the Fur, killing, looting, burning shops, and rustling livestock.

Obviously, there are many social, political, historical, and cultural dimensions to the conflict in the Sudan that cannot easily be resolved. It is equally obvious that the ruling government of Sudan has fostered and perpetuated genocide against the people of Darfur. Apsel (2009: 257) divides the cycle of violence in Darfur into several stages. During the first stage, the gestation period before 2002, indigenous Africans suffered from discrimination and neglect, while environmental degradation increased competition for scarce resources. The initial stage (2003–05) was the time of mass killings, destruction of villages, and displacement of millions of people. The slow motion stage (2005–08) saw periodic attacks on villages and refugee camps. Sexual violence and human rights abuses were rampant during this period, and the displaced persons suffered from malnutrition, disease, and high mortality rates due to lack of security and few resources. The situation in Darfur remains extremely volatile, with continuing political instability, land, water, and food shortages, a proliferation of arms in the possession of ruthless thugs, and an Arab-Muslim ideology that threatens the cultural diversity of the region.

"Kaltoma Idris, 23, was inside her hut when the *janjaweed* arrived. Outside her sister was boiling water ..., her recently born twins next to her. 'The *janjaweed* came and took the water and poured it over the babies.... They tied my sister up.' Idris fled out the back ..., she saw children being thrown into flaming huts. Two hours later, she returned to find her sister still tied up. 'The babies were dead inside the pot.' She untied her sister. They took her babies and buried them.... Her sister later told her she was whipped and gang raped twice." Raghaven (2004), quoted in Apsel (2009)

The issue of humanitarian intervention has been raised numerous times, though little has been accomplished. Anthropologists have been vocal in their support of "a more vigorous international humanitarian response" as well as international pressure to bring peace to the region (AAA 2004: n.p.). However, anthropologists also feel strongly that any humanitarian intervention should come from African nations with support from Europe and the United States, and that the Sudanese government must be held accountable for its role in perpetuating and facilitating the conflict (AAA 2004). The role of anthropologists in this crisis has been predominantly research and dissemination of information, especially given the reluctance of Western media to publicize this crisis, and the apathy, lack of compassion, and disinterest of the public[5] in this humanitarian crisis. Yet anthropologists are uniquely situated to understand ethnic conflict and genocide, and they are able to give voice to the people and their suffering. In the future this may become a vital role in mediating resolutions or mitigating conflict crises.

In January 2011, after two decades of civil war, the people of south Sudan voted in a referendum to separate from Khartoum-controlled northern Sudan (Avlon 2011). Whether this will lead to peace and security for the people of Darfur remains an open question.

REFUGEES AND HUMANITARIAN CRISIS

Populations of displaced persons are one of the tragic consequences of ethnic conflict. Seventy-eight percent of the world's refugees come from 10 countries: Afghanistan, Angola, Myanmar, Burundi, Congo-Kinshasa, Eritrea, Iraq, Palestine, Somalia, and Sudan (Human Rights Watch 2004). In the twentieth century, the preponderance of

---

5 Mainly referring to North Americans and Europeans.

FIGURE 5.2 DARFURI REFUGEES IN BAHAI, CHAD

refugees created a vast network of permanent international aid agencies. The most obvious form of aid is establishing refugee camps in "trouble spots" to accommodate displaced people. Conditions in these camps vary greatly, but most anthropologists agree that refugee camps are part of the problem, not the solution, because they disempower people and perpetuate a culture of dependency.

According to Waldron (1988), anthropologists are urgently needed to serve as cultural brokers—i.e., speaking on behalf of refugees or, preferably, serving as conduits for refugees to speak for themselves. Ethnographic research often leads to greater understanding of a situation, and anthropologists who document and interpret cultural diversity through ethnographic fieldwork are ideally situated to study the implications of forced migration and the adaptations that refugees must make to survive in the camps. For example, Gadi Ben-Ezer (1990) applied an anthropological approach to his study of Ethiopian refugees in Israel and their problems with authorities. He found that clashes were due to differing social norms and to the way in which the Ethiopians perceived proper interaction between people of differing status: "When children who had stopped eating were referred to him, he was able to identify their 'abnormal' behaviour (eating disorders), caused by the uprooting and the tensions experienced in the process of adapting. He learned that the Ethiopians identified the abdomen as a 'container' of

"Beyond the short-term deprivations and degradations of becoming a refugee, and of sometimes being exploited by middlemen, lies the (possibly lifelong) traumatic reality of never belonging, of being permanently dispossessed of homeland and rights. The practical effects of what this entails is under-researched; recent findings, however, indicate that fear, depression, and the loneliness of having no roots—often being cut off from relatives, friends, community support, culture, and means of livelihood—can have profound effects which are sometimes only apparent in refugees and their children long after resettlement." D'Souza (1981: 5)

emotions. When it became 'too full' of troubles and sorrows, the children were unable to eat" (Harrell-Bond & Voutira 1992: 8).

In Darfur, over one-third of the population has been displaced by the ongoing conflicts, and many more are directly affected by this population displacement. As a result, many refugee camps have been established in the Darfur region. Yet these refugee camps are beneficial to the Sudan government because they attract relief aid and create a pool of recruits for the Sudanese army and cheap labour.

Land degradation and water and firewood scarcity are serious problems around large camps in Darfur (Apsel 2009), as is poor sanitation. Conditions continue to deteriorate in 2012; camps are crowded, and many refugees suffer from acute malnutrition and infectious diseases such as yellow fever and malaria (Welling 2007). Tensions run high over access to scarce resources within the camps, there is constant danger of conflicts with neighbouring communities, and women and children face sexual violence when they leave the camps in search of firewood. The camps are recruiting grounds for various factions and militias. Loss of traditional family and societal structure, poverty, and trauma have resulted in increased violence in the camps, from rape to extortion (Apsel 2009). Individuals in positions of power and celebrity, such as actor George Clooney, have tried to draw attention to the plight of the Darfurian people, but still the problems persist.

For anthropologists, the study of refugees offers a chance to record and interpret the processes of culture change that reach far beyond systems of transition found within a small-scale society. They have the opportunity to witness the cultural adaptations and coping strategies of refugees in a new social, economic, and physical environment (Harrell-Bond & Voutira 1992), and can contribute to understanding the social meanings attached to refugee status. For example, when Malkki (1990) conducted an ethnographic study of a refugee camp in Tanzania, she found that the camps provided people of the same ethnicity with a sense of cohesiveness not found among refugees settled in urban centres.

"We are not able to go back to our villages and we are not able to stay here safely, so we are not thinking about life now." Khaled Abdel Muti All, a displaced person in Abu Shouk camp on the outskirts of El-Fasher, North Darfur (Henshaw 2008)

As a result, studying refugees and forced migration has become a major field within anthropology. The role of anthropologists as cultural brokers has been undervalued to date; however, the potential for their contributions to refugee studies and situations is significant. Anthropologists are also working to provide solutions to refugee plights by creating agencies such as Cultural Survival that give voice to the refugees.

CONCLUSION

This chapter began with the question, what are the underlying reasons for ethnic conflict? Obviously, ethnic conflict is a complex issue embedded in political, social, religious, and economic factors. Although ethnic groups are at the centre of these conflicts, the underlying reasons have little to do with ethnicity and everything to do with power struggles over people, resources, and land, which is why these conflicts continue to be perpetuated around the world, and why solutions to ethnic conflict remain elusive.

The most devastating consequence of ethnic conflict is the displaced persons that lose their socio-economic and political status at the same time as they lose their "place." Throughout the twentieth century and into the twenty-first century, genocide has been perpetuated against ethnic groups—this is a global crisis, not a regional one. The conflict in Darfur is an example of the devastation that is wrought when state authorities seek to marginalize or destroy an ethnic group for economic gain, religious ideology, or ethnic imperialism. The United Nations aptly describes the Darfur conflict as one of "the world's worst humanitarian crises" (AlertNet 2011: n.p.).

What is anthropology's role in addressing worldwide ethnic conflict? According to Harrell-Bond and Voutira (1992), recognizing that survival, loss, and suffering are part of the permanent human condition in pluralistic societies could make anthropology politically relevant and remove the aura of detachment still prevalent in academic anthropology. As well, anthropologists have an ethical responsibility to work as mediators during ethnic conflicts and advocate for the millions of people that have been displaced by ethnic conflict.

QUESTIONS FOR CONSIDERATION AND CLASSROOM ACTIVITIES

1. The question is often asked whether conflict can be reduced if ethnic minority groups are encouraged to assimilate into mainstream society. Do you agree or disagree with a policy of assimilation? Research the meaning and application of assimilation policy, and then respond to the above question. What would we gain if everyone identified with one homogenous "ethnic" group? What would we lose?

2. We have all heard a great deal about the harmful effects of racism and ethnic prejudice on the victims. But have you ever thought about the perpetrators—the people who hold these views, and how these attitudes affect their lives? In other words, have you ever met a happy bigot? Create a list of the ways in which racists limit their lives because of their views.

3. What does ethnicity mean to you? Do you identify with an ethnic group? Why or why not?

4. Choose a nation and research its history of ethnic conflict. What are the underlying causes of this conflict? What level has this conflict reached, and have any of the issues been resolved?

5. Research the term "race." What criteria have been used to categorize people into different races? Examine the weaknesses with these criteria. Why have these criteria failed to work for every group?

6. Locate a refugee camp (e.g., in Darfur) and research the economic, social, political, and religious systems found within this camp. How do these systems of culture enable the refugees to survive camp life? Are these systems as well developed as in cultures outside a camp environment?

7. Actor George Clooney has visited refugee camps in Darfur several times, and has been a vocal proponent for international aid in the region. What impact(s) do you think his activism has had on the situation? What can you (e.g., you and your fellow students) do to help the people of Darfur?

8. Debate topic: Should international military forces move into Darfur and "clear out" the *janjaweed*?

SUGGESTED READINGS

Bringa, T. (1995). *Being Muslim the Bosnian way.* Princeton, NJ: Princeton University Press.

This book is an ethnographic account of Bosnian Muslims living in a rural village near Sarajevo. Bringa focuses on religion as a boundary marker for ethnic identity, and the role of individual households in creating this identity. The issues of ethnicity and nationality are explored through the struggles of a small community dealing with the horrors of conflict and war.

Hecht, J. (2005). *The journey of the lost boys: A story of courage, faith and the sheer determination to survive by a group of young boys called "The Lost Boys of Sudan."* Jacksonville, FL: Allswell Press.

This award-winning book recounts the struggle of orphaned boys in war-torn southern Sudan, where their lives were in danger, walking a thousand miles to safety. This book also discusses political and historical events that led to the civil war in Sudan.

Chapter 6

HOW DOES BODY IMAGE AFFECT SELF-ESTEEM, WELL-BEING, AND IDENTITY?

Key Terms: androcentrism, body dissatisfaction, body image, body modification, cyberpunks, eating disorders, ethnicity, gender, Modern Primitives, queer subculture, ritual, symbolic capital

---

INTRODUCTION

The perfect body—what does this mean? Is it a size-two woman with an impossibly small waist and large breasts, or a woman whose neck has been artificially elongated with brass rings? Is it a man with bulging muscles and a flat stomach, or a man covered with intricate scarification? Every society has its own image of beauty, and in every society men and women are, to a certain extent, defined by their body image. In North America, tall, blond, thin women continue to represent the body ideal. This narrow, "Barbie-doll" beauty standard is perpetuated by media—television, magazines, and the Internet glamorize thinness and equate it with perfection. Women are inundated with advertisements for Botox, cosmetic surgery, diets, exercise equipment, and "self-help" programs that feature ways to "improve" their appearance—what Nichter and Vuckovic (1994) call "body work."

Despite some rather convoluted psychological definitions, quite simply **body image** is the way we think our body looks, and how we think our body *should* look—a mental image of an ideal body that is culturally constructed (van Esterik 2001: 20) and learned from birth. In this chapter we will investigate the social, economic, and cultural influences that perpetuate an ideal body image. Obsession with the ideal body has led many women and men in Western societies to feel inadequate and dissatisfied with their bodies. Body dissatisfaction refers to "a negative self-evaluation of one's own appearance and desire to be more physically attractive" (Cash & Pruzinsky 2002, quoted in Ferguson et al. 2011: 458). The psychological and physical problems that can result from body dissatisfaction will be addressed, including the increase in eating disorders in many societies. The transnational flow of people and ideas is spreading Western perceptions of beauty to other countries, resulting in many of the same body-image issues as seen in the West. We will consider the consequences of this globalization of the West's body image.

Not all cultural groups agree with the North American perception of beauty, especially the view that a thin woman's body is ideal. In some non-Western cultures, the body is considered the means by which women carry out social, economic, and reproductive roles. For a very different perspective on the ideal body, we will explore the concept of "fatness" as symbolic capital among the Tuareg of northern Niger and northern Mali. We will also explore body-modification practices as a means to defy oppression and assert sexuality, identity, and political resistance in the queer, cyberpunk, and Modern Primitive subcultures.

ANTHROPOLOGISTS AND BODY IMAGE

Although anthropologists have traditionally concentrated on the body rather than on body image, some anthropologists have turned their attention to body politics and power relations, the social and cultural aspects of body image, and the significance of sex and gender on body image (Kaplan-Myrth 2000). In fact, anthropologists bring a cross-cultural perspective to the study of the meaning of body image and the concept of beauty in cultural systems. Beliefs and behaviours regarding body image can vary significantly from one culture to another. For example, Rasmussen (2010) conducted an ethnographic study in the Tuareg culture to explore the full range of meanings assigned to female fatness, comparing the nomadic herding Tuareg and the more sedentary oasis-gardening Tuareg communities.

Contemporary anthropologists apply their cross-cultural knowledge when they join the ongoing discourse concerning body image. This is particularly evident in medical anthropology, where the cultural meanings and social dynamics of fasting, overeating, and body modification have been studied. For example, Massara (1989) investigated the cultural meaning and the social implications of being overweight among older Puerto Rican women. This study was particularly relevant because Massara employed ethnographic research methods and, in doing so, provided a model for medical professionals to understand their patients within a cultural context (Mackenzie 1991). Researchers are also taking more notice of male body image, especially since adolescent boys often have body-image issues similar to those of girls. Viviani, Lavazza, and Gallo (2004), for instance, investigated whether body image is linked to biological maturity, intellectual development, or mood among adolescent male basketball players in Italy.

THE NATURE OF BODY IMAGE

In *The Body Image Trap*, psychologist Marion Crook (1991) defines the perfect female body as tall, blond, and size 10—an outdated image, considering that most twenty-first-century North American women preoccupied with thinness would be horrified to reach a size 10. The pursuit of thinness among women is a highly valued behaviour, especially in Western countries, and even though there are other places where thinness is preferred, anthropologist C. Counihan (1999) has never encountered a cultural group where it is acceptable to starve oneself in order to become thin, and contends that the self-destructive relationship that many Western women have with their bodies differs from that of women in non-Western cultures.

Hesse-Biber (1996) likens the quest for thinness to a religious cult, with all the requisite characteristics—isolation, obsession, and excessive **ritual** (dieting, exercise, daily weigh-ins, and calorie counting). The media and entertainment industry provides icons to worship (e.g., Jennifer Aniston) and ceremonies, such as beauty pageants, to reaffirm the ideal. Diet clubs (e.g., Weight Watchers), sages (e.g., Dr. Atkins), and gurus (e.g., Oprah Winfrey) often take on a quasi-religious connotation. It is difficult to shed the attitude that the perfect body and weight are not important when shows such as *Entertainment Tonight* (CBS) feature at least one and sometimes several vignettes on a celebrity's rising or falling weight. Consequently, weight loss and cosmetic surgery have become big business as women struggle to emulate the North American ideal body. Women with bodies outside the ideal often suffer from society's disapproval and become marginalized. They experience difficulty finding jobs and are considered lazy and lacking in self-discipline and willpower.

Ethnicity may also play a role in body image (Kawamura 2002). Western media tends to stereotype the features of minority groups and seldom uses them as role models to exemplify beauty. Discrimination based on physical characteristics can be harmful to self-esteem, leading young people to dislike the physical features they inherited.

"We urban, Jewish, black, Asian and Latina girls began to realize slowly and painfully that if you didn't look like Barbie, you didn't fit in. Your status was diminished. You were less beautiful, less valuable, less worthy. If you didn't look like Barbie, companies would discontinue you. You simply couldn't compete." Gilman (1998: 236)

Body image (negative or positive) is shaped by the way others see us, or the way we *think* they see us. Kaplan-Myrth (2000) discovered that even visually impaired people are self-conscious about their appearance, despite not being able to see their own image. They find their body image through the eyes of friends and family around them. Ferguson et al. (2011) also found that the most powerful influences on **body dissatisfaction** are peer pressure and criticism, although media images of idealized body types may contribute to a sense of inferiority. Peer influences can be active (a conversation with peers about the ideal body, or bullying because of appearance) or passive (the presence of competition). Indeed, this study found that body dissatisfaction increased in the presence of competitive females, especially if an attractive male was present. Thus, from an evolutionary perspective, body dissatisfaction is one ramification of females competing for males. Other studies have found that individuals respond to media hype in different ways, although women who already suffer from body dissatisfaction are more influenced by media ideals of female beauty (Trampe, Stapel, & Siero 2007).

The ideal body image is culturally defined (Sault 1994). For example, Chinese foot binding involved bending the toes under the sole, and making a pointed front—arching the foot like a small hook (Ping 2000). This practice was popular in tenth-century China and for a thousand years afterward, but it eventually faded out when Mao Zedong and the Cultural Revolution transformed China's political and social environments. Most

North Americans find foot binding cruel, yet this symbol of traditional Chinese femininity and beauty[1] is remarkably similar to the current Western practice of young women undergoing breast augmentation, or the historic practice of wearing a tightly cinched and physically damaging corset. In a similar example, the Kayan women of northern Thailand wear brass neck coils that reduce their clavicle and create an image of an elongated neck. This body modification gives women their cultural identity and sense of beauty (Mirante 2006).

Although body-image dissatisfaction is more prevalent among women, this pattern is not age- or gender-restricted—both males and females are concerned with their appearance and expend enormous time, energy, and money in achieving the perfect body. Hesse-Biber (1996) found that men are also concerned about their weight. This body dissatisfaction has opened up a huge market for weight-loss programs, exercise equipment, health spas, and various men's products. The strategy appears to be working, because the rate of body dissatisfaction among men is increasing.

Language may also reflect body image. Nichter and Vuckovic (1994) commonly encountered the phrase "I'm so fat" during their ethnographic research on body image and dieting among adolescent North American girls. This "ritualized talk" signals unhappiness, a call for peer support, and apology for bad behaviour. Whether the body is viewed as the sum of its parts or as a whole entity is also reflected in language choice. In North America, where the body is viewed in parts (e.g., breasts, head, etc.), we would say "my head aches." Among the Wintu of California, by contrast, where the body is viewed as a whole, they may say "I head ache" (Sault 1994: 13, from Lee 1959: 124).

FIGURE 6.1 MEDIA PORTRAYAL OF YOUNG, BEAUTIFUL, "PERFECT" WOMEN HAS LED MANY WOMEN TO FEEL INADEQUATE

The first recorded weight-loss program took place in 1558, when Italian Luigi Coronaro ate sparingly to change his overall health. He became thin and energetic, and his writings on the value of "dieting" convinced others to try losing weight to improve their health (Crook 1991). The Western obsession with thinness began in the 1960s,

---

1 Foot binding also served to isolate and control women, who were thus unable to walk very far from home.

in part due to media adulation of British fashion model Twiggy. Before this time, the ideal woman was full-figured and healthy looking, signifying her ability to bear children. Then Twiggy appeared, and the desperate quest for thinness began. At about the same time, Barbie, the fashion doll, appeared on store shelves. This doll inspired young girls and women to strive for her impossible-to-emulate beauty standard—what Gilman (1998) calls the Barbie doll syndrome.

Despite their symbolism, Barbie and Twiggy were merely physical manifestations of the fashionable emphasis on thinness, at a time when other equally significant socio-cultural transformations were taking place. During the 1960s, young women were being inundated with conflicting demands that created an identity crisis (Bruch 1978). New education and career opportunities conflicted with women's traditional roles as nurturers and homemakers, thereby creating confusion and a feeling of powerlessness (Gordon 2000) that eventually led to a rise in eating disorders.

FIGURE 6.2 THIS EXTENSIVE COLLECTION OF BARBIE DOLLS SYMBOLIZES NOT ONLY AN IMPOSSIBLE-TO-ACHIEVE STANDARD OF BEAUTY BUT ALSO OUR OBSESSION WITH HER TYPE OF BEAUTY

EATING DISORDERS

North American children as young as seven are aware of whether eating a particular food will make them fat, and they judge their self-worth according to their body size. This all-consuming desire to achieve a perfect body has led to serious psychological, socio-cultural, economic, and health consequences in the West and, increasingly, in other parts of the world. **Eating disorders** are symptomatic of cultural expectations and revolve around identity issues and body image (Gordon 2000). Anorexia nervosa, the avoidance of food to the point of starvation, and bulimia, binge eating followed by self-induced vomiting, are two of the most common types of eating disorder (Holmberg 1998).

"You're busted, Babs. You've been found guilty of inspiring fourth-grade girls to diet, of modeling an impossible beauty standard, of clinging to homogeneity in a diverse new world." Edut (1998: 1)

"When I'm out of control of my eating and my weight, I'm out of control of my life!" Quoted in Mackenzie (1991: 408)

As mentioned earlier, body image is about power. Brumberg (1989) found that fasting is one of the few forms of protest available to young women. In other words, refusing to eat offers a sense of empowerment—a way for women to gain control and autonomy over their lives (Hesse-Biber 1996). Fasting is also symptomatic of a concern for virtue, feelings of being unlovable, and a desire to improve self-esteem by losing weight (Mackenzie 1991). With the reduction in women's domestic role as mothers and housewives and the splintering of kinship, women's social roles and status have changed, and attractiveness has become a measure and mechanism for success (Littlewood 2004).

Eating disorders are shaped by social and cultural phenomena (Pike & Borovoy 2004), meaning they arise because of unique cultural experiences stemming not from a fear of fatness, but from a fear of loss of control (Lee 2001). Risk factors for developing eating disorders include female sex, adolescence, rapidly changing social conditions, and living in the West. Concern with eating and body image is increasingly a global phenomenon, however. Changing **gender** roles and beauty ideals have had an impact on women in Japan, for example, where the incidence of eating disorders and an obsession with thinness have been rising throughout the twentieth century (Pike & Borovoy 2004). Japanese women have been exposed to Western ideals of beauty, while also having to deal with Japanese cultural values and changing gender-role expectations and social pressures in Japanese culture and society (Pike & Borovoy 2004).

> "Anorexia nervosa (and other eating disorders) is not really about losing weight, eating or not, exercising like a maniac or not, it is about self-esteem, it is about how you feel about yourself." Judy, a recovering anorexic, quoted in Sargent (n.d.)

In Florence, Italy, Florentines view the body as a source of pleasure and a reflection of family (Counihan 1999). Both men and women love food (*gola*) and love to nurture their bodies. Though they enjoy eating, Florentines also believe in control—gluttony destroys the pleasure of eating and leads to obesity. Therefore, Florentines believe in "enjoying food greatly but consuming it moderately" (Counihan 1999: 182). Unlike North Americans, who may feel guilty after a day of overeating and resort to strenuous exercise and dieting, Florentines do not. A plump body signifies health and fertility, while a thin body may mean physical illness or emotional upset. Despite their healthy relationship with food and their bodies, however, Western influence is seeping into the Italian consciousness. Florentine women are being bombarded with North American images of thin women, which are affecting the way young Florentine women view themselves. Counihan (1999) also found that eating disorders in Italy were on the upswing in the 1990s.

In many Asian countries, plumpness was once a sign of prosperity, good health, and beauty. Recent studies have shown that this is no longer the case; the North American quest for thinness has spread to these regions as well (Kawamura 2002). In Vietnam, the newly infused Westernized perception of the proper height for humans lies at the root of a dangerous fad: leg-lengthening surgeries (Cudd 2005). This new body image has even influenced employment opportunities: some companies have set height restrictions and will not hire individuals who do not fit within this ideal height. Some Asian women are even resorting to cosmetic surgery to remove their epicanthic folds and create a double eyelid in order to meet Western standards of beauty. The same holds true for Latino cultures. Latin American women have been exposed to Western ideals of thinness, which has led to a dramatic increase in eating disorders—girls in private schools in Brazil, for instance, have adopted Western body ideals, leading to abuse of laxatives and diuretics (Altabe & O'Garo 2002).

The more acculturated a group becomes to North American values, the more body dissatisfaction they experience. Even in relatively isolated regions, Western influences are being felt. In Samoa, feeding of the body to make it plump is a sign of social success. However, as Brewis (1999) discovered, those Samoans living in an urban setting in Auckland, New Zealand (and consequently more exposed to Western ideals), possessed slimmer body ideals than those still living in Samoa. Katzman et al. (2004) also found that women suffering from anorexia nervosa in Curaçao had lived away from the island for some time, learning a new body-image ideal.

THE CONCEPT OF "FATNESS"

Although this discussion has focused on North American body image and the spread of this ideal to other cultures, the pressures to conform to a certain body image are not the sole domain of Westerners. Southeastern Nigerians consider curvaceous women the ideal. They see a plump woman as healthy, her family as prosperous, and her sexuality alluring (Simmons 1998). To this end, young women undergo an age-old rite of passage when they are isolated in a fattening room, fed forcefully to gain weight, and instructed in the ways of a proper wife and mother. The age when girls enter the fattening room varies, from as young as seven to just before marriage. The general guideline is "the bigger the better," although today most families can afford to support their daughters in the fattening room for only a few months rather than the traditional two years.

"We now have damning evidence from Fiji of the impact of Western ideals of beauty where, in a three-year period after the introduction of TV (mainly US programmes), 15 per cent of the teenage girls developed bulimia. The penetration of Western images coupled with an economic onslaught, had destabilised Fijian girls' sense of beauty, infecting them with a virus more lethal than the measles Britain exported to the colonies 100 years ago." Orbach (2001: 1), quoted in Wykes and Gunter (2005: 14)

In the northern regions of Niger and northern Mali, female fatness is also valued; however, changing political and economic conditions and patterns of settlement have affected this idealized body image. The Tuareg are a socially stratified Muslim people living in the Sahara. In former times, adolescent females of noble families underwent fattening rituals in their mothers' tents before marriage; however, conflicts and droughts have reduced the prosperity in these regions, leading to a decline in the fattening ritual. Anthropologist Susan J. Rasmussen[2] (2010) explored the changing meanings of female fatness and the ambivalence that some Tuareg now feel toward body fat. Rasmussen compared two communities, one a nomadic group practising pastoral transhumance, the other, agropastoralists settled on an oasis. Rasmussen analysed the cultural, medical, and psychosocial meanings of body image and body politics, and how attitudes have changed over time.

Contemporary Tuareg noble women still feel pressure to gain weight to earn prestige and identity, to appear healthy and fertile, and to maintain a separation from women of lower status. This is particularly true of the nomadic community. Indeed, fatness is symbolic of their aristocratic status and is a sign of social strength (Bourdieu 1977). "Soft" fat, based on eating milk and meat, symbolizes purity, happiness, and abundance, while hard muscles are associated with physical labour and having to eat grains. In the more sedentary oasis community, attitudes toward female fatness

---

2 All information on the Tuareg is taken from Rasmussen (2010) unless otherwise noted.

FIGURE 6.3 AMONG THE TUAREG, BODY FAT IS HIGHLY VALUED

are more ambivalent; some still value fatness, while others feel it interferes with the physical labour necessary in a farming community. Tuareg women in the oasis gardening community work hard to become an economic asset to their husbands. This presents what Rasmussen (2010) calls a double-bind dilemma for the women: refrain from heavy work and gain weight, but risk their husbands acquiring more wives to do the work; work hard and risk becoming thin, infertile, and unattractive to their husbands, who will then take younger wives.

The conjugal and reproductive roles of women are very important in Tuareg society. Traditionally, a woman's role in the matrilineal nomadic pastoral culture was as a mother and educator of Tuareg children, while in the oasis, where matriliny is weakening, men have become the educators, and emphasis is now placed on women's fertility. Fear of hunger also accounts for the value placed on bodily fat; however, Rasmussen cautions that the fat aesthetic holds many other meanings, especially since status from fatness applies only to noble women. Female fatness also signifies a man's role as a productive husband, father, and son-in-law to his affines. Therefore, the condition of a woman's body represents a man's economic success or failure.

Thus, cultural, social, and economic processes encourage attitudes and meanings assigned to fatness. In both communities, fatness is a sign of mastery of cultural and political-economic challenges, and represents **symbolic capital**. Fatness is considered a sign of free choice, independence, and prestigious social and gender status. Among the nomadic herders, fatness represents prosperity and freedom from having to do any heavy physical labour. The Tuareg believe that not eating enough decreases sexual appetite; therefore, a woman eating well and growing fat increases her sexuality and fertility. In the oasis, on the other hand, women would prefer to be fat, but physical labour prevents them from gaining weight. As well, many members of this community now disdain fat because it impedes the physical labour necessary for oasis gardening and cereal processing. Despite this ambivalence toward female fatness and labour, psychologically the ideal body image still remains a fat woman.

> "Fatness envelops and comforts women, fortresslike, in 'layers' of protection, from several dangers: literal hunger; diminution of prestige and self-respect of noble, mother and wife and, also, violence and hunger." Rasmussen (2010: 632)

BODY MODIFICATION

Body politics and power relations, including identity, ethnicity, class, gender, and sexuality, have become important themes in the study of the human condition, from the quest for women's body rights to self-expression, activism, and resistance communicated through body modification. **Body modification** is the alteration of body parts in a non-medical way, most typically through tattooing, piercing, and cutting, but also involves scarification, branding, and implants. Although some body modifications (e.g., tattoos and piercings) have gained increasing acceptance in mainstream society, many of the practices remain neo-tribal—the domain of indigenous cultures. Among the Rashaayda Bedouin of eastern Sudan, tattooing is used to communicate identity and symbolize relations with others. Rashiidi women tattoo their bodies in three places: the forearms, the lower half of the face, and the upper legs and thighs (Young 1994). Arm tattoos are merely decorative, while face and leg tattoos are private symbols reserved for the eyes of their loved ones. An unmarried girl may have her thigh tattooed with a man's camel brand to announce her love for him. Only the women's husbands will ever see the tattoos, because their faces are covered with veils and their legs with long skirts.

> "If people were using beads, they were using them to convey a message about themselves, I believe that implies there was language, which does much the same thing." Henderson (2006: n.p.)

According to sociologist Victoria Pitts (2003: 21), body modification is still considered outside normal behaviour and a social problem. This has encouraged the development of body-modification subcultures, such as cyberpunks who merge the body with technology. Indeed, body modification performed with others may create a sense of community, empowering the performers and fostering feelings of self-assertion

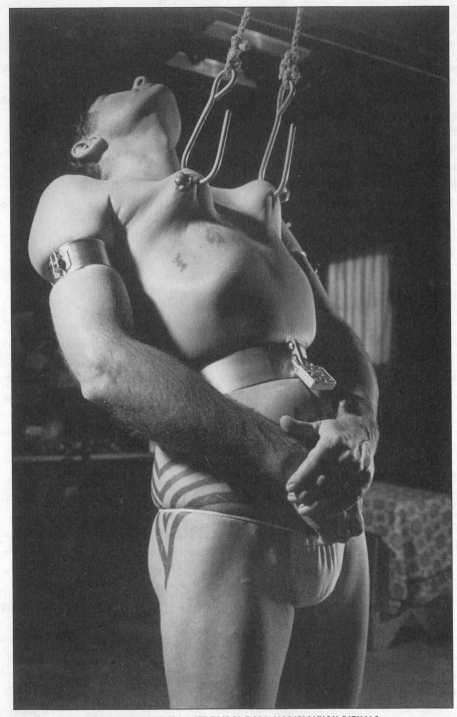

FIGURE 6.4   MODERN PRIMITIVES EMULATE TRIBAL BODY MODIFICATION RITUALS

and a means for coping with stress. Body modification is a way of expressing resistance to mainstream society for those who are or feel they are marginalized.

For female body modifiers, modification is a way to reclaim their bodies, often in response to sexual abuse or violence, and a way of contesting patriarchy. Body modification also challenges **androcentric**, racist, and classist concepts of beauty and body image. Thus, body modification should be viewed as a feminist, cultural, and political act (Kleese 2007: 277) that gives voice to the marginalized.

This holds true in **queer subculture**, where body modification expresses and symbolizes resistance to oppression and marginalization in modern society. The most prominent forms of body modification among queers are piercing, branding, cutting, tattooing, stretching, various forms of surgery, and body alterations for BDSM[3] or fetish play. Body modification articulates queer identity and is an expression of rebellion or disobedience (Kleese 2007). This transgression is often sexual among queers, exceeding the boundaries of permissible or imaginable behaviour in the eyes of mainstream society (Jenks 2003). Body modification, then, contests heteronormativity—behavioural norms that place people in a society's "normal" gender identities (e.g., men and women). By provoking shock with their distinctive tattoos, scars, and brandings, queer body modifiers emphasize the symbolism of the body (Pitts 2000) and challenge mainstream concepts of beauty.

> "All sensual experience functions to free us from 'normal' social restraints, to awaken our deadened bodies to life." V. Vale and A. Juno, quoted by D. Bonetti in a review of *Modern Primitives* (1989)

Modern Primitives are a small countercultural movement that originated in the 1970s and 1980s in the United States and continues to grow in popularity (Kleese 2007). These white, middle-class individuals adopt neo-tribal rituals and practices, such as the traditional Sun Dance of Plains First Nations, which involves hanging from piercings in the chest muscles and requires displays of stoicism and bravery. The rituals signify "spiritual enhancement, sexual liberation and embodied cultural dissidence" (Kleese 2007: 279). Modern Primitives attempt to "rescue the body and self from the problems of the world" (Pitts 2003: 3). Therefore, this group is using body modification to stretch cultural boundaries of what is appropriate to display in public. There are socio-economic implications from this movement, since modern "primitiveness" has become trendy, with some members of mainstream society, especially youth, becoming consumers of Modern Primitive lifestyle and ritual.

> "The magnetic implant is not the most sophisticated or rich sensation, it was just the easiest to implement with our available technology." Unidentified cyberpunk following implant of a small magnet in his thumb (Cyberpunkreview.com 2006)

Cyberpunks, a high-tech counterculture, use implants and technological invasion of the body (e.g., prosthetics) to create hybrid humans or "cyborgian bodies" (Pitts 2003: 152). Like the Modern Primitives, cyberpunks have cyber-communities of body modifiers and ezines to maintain communication. Cyberculture and its dystopian view of the near future is growing in popularity,

---

3 Bondage and Discipline, Dominance and Submission, Sadism and Masochism.

especially among curious youth who feel disenfranchised from society. Although body modification is an important component of cyberpunk counterculture, science fiction literature featuring dystopian near-futures where machines rule and human life has been devalued is also a hallmark of this counterculture.

These three examples of body modifiers—queers, Modern Primitives, and cyberpunks—use the body as a space for resistance and empowerment through body modification. The body, then, becomes a site of social, political, and cultural contestation for marginalized people (Pitts 2003).

CONCLUSION

The ideal body, body image, body modification—these are all concepts that symbolize the quest for acceptance and worthiness. Indeed, body image, and by association the ideal body, are cultural constructs. Human identity and sense of belonging are revealed through body image; thus, men and women are willing to endure all sorts of inconvenience and discomfort to attain the ideal body in order to earn the status and approval of their society.

In the last half-century, Westerners, particularly women, have developed a distorted sense of the ideal body that has created emotional and physical problems. Eating disorders have increased dramatically since the 1960s, especially in North America and Western Europe. But the Western body ideal is permeating other cultures as well. Young people the world over are adopting the Western ideal of beauty and developing similar body-image problems and eating disorders as in the West. However, culture is dynamic, and even the obsession with thinness may be shifting; for example, Israeli authorities have banned thin models from the runway in the hope of reducing the exposure of young girls to extreme thinness (*The Talk* 2012).

A continuing theme running through this chapter has been the influence of culture and the social relations within a culture on body image. As is obvious, North American society stresses thinness as the ideal body. In other cultures, health and child-bearing capabilities are the ideal. Among the Tuareg, fatness is a symbol of beauty, prosperity, high status, and represents a woman's value as a mother and educator—fatness, not thinness, becomes symbolic capital.

Body modification is often used to signify resistance to the status quo. For more hardcore body modification like scarification, counter-cultural movements such as the Modern Primitives use body modification as a medium for expressing their discontent and to create a sense of belonging with other modifiers. Body image, then, the different forms of body modification, and the many meanings of "the ideal body" are extremely complex issues embedded in body politics and power relations.

QUESTIONS FOR CONSIDERATION AND CLASSROOM ACTIVITIES

1. Diffusion of the Western ideal of beauty to other parts of the world is affecting young women's sense of well-being. Choose a country and investigate the influence of Western ideals on people's perception of beauty and how they have responded to these changes.

2. How prevalent are eating disorders in your network of friends and family? Identify the symptoms and behaviours of someone with an eating disorder.

3. Conduct an honest self-analysis of your body image and the efforts you expend to improve your appearance. Analyse the reasons for your behaviour.

4. Class debate: How thin is too thin? Should models be forced to maintain a healthy weight? Should employers have the right to fire employees (e.g., cocktail waitresses, flight attendants) if they gain weight?

5. Keep a journal for one week, noting everything you eat, when, and why. Based on your journal, do you eat when stressed, sad, lonely, tired? Are you an emotional eater?

6. Conduct an in-depth study of cyberpunks, Modern Primitives, or queer subculture. What are the underlying reasons for their rejection of so-called mainstream behaviour?

7. Debate question: Eating disorders appear to be on the increase in developed countries. What are the likely reasons for this phenomenon? While these disorders are rising in prevalence around the world, is it possible that their incidence could be levelling off or even declining in the West, and why?

SUGGESTED READINGS

Edut, O. (Ed.). (1998). *Adios, Barbie: Young women write about body image and identity.* Seattle: Seal Press.

A delightful collection of cross-cultural essays that consider the social impact of the Barbie doll. The young women featured in this book show little interest in resembling a Barbie doll, yet they address many of the body-image concerns and issues faced by women.

Nasser, M., Katzman, M.A., & Gordon, R.A. (Eds.). (2001). *Eating disorders and cultures in transition.* New York: Brunner-Routledge.

An exploration of the cross-cultural factors in eating disorders in South America, Asia, Africa, and Eastern Europe. This book examines cultural transformation and its impact on emotional issues.

Chapter 7

IS FEMALE CIRCUMCISION A VIOLATION OF HUMAN RIGHTS OR A CHERISHED CULTURAL TRADITION?

Key Terms: clitoridectomy, cultural imperialism, cultural relativism, development and modernization approach, engaged anthropology, ethical dilemma, ethnic identity, ethnocentrism, female circumcision, gender equality, gender identity, human rights, infibulation, pharaonic circumcision, rite of passage, ritual, sexuality, sunna circumcision, symbolic circumcision, universalism

---

INTRODUCTION

Perhaps no other cultural practice has raised the ire of the international community more than female circumcision. Feminist and human rights groups, medical practitioners, religious and political organizations, the media, and many others have voiced their opposition to this ancient practice. Yet some anthropologists believe we must look beyond the "shock" value of female circumcision to understand the deeply rooted and divergent reasons behind this practice. We must ask what meaning(s) female circumcision holds for individuals and communities and why this ritual is so persistent, despite global condemnation. Only then will we begin to understand female circumcision through the eyes of its practitioners. This does not mean that anthropologists condone female circumcision, nor does it mean they champion the rights of cultural groups to continue the practice. Rather, we cannot understand the cultural meanings behind this ritual without *listening* to why people practise female circumcision, what the ceremony accomplishes in their eyes, and why it is important in their everyday lives. Only then can anthropologists offer an informed opinion, and as anthropologist Dave Smith states, "It's fine to want to help people, but you need to wait to be asked" (Erikson et al. 2001).

In this chapter we will enter the debate surrounding female circumcision and the politics of reproduction, a debate that often pits cultural relativism against universalism and advocacy for human rights. **Cultural relativism** holds that every culture is equally valid and should not be judged against other cultures, while **universalism** suggests there are universal human rights that must be followed, regardless of culture. Anthropologists tend to focus on protecting and supporting cultural groups, rather than promoting Western values, which is a goal of human rights groups. Anthropologists, then, are integral to this discussion as they investigate the political, socio-economic, and historical factors that contribute to the persistence of female circumcision. The controversy attached to the practice, the opposition to female circumcision, and the reasons behind this opposition will also be addressed.

"There is an unfortunate and perturbing silence among African women intellectuals who have experienced initiation and 'circumcision.' This is understandable, given the venomous tone of the debate and unswerving demand that a definitive stance be taken—evidently, if one is educated—*against* the practice."
Anthropologist Fuambai Ahmadu (2000: 283), quoted in Moruzzi (2005: 216)

To offer insight into the complexity of this issue, several narratives are presented in the margins. Readers should note that while it is easy to find people who hold negative views on female circumcision, giving voice to people who support this practice is more challenging. The reasons for this one-sided debate are many: the researchers, usually of Western origin, may be unconsciously showing their bias by seeking out those who reject female circumcision; those who practise female circumcision may be less willing to speak out for fear of reprisals from government officials or condemnation from the interviewer, or they may feel no need to justify female circumcision to outsiders.

DEFINITION OF FEMALE CIRCUMCISION

Female circumcision is the ritual cutting, removal, or altering of external genitalia. The procedure is performed by traditional or government-trained midwives living in the community. Although popular media tends to lump all forms of female circumcision together, there are several types; the choice of which type is practised is influenced by differing socio-cultural, political, and historical contexts (Shell-Duncan 2001: 2). The least invasive procedure is **sunna circumcision**, where only the clitoral prepuce (hood) is removed (Gordon 1991). The second and most common type of circumcision is known as excision or **clitoridectomy**, where part or the entire clitoris is removed, as well as part or all of the labia minora.[1] **Pharaonic circumcision** involves the complete removal of the clitoris, labia minora, and most or all of the labia majora.[2] In pharaonic circumcision, the cut edges are then stitched together, leaving a small opening for urine and menstrual flow. This stitching is known as **infibulation**. Before intercourse, an infibulated woman may have to be cut open, then re-infibulated after the birth of her child. The type of circumcision performed is determined by the underlying reasons for the procedure, as is the age at which circumcision is performed. The most common times are soon after birth, before puberty, at the onset of puberty, just before marriage, in the seventh month of a first pregnancy, or after the first birth (Mackie 2000).

---

1 Inner lips of the vulva.
2 Outside lips of the vulva.

Historically, colonial efforts to eradicate the practice met with stiff resistance and failed miserably. Indeed, such efforts, predicated on a notion of moral superiority, often served to further entrench the practice (Martinez 2005: 33). In northern Sudan in the late 1940s, the British colonial government passed a law that prohibited pharaonic circumcision (Abusharaf 2006: 209). Because of their desire to eradicate female circumcision, the British established themselves as authority figures in family matters and ultimately reinforced male dominance in Sudanese society by encouraging "colonial surveillance and the policing of women by their male relatives under the direction of colonial authorities" (Abusharaf 2006: 219). They were horrified that women had control over circumcision—what they called female sadism, but the real problem stemmed from the power of Sudanese women to make decisions, something that contradicted the male-centred society of early-twentieth-century Britain. The end result was that the power and authority of Sudanese women in cultural and ritual life were weakened.

"In their attempt to outlaw customs the European rulers considered cruel, it was not the concern with indigenous suffering that dominated their thinking, but the desire to impose what they considered civilized standards of justice and humanity on a subject population, that is, the desire to create new subjects." Talal Asad (1996: 1091), quoted in Abusharaf (2006: 214)

The British ignored the importance of female circumcision to Sudanese **ethnic** and **gender identity**, instead labelling it a "crime against humanity" (Abusharaf 2006: 216). They even sought a Muslim *fatwa*[3] to lend credibility to their legislation.[4] The British attempt to legislate (Western) morality was viewed as an attack on Sudanese identity and self-determination that led to what Abusharaf (2006) calls cultural wars between British colonial authorities and northern Sudanese society, and a surge in Sudanese cultural nationalism: women's bodies became synonymous with nation.

ANTHROPOLOGISTS AND FEMALE CIRCUMCISION

Anthropologists have much to offer the discourse on female circumcision. As researchers, they use their fieldwork skills to gather detailed descriptions and contribute to analysis of the controversy. This is where participant observation proves valuable; anthropologists immerse themselves in a culture in order to better understand female circumcision. Although anthropologists often encounter restrictions when it comes to highly sensitive practices such as this, living within a culture affords them a clearer picture of the purpose and value of the ritual.

A great deal of debate rages within the field of anthropology regarding female circumcision. Most anthropologists would agree that the practice is a highly valued

---

3 Religious decree or opinion.

4 In 2010, Muslim clerics and scholars in Mauritania declared a *fatwa* against female circumcision, even though 72 per cent of Mauritanian women are circumcised.

tradition embedded in a society's cultural system; however, this is likely the only point on which anthropologists agree. Indeed, the practice represents an **ethical dilemma** in anthropology; anthropologists grapple with the intellectual, emotional, and moral issues attached to female circumcision. Some anthropologists, including feminist anthropologists, view the practice as oppressive and symptomatic of a male-dominated, patriarchal society. Others believe that outsiders, including anthropologists themselves, have no business interfering with this ancient cultural practice. Both of these perspectives are one-dimensional and have prevented anthropologists from becoming fully involved in what Howell (2010: S269) refers to as **engaged anthropology**. According to Low and Merry (2010: S214), engaged anthropology ranges "from basic commitment to our informants, to sharing and support with the communities with which we work, to teaching and public education, to social critique in academic and public forums, to more commonly understood forms of engagement such as collaboration, advocacy, and activism." In an issue as sensitive as female circumcision, not to become engaged makes anthropology somewhat irrelevant (Martinez 2005: 31).

Those anthropologists attempting to maintain a culturally relativistic perspective are accused of validating female circumcision, and of over-compensating for Western **ethnocentrism**. The first part of this accusation misses the point. Anthropologists are not supporters of female circumcision; indeed, it is safe to say that virtually all anthropologists are against the practice. Unfortunately, ethnocentrism has coloured the discourse on the topic. What many anthropologists do advocate is the freedom of cultural groups to choose this practice or not, without pressure from outsiders. However, the word *choice* is a vague term that often fails to recognize that the girls and their families may not have much in the way of a choice if they are to meet the social expectations of their community and avoid ostracism if they refuse to follow group norms. As far as group choice is concerned, the issue becomes even more complicated—who in the group makes the decision? Are the women of the community equal decision makers or is tradition established by men? Are opponents to the ruling hierarchy silenced, or do all members have a say in group decisions? There does appear to be some community autonomy. When I discussed this issue with my male students from Nigeria, they pointed out that their village no longer practises female circumcision, while the village down the road still does.

"Protecting the rights of a minority of women who oppose the practice is a legitimate and noble cause ... mounting an international campaign to coerce 80 million African women to give up their tradition is unjustified." Anthropologist Fuambai Ahmadu (2000: 45), quoted in Shell-Duncan and Hernlund (2000: 2)

The second part of the criticism may have some merit. Certainly, I find myself explaining traditions and beliefs from a culture's point of view, and perhaps over-emphasizing the validity of customs and traditions because students have been exposed to only a very limited and ethnocentric Western point of view. This approach should not lead to advocacy for continuing a ritual, only recognition of its place in a community. As conflicted as others, anthropologists recognize that any attempt to end this practice must take into consideration its cultural meaning and context. Janice Boddy

(1982) is one anthropologist who looked beyond her cultural biases to understand the cultural meanings and value of female circumcision. In northern Sudan, 98 per cent of the women are circumcised. Boddy knew that her responsibility was to the Sudanese women—to tell their story in their words. Not surprisingly, Boddy's perspective has drawn the wrath of feminists bent on eradicating the practice. However, the issue is respect—having enough respect for these women to listen to their point of view and attempt to understand the importance of female circumcision to their physical, spiritual, and cultural identity (Blackburn-Evans 2002).

> "Ultimately, the thing I try to do in my research as well as in my teaching is to emphasize the need to really explore what it is we're trying to understand—from as many angles as possible—so that we're informed of the complexities."
> Janice Boddy, quoted in Blackburn-Evans (2002: 1)

The question then becomes, what next? After listening to all sides, should anthropologists express their opinion regarding the practice? Can they ethically support or reject female circumcision? Some anthropologists feel that they have an obligation to speak their mind, to become involved, while others feel that supporting or rejecting cultural practices outside of their home culture is not the role of anthropologists, unless asked to do so by the community.

THE NATURE OF FEMALE CIRCUMCISION

Female circumcision is an ancient and widespread **ritual**, although in some nations (e.g., Chad) it has been adopted only recently. The World Health Organization (WHO) estimates that 130 million females living in 28 countries have been circumcised at a rate of two million per year (Rahlenbeck, Mekonnen, & Melkamu 2010: 867). It is practised extensively in Africa, and in some regions of Indonesia, Malaysia, and the Arabian peninsula. The practice has also found its way to North America with immigrants from these regions. Toubia and Izette (1998) point out that 85 per cent of all circumcisions involve sunna circumcision or clitoridectomies, while infibulation is practised mainly in Somalia, Sudan, northeastern Kenya, Eritrea, parts of Mali, and a small region in northern Nigeria. In Djibouti, Mali, Egypt, and Somalia, the practice is nearly universal, while in other countries, such as Tanzania, Uganda, and Niger, fewer than 20 per cent of women are circumcised. Female circumcision appears to be declining in some regions, while in others it is spreading, partly as a backlash against Western interference. However, statistics on the extent of the practice are unreliable, since much of the data are anecdotal and government-released statistics are often questionable.

The origin of female circumcision is lost in time, although the practice is at least 3,000 years old. Mackie (2000) believes that female circumcision began in ancient Sudan, where it ensured fidelity and paternity. The practice may have developed independently in several regions of sub-Saharan Africa in tandem with male circumcision, beginning as a puberty or initiation rite. Boddy (1982: 685) points out that knowing this "custom's remote historical origin [does not] contribute to our understanding of

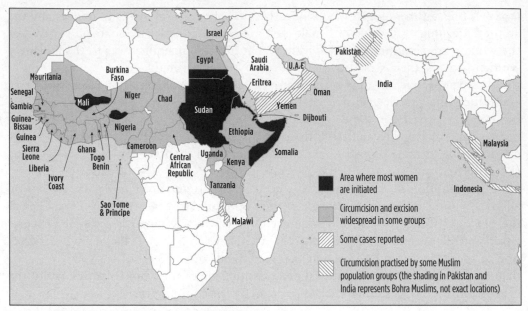

MAP 7.1 COUNTRIES PRACTISING FEMALE CIRCUMCISION

its present significance." Nevertheless, for those who believe in this practice, and find themselves continually having to justify it, an ancient origin may be significant.

HEALTH RISKS ASSOCIATED WITH FEMALE CIRCUMCISION

Any discussion of female circumcision would be incomplete without consideration of the potential health risks and complications. These health risks are used as medical justification for stamping out the practice, although much of the information on complications is dated, originating with British colonial medical practitioners in the 1930s and 1940s (Shell-Duncan & Hernlund 2000). These "facts" are often not supported by the experiences of women in communities that practise female circumcision; the "medical view" that female circumcision is a pathological practice, given the risks to health and even to life, has not resonated with people who engage in it. Gruenbaum (1982) notes that medical complications have little relevance for changing or ending the practice. Most of the problems described are the result of bungled infibulations, not the far more common and less invasive clitoridectomy or sunna circumcision. In other words, we need to view Western propaganda against female circumcision with caution.[5]

Female circumcision is usually performed without anaesthetic. In some cultures, such as the Mandinga of Guinea-Bissau, the ability to bear pain with courage and fortitude is an important part of the ceremony, bringing honour to the girl and her family

---

5 The proliferation of articles on the "evils" of female circumcision on the Internet is an example of this one-sided debate.

TABLE 7.1 COUNTRIES WHERE FEMALE CIRCUMCISION IS DOCUMENTED[a]

COUNTRY	PREVALENCE	YEAR OF DATA	TYPE[b]
Benin	16.8%	2001	excision
Burkina Faso	72.5%	2005	excision
Cameroon	1.4%	2004	clitoridectomy, excision
Central African Republic	2.5%	2005	clitoridectomy, excision
Chad	44.9%	2004	excision, infibulation
Côte d'Ivoire	41.9%	2005	excision
Djibouti	93.1%	2006	excision, infibulation
Egypt	95.8%	2005	excision, clitoridectomy
Eritrea	88.7%	2002	excision, clitoridectomy, infibulation
Ethiopia	74.3%	2005	clitoridectomy, excision
The Gambia	78.3%	2005	excision, infibulation
Ghana	3.8%	2005	excision
Guinea	95.6%	2005	clitoridectomy, excision, infibulation
Guinea-Bissau	44.5%	2005	clitoridectomy, excision
Kenya	32.2%	2003	clitoridectomy, excision, infibulation
Liberia	45%		excision
Mali	91.6%	2001	clitoridectomy, excision, infibulation
Mauritania	71.3%	2001	clitoridectomy, excision
Niger	2.2%	2006	excision
Nigeria	19%	2003	clitoridectomy, excision, infibulation
Senegal	28.2%	2005	excision
Sierra Leone	94%	2005	excision
Somalia	97.9%	2005	infibulation
Sudan (Northern)	80%	2000	excision, infibulation
Tanzania	14.6%	2004	excision, infibulation
Togo	5.8%	2005	excision
Uganda	0.6%	2006	clitoridectomy, excision
Yemen	22.6%	1997	*no information*

a World Health Organization (2008), *Eliminating female genital mutilation. An interagency statement.* OHCHR, UNAIDS, UNDP, UNECA, UNESCO, UNFP, UHCR, UNICEF, UNIFEM, WHO. Retrieved 15 November 2011 from http://www.unfpa.org/webdav/site/global/shared/documents/publications/2008/eliminating_fgm.pdf. These estimates were derived from national survey data (the Demographic and Health Survey [DHS] published by Macro, or the Multiple Cluster Indicator Surveys [MKS] published by UNICEF).

b Type of female circumcision was taken from Amnesty International (1997), *Female genital mutilation in Africa: Information by country.* Retrieved 17 March 2006 from http://www.amnesty.org/library/indesc/ENGACT770071997.

Colombia, Democratic Republic of Congo, India, Indonesia, Iraq, Israel, Malaysia, Oman, Peru, and Sri Lanka, and the United Arab Emirates also practise female circumcision, but statistics are unavailable.

(Johnson 2000). For the Gikuyu of Kenya, the pain from circumcision is ritualized, and it is considered one marker on the path to adulthood (Moruzzi 2005). However, in areas where medical services are available, anaesthetic may be used, as well as antibiotics to prevent infection, and if infibulation is practised, cat gut or silk sutures are used rather than the more traditional thorns.

The actual prevalence of complications is difficult to assess; the women are often unwilling to seek medical care, or they may not associate their medical problems with circumcision. Shortly after the procedure, some women have experienced hemorrhaging, severe pain, local and systemic infections, shock, and in extreme cases, death. Young girls may refuse to urinate for fear of stinging, which can lead to urinary tract infections. Infections at the wound site are also common. Infibulation may lead to chronic complications, such as difficulties in passing urine and menstrual flow, renal failure or septicaemia from untreated urinary tract infections, and serious pelvic infections that may cause infertility. The inelasticity of the scar tissue may prolong labour and delivery, risking the life of infant and mother. Despite the possible problems, Obermeyer (2003) determined, through an intensive review of the literature, that medical complications are the exception rather than the rule.[6] Female circumcision may also cause psychological injury, although this is impossible to assess. Indeed, Gruenbaum (2000) found that circumcised women remembered the pain and fear, but refused to dwell on it, and even laughed about it.

Boddy (1982) looked beyond the medical issues that consume Western activists, and instead focused on the social role that female circumcision plays in the lives of Sudanese women. To the Sudanese, this is a time of celebration—gift giving, feasting, and visiting with well-wishers. The identity of women as sexual beings is downplayed and their role as future mothers of men is emphasized. Lutkekaus and Roscoe (1995) agree: the Sudanese believe that circumcision marks a transition from an androgynous childhood into a distinct female gender. Thus, female circumcision is an integral part of Sudanese gender identity. This is also true among the Kono of Sierra Leone, where female and male circumcision (*bondo*) and other initiation rites are cultural and symbolic processes that celebrate the transition from boyhood and girlhood to manhood and womanhood (Ahmadu, quoted in Shweder 2009). The prepuce and foreskin of the penis are associated with femininity, so their removal masculinizes boys; the exposed clitoris represents the male organ, and its removal feminizes girls.

Although decreased sexual pleasure is cited by opponents as a consequence of circumcision, Toubia and Izette (1998) report that up to 90 per cent of infibulated women enjoy sex and experience orgasms. Indeed, interviewees who have been excised claim they enjoy sex and achieve orgasm as much as "intact" women (Londoño-Sulkin 2009: 18). On the other hand, El Dareer (1982) found that up to 50 per cent of his respondents experienced reduced sexual enjoyment. These conflicting statistics add to the debate surrounding female circumcision.

REASONS FOR FEMALE CIRCUMCISION

Given the possibility of complications and the painful nature of the procedure, the question uppermost in readers' minds might be, why? For what reasons would parents put their daughters through the ordeal and dangers of this procedure? This is where examining female circumcision becomes complex because the issue is hampered by assumptions, Western notions of human rights, **sexuality**, and **gender equality**, and a

---

6 Obermeyer's review, as well as other studies that run counter to the ruling notions of medical complications, have been largely ignored by Western media (Shweder 2009).

lack of consensus regarding the practice—what it means, the way it is done, and the value it holds for the people who practise it.

Female circumcision is governed by tradition, religious beliefs, honour, prestige, ethnic identity, gender, aesthetics, and sexuality (Gruenbaum 2005: 435). Although groups or clusters of societies may share similar reasons, for example, a gendered identity marker, other societies and even individuals may have different reasons or multiple motivations for continuing the practice despite mounting pressure to stop.

The most common reason given for female circumcision is to ensure that a young woman remains a virgin until marriage and that any children born of the marriage are the husband's progeny. Among northern Sudanese, circumcised and infibulated women are considered a preferred marriage choice that will increase family honour (Gruenbaum 2000). Although women contribute significantly to the household economy, they gain most of their economic security from their husbands (e.g., access to land and livestock), and in old age from their sons. Thus, female circumcision may ensure socio-economic well-being for a woman, and it is often her only path to social status, acceptance, and security. The question needs to be asked, then: If women gain economic independence through education and employment, will female circumcision decrease in frequency?

"Of course, I shall have them circumcised exactly as their parents, grandparents, and sisters were circumcised. This is our custom, our boys and girls must get circumcised. We don't want our girls to be like men. Men derive pleasure only from circumcised women. Both my older girls were circumcised at the age of 6. A woman circumcised them at home, before circumcision it was I who told them, 'We want to celebrate your circumcision, have a feast and prepare you a chicken.'" Fatma, an Egyptian mother quoted in Assaad (1980: 13)

For many groups, the answer would be no, since maintaining an age-old tradition is the underlying reason. The practice continues because the women do not want to break with their grandmothers' tradition (Hernlund 2000). A bond of solidarity is forged between generations of women when everyone has undergone the ritual. Female circumcision is a **rite of passage**, symbolizing the passing from girlhood to womanhood. Once circumcised, a girl is considered pure, clean, and womanly, and her status increases (Althaus 1997). Among the Sudanese, pharaonic circumcision reinforces class distinctions and is a symbol of northern Sudanese ethnic and class identity that distinguishes them from other Sudanese.

Various beliefs, whether substantiated or not, also influence the prevalence of female circumcision. The Yoruba believe that if the clitoris touches the baby's head during birth, it will die; therefore, the Yoruba practise female circumcision to ensure the survival of their children (Orubuloye, Caldwell, & Caldwell 2000). In addition, clitoridectomies and sunna circumcision are believed to reduce a woman's sexual desire, preventing her from becoming sexually active before marriage or seeking extramarital affairs during marriage. Infibulation prevents sexual intercourse outside of marriage and is alleged to increase a man's sexual pleasure. However, Shandall (1967) found that Sudanese men who practised polygyny preferred sex with their uncircumcised wives.

Female circumcision is often associated with Islam. Despite pharaonic circumcision predating Islam by hundreds or even thousands of years, the practice has been incorporated into Islamic beliefs (Gruenbaum 1982). This incorporation ignores the fact that Islamic scholars are adamant that the Qur'an does not promote female circumcision. It also ignores the fact that some form of the practice occurs among Coptic Christians, Ethiopian Jews, traditional spiritualists, and Christian converts (Moruzzi 2005: 208). Those who link female circumcision with Islam see the practice as a cleansing rite that marks the woman as a Muslim and gives her the right to pray (Johnson 2000). Regardless of whether the connection to Islam is legitimate or not, if people believe that their religion commands it, then it is an important religious practice.

GLOBAL OPPOSITION TO FEMALE CIRCUMCISION

When Hillary Rodham Clinton addressed the 1995 United Nations Fourth World Conference on Women in Beijing, she stated unequivocally: "It is a violation of human rights when young girls are brutalized by the painful and degrading practice of female genital mutilation" (Equality Now 1996: n.p.). Clinton's forceful statement is understandable, given that it comes from a woman living in the West, where there are strong opinions about **human rights**, especially the right to health and safety. However, this is a Western position and does not take into consideration the way other cultures perceive female circumcision or how they define human rights. The whole issue of human rights, though based on a desire to ensure that everyone, the world over, is free from harm, is a vaguely understood and by no means universally acknowledged concept used to justify "making people over in the Western image"—what Shell-Duncan and Hernlund (2000: 34) label the **development and modernization approach**.

"Foreigners from America, from London, who call us bad names, call us primitive and call our circumcision rites genital mutilation ... It makes us want to do more." Kapchorwa magistrate Albert Laigiya, a Ugandan elder, quoted in Masland (1999: 9)

As is obvious from Clinton's statement, the terms we use provide a barometer for attitudes. The "politics of names" is particularly evident when it comes to female circumcision. In the West, the practice is called "female genital mutilation" in order to symbolize Western disapproval. However, "mutilation" is a judgemental term and does not belong in an intellectual discussion of this topic. Even when the term "female circumcision" is used, the word "circumcision" is often placed in quotation marks to distinguish it from male circumcision, which is still practised in North America and considered a legitimate custom.[7] Opponents also object to the word "circumcision" itself because it detracts from the severity of the procedure. To avoid a judgemental tone, but to separate the practice from male circumcision, some researchers prefer to use the term "female genital cutting."

---

7 Therefore, the term male genital mutilation should also be used.

Opponents of the practice believe that female circumcision "violates a minor child's human right to bodily integrity" (Gruenbaum 2005: 430). Yet to practitioners, female circumcision is not an act of cruelty or child abuse. Indeed, parents who have their daughters circumcised care about their well-being as much as any parents do, so to characterize circumcised women as victims is simplistic and condescending. Whether female circumcision is a violation of human rights depends on how we define the concept of human rights. As some of my more insightful students have pointed out, taking away a woman's right to be circumcised and enjoy higher status in the community, her right to marry well and bear sons, thereby ensuring her security in old age, is in itself an infringement on her human rights.

Female circumcision is often blamed on men and their need to oppress and control women. Although some men are purported to prefer circumcised women, this is by no means universal, and the procedure itself is controlled and perpetuated by women. Banning circumcision has not improved the status of women; indeed, it often has the opposite effect, and there is growing evidence that female circumcision actually empowers women, although this is a contested stand. Furthermore, to suggest that these women are submissive and "brainwashed" into thinking circumcision is a good practice is an insult to the intelligence and strength of all women.

Opponents of female circumcision are often accused of Western **cultural imperialism**—the promotion of Western values, beliefs, and behaviours. Campaigns against female circumcision, funded by the West and often cocooned in development projects, are well entrenched in most African communities, although they have met with limited success. These campaigns have failed because the goal has been to change women's minds about female circumcision with little consideration given to what the practice means to them socially, economically, and culturally. As well, the assumption that education and awareness programs will put an end to the practice once people realize the health risks is naive, and except for isolated cases, practitioners are far more aware of the dangers than outsiders. Toubia (1988) asserts that female circumcision is not a medical problem; rather, it is part of women's social sphere, where cultural pressures (e.g., peer, parental, societal) and marriageability supersede any perceived risks. Furthermore, the suggestion that female circumcision must be eradicated as if it were a disease reeks of medical imperialism.

"Over the last decade the West has acted as though they have suddenly discovered a dangerous epidemic which they then sensationalized in international women's forums creating a backlash of over-sensitivity in the concerned communities. They have portrayed it as irrefutable evidence of the barbarism and vulgarity of underdeveloped countries ... [and] the primitiveness of Arabs, Muslims, and Africans all in one blow." Toubia (1988: 101)

The main and most damaging impact of anti-circumcision movements has been to bring to light the pervasiveness of the practice, which, in turn, has resulted in unwanted international attention (Ginsburg 1991), especially since the 1970s when international organizations such as WHO and the United Nations took notice. These movements have outraged women in the countries where female circumcision is practised. Women,

"The voices of the many East and West African women who value the practice of genital modification for girls and boys have not been audible in North America and European media accounts of the practice." Shweder (2009)

such as anthropologist Soheir Morsy, have expressed indignation over Western interference. The paternalistic concept of "helping" other people—what Morsy (1991) calls "rescue and civilizational missions," really amounts to an attack on their cultural values and has resulted in silencing and alienating the very women who could bring about change.

Not all opposition to female circumcision comes from Westerners, however. African women's organizations, such as the Inter African Committee Against Harmful Traditional Practices, was formed in 1984 and now has national committees in more than 20 countries (Althaus 1997). Their mandate has been to bring the harmful effects of the procedure to the attention of African governments and thereby have the practice banned. Grassroots self-help movements, such as Abandon the Knife in the Pokot community of highland Kenya, struggle to change the community's perception of female circumcision (*Al Jazeera* English 2011). Most of their efforts focus on convincing parents that allowing their daughters to get an education is of more economic value than cutting followed by marriage for a dowry.

Some activists promote the criminalization of female circumcision to counter social pressures to continue the practice. In 1994, for example, a law was passed in Sudan banning female circumcision. It caused a public furor and a backlash that actually increased the incidence of the practice (Shell-Duncan & Hernlund 2000). As an example of how extreme the resistance became, a ban on clitoridectomies in Kenya's Meru District resulted in adolescent girls excising each other (Thomas 2000). Another worry is that legislation may force the practice underground where sanitation and quality of care are poor. Circumcised women experiencing difficulties might then be unwilling to seek medical assistance for fear of prosecution, similar to young women having illegal abortions in Canada prior to 1969, then refusing to go to a hospital if they became ill after the procedure. Even Amnesty International has acknowledged that efforts to ban female circumcision through legislation have backfired (Amnesty International 1997). Some Western countries have threatened to make international aid conditional to the country's banning of female circumcision. Governments may yield to Western pressure, but if the ban is not enforceable, then it is irrelevant.

"What's important is that I become empowered and help myself and people like me. My parents want me to be cut and married off for a dowry .... Boys and girls are equal ... I can see a flood coming and all you people just want to hold us back. I'm moving forward. I'm heading for the land of milk and honey. My passion for education is driving me. Look for someone else to cut, so long as it's not me." Nancy, a 17-year-old Kenyan from the Pokot community (*Al Jazeera* English broadcast 2011)

Both opponents and defenders of female circumcision have raised alarms over efforts to medicalize the procedure (Shell-Duncan, Obiero, & Muruli 2000). If female circumcision became institutionalized—performed in medical institutions by licensed doctors—opponents fear that this would amount to tacit approval that would stymie efforts to eliminate the practice. Others suggest that if medicalization improved the health and saved the lives of women, then it would be worth the risk. On the other hand, defenders of female circumcision fear that medicalization would shift control of female circumcision from women in the community to male practitioners in biomedical facilities (Shell-Duncan & Hernlund 2000). Johnson (2000: 230) found that among the Mandinga of Guinea-Bissau, women refused a hospital circumcision because the cutting is "not the same."

Recent efforts to find alternative rituals in The Gambia and Kenya, where the clitoris is only nicked, have met with limited success. Practitioners seem not to value **symbolic circumcision** in the same way as traditional cutting. Some of the reasons for female circumcision—for example, ensuring chastity—are not served by symbolic circumcision. In North America, where symbolic circumcision would offer immigrants an alternative to more invasive procedures, activists have protested that even that practice is oppressive and have effectively shut down the programs with their protests. These activists fail to appreciate that male circumcision is still performed in North American hospitals and is much more invasive than symbolic circumcision (Coleman 1998). Ironically, many of the reasons for justifying male circumcision in the West are the same as those given for female circumcision (e.g., cleanliness, aesthetics, family tradition, religious beliefs) (Ahmadu, quoted in Shweder 2009).

> "You simply can't outlaw cultural practices.... It is not possible to criminalize the entirety of a population, or the entirety of a discrete and insular minority of the population, without methods of mass terror. People have to decide to stop on their own." Mackie, quoted in *The Economist* (1999: 450)

CONCLUSION

Obviously, it is extremely difficult to step outside our Western bias when examining an issue as sensitive as female circumcision. Yet, to comprehend the symbolic complexities of this practice, this is what we must do. Female circumcision holds meaning for millions of people; this cannot be taken away without causing harm equal to or surpassing the perceived harm of the original ritual. We will never eliminate female circumcision if we do not understand why it is so important and why it continues to be practised despite international condemnation. Herein lies the challenge: to respect cultural traditions, values, and autonomy while promoting global human rights.

Yet cultures are not static; they change to meet changing needs. If the meaning of female circumcision to a community changes, then its value and continued practice would likely change as well. Anthropologist Carolyn Sargent (1991) believes that efforts to change or end this custom must come from within the cultures themselves, and will happen only when women have opportunities for economic security other than marriage and childbearing. A refreshing example of this is the Senegal-based NGO Tostan, which has

> "If they [cutting practices] are to disappear, let it not be as a result of impositions from powerful outsiders with unquestioning faith in their own understandings of personhood, cosmology, and sociality." Londoño-Sulkin (2009)

established literacy and leadership skills programs and promotes social development, giving women the power to decide for themselves if female circumcision is necessary in their community (Gruenbaum 2005: 438). In addition, Rahlenbeck, Mekonnen, and Melkamu (2010: 868) found among the Oromia of Ethiopia that "a woman's feeling of self-empowerment is proportional to the degree to which she takes a stance against the practice." In this study, those with a higher education opposed the practice, as did those who rejected any form of domestic violence as being normal. This runs counter to many upper-class urban families in Egypt, where women tend to have higher education yet the practice is common, even to the point of taking their educated, sophisticated daughters back to traditional villages to have the procedure done. Indeed, in quite a few cases, women of middle and upper classes are more likely to be circumcised than are those from the poorer classes.

Anthropologists have found that the practice is spreading in the face of modernization—oftentimes the poorer social classes are adopting infibulations in the hopes that their circumcised daughters will make a good marriage, thereby increasing their status and economic well-being (Leonard 2000). Certainly, Western interference has been met with strong resistance—both from within the cultures that practise female circumcision and from others who resent this Western intrusion.

While hopes for eradication remain high, in reality there is little evidence that female circumcision is on the decline, despite community "successes." Although Westerners may believe eradication of female circumcision is a priority, women in developing nations have more serious concerns on their minds—like poverty, childhood diseases and malnutrition, ethnic conflict and war, and a lack of resources due to decades of exploitation by the very Westerners bent on changing their traditions. Young people, such as the women in Pokot, Kenya, appear more amenable to ending the practice than older people; however, this does not mean that, as they mature, this generation will continue to reject the custom—honouring the traditions of forbears is a very powerful force. Legislation appears ineffective and difficult to enforce, and if the people value the custom, it will continue despite any illegality.

Will female circumcision ever be eradicated? The question itself is controversial because it harkens back to the West's desire to eliminate any cultural practice considered wrong, as well as to the political implications of colonialism and imperialism. The issue is incredibly complex because it seems natural, even fundamentally human, to want everyone to enjoy the rights and freedoms we enjoy in the West. Some argue that in the West we honour human life, individuality, and freedom, and that we want to give other people the same quality of life—a laudable sentiment, but if examined closely, somewhat hollow and based on a sense of cultural superiority and over-dramatization of questionable information. To barge in and demand that people change because we consider these acts cruel and barbaric is unethical and immoral to say the least.

So how do anthropologists reconcile their responsibilities as scientists and researchers with their sense of human rights? Should anthropologists in their role as advocates work to end female circumcision, or should they continue to advocate for the freedom of cultural self-determination? There is no easy answer. Fuambai S. Ahmadu sums up the politics of reproduction: "There are different and contested views and experiences and ... no one is more right than the other" (Ahmadu, quoted in Shweder 2009: 17).

QUESTIONS FOR CONSIDERATION AND CLASSROOM ACTIVITIES

1. In your opinion, should Westerners attempt to eradicate the practice of female circumcision? If yes, what is the best way to go about ending this practice? If no, why do you feel this way? Create a student blog to open debate on the pros and cons of Westerners interfering with female circumcision.
2. Immigrants to Western countries (e.g., Canada) may wish to continue this practice. How should this issue be addressed in Canada? Consider the implications of the options and address them in your response.
3. In Chapter 6, the issue of body image is addressed. How is the practice of female circumcision connected to body image? How is female circumcision similar to North American cosmetic surgery, such as breast implants? How is it different—or is it?
4. Compare female circumcision to male circumcision. How are these procedures alike and how are they different? Create a comparative analysis of reasons given for practising male and female circumcision, and then enter into a class debate. Each group must provide five reasons to justify either female or male circumcision and be able to argue the merits of each reason.
5. The Kenyan woman in Pokot wanted an education and employment opportunities rather than circumcision and marriage. If she, and other young people like her, are successful, how will this change their community—socially, economically, and politically?
6. Imagine an anthropologist from another country studying your community and negatively judging your lifestyle choices (e.g., rodeos, compulsory school attendance for girls, ear piercing, alcohol consumption, androgynous or scanty clothing, and teen dating). How would you and the rest of your community react? Would this condemnation make you stop these practices? Why or why not?
7. It is extremely difficult to maintain a culturally relativistic stance when confronted with what we perceive to be a harmful cultural practice. How do we reconcile our ideas of right and wrong with the needs of cultural groups for self-determination?
8. Why do you suppose Western media has ignored research that suggests medical complications from female circumcision are not that common?
9. "The operation was usually performed by untrained midwives, old and dirty, who used the blade of a cut-throat razor or some locally made instrument, often

blunt and always unsterilized. No injections were given at the time" (Hills-Young 1943: 13). In this quotation, identify the biased language that perpetuates images of horror, fear, disgust, etc. Discuss why these particular words might have been chosen, and describe the message they convey. Now try re-writing the quotation, taking out the biased language and using neutral terms to explain the practice, and then discuss how the rewritten statement changes your views.

10. Create a PowerPoint presentation on female circumcision that includes the voice of practitioners, thus providing the cultural logic of this practice and how it makes sense to the practitioners.

11. Conduct research on the Universal Declaration of Human Rights. In groups of three or four, focus on one section of the declaration. Argue how female circumcision violates this right and/or how forcefully stopping female circumcision violates this right.

SUGGESTED READINGS

Barnes, V.L. (1994). *Aman: The story of a Somali girl—As told to Virginia Lee Barnes and Janice Boddy.* London: Bloomsbury Publishing.

This book presents the personal account of a 17-year-old girl living in Somalia. She describes being circumcised at age eight, and married to a much older man at age 13. By 17, she has endured rape, divorced twice, and had two children, one of whom died. Anthropologists Virginia Barnes and Janice Boddy present a straightforward, objective account of Aman's life and the patriarchal society in which she lives.

Little, C.M. (2003, Spring). **Female genital circumcision: Medical and cultural considerations.** *Journal of Cultural Diversity.* **Retrieved 10 March 2006 from** http://www.findarticles.com/p/articles/mi_m0MJU/is_1_10/ai_102025141.

A comprehensive discussion of the medical and cultural implications of female circumcision. Presents a fairly balanced discussion and is easily accessible to students. The site also provides numerous links to related articles.

Chapter 8

WHAT ARE THE SOCIO-ECONOMIC, RELIGIOUS, AND POLITICAL IMPLICATIONS OF SAME-SEX MARRIAGE AND CHANGING FAMILY STRUCTURE?

Key Terms: division of labour, family, gender identity, gender variant roles, homosexuality, marriage, same-sex marriage

---

INTRODUCTION

On June 28, 2005, the Canadian parliament passed Bill C-38, and Canada became the fourth country in the world to legitimize same-sex marriages. The Bill changed the definition of marriage to a union between two people rather than between a man and a woman. The long battle leading up to this historic vote was both disturbing and divisive. The struggle for same-sex marriage rights came to a head in 2003, when Ontario's Court of Appeal ruled that the current Canadian definition of marriage was unconstitutional. This opened the door for gays and lesbians to legally marry and signalled a Western shift in acceptance of same-sex marriage.

> "This is about the Charter of Rights. We are a nation of minorities. And in a nation of minorities, it is important that you don't cherry-pick rights. A right is a right and that is what this vote tonight is all about." Former Canadian prime minister Paul Martin, quoted in Whittington and Gordon (2005)

The politicization of marriage is not a new phenomenon; indeed, societal rules and restrictions have been a part of marriage systems for a very long time. In the West, state authorities have increasingly weighed in on issues of family and private life (Baskerville 2006). Changes in family structure, such as the rise of single-parent families, have increased the political influence on what used to be a private matter, and now the cacophony surrounding the legalization of gay and lesbian marriages has pushed the debate into the larger political sphere.

Same-sex marriage is the marriage of two people who are of the same biological sex. The contested issues surrounding same-sex marriage are complex. First, religious and social conservatives morally object to **homosexuality** as a lifestyle. Second, there is strong opposition from many walks of life to changing the "traditional" definition of **marriage** as between a man and a woman. Third, feminists reject marriage of any kind, including same-sex marriage, for perpetuating a patriarchal and oppressive system on gays and lesbians as well as other women. Those opposed to same-sex marriages and the redefinition of marriage fear that marriage is being threatened, and that ultimately **family** structure and society will break down.

Yet, as anthropologists point out, same-sex marriages have been accepted in other cultures without dire consequences; marriage is practised in a variety of ways around the world and is a dynamic institution that has changed considerably over time. Therefore, to cite any one form of marriage as "traditional" is misleading. In this chapter we will consider both what marriage means and the way in which marriage has been culturally constructed to meet the needs of various groups of people, including gays and lesbians. The socio-economic, religious, and political implications of legalizing same-sex marriages will be explored, including this question: will same-sex marriage, as it gains legal and social acceptance, transform both the queer and traditional meanings of marriage? Marriage, regardless of its form, creates a family; we will also examine the impact of same-sex marriages on the concept of family.

The question often arises whether marriage is a religious or a social institution. Anthropologists respond that it is both, and much more. Long before the institutionalized religions (e.g., Christianity, Islam, Judaism) of today, people were joining together in what even the most limited definition would consider a marriage. They were doing so for many reasons—to regulate sexual behaviour and create families, of course, but even more significant were the economic benefits of marriage. The roles that marriage plays in society, now and then, will be discussed in this chapter through the lens of same-sex marriage and from several schools of thought, including social conservative, critical feminist/queer, and gay and lesbian assimilationist. In this discussion, marriage will be examined from sociological, political, historical, and anthropological perspectives.

ANTHROPOLOGISTS AND SAME-SEX MARRIAGE

Until recently, the issue of same-sex relations and/or marriage did not earn much attention from anthropologists. Indeed, there seemed to be a stigma attached to studying homosexuality as a behaviour regulated by desire, especially as it is found in the West. This stigma translated into a lack of funding for ethnographic research into homosexual behaviour. The reasons for this oversight or "slighting" are manifold. Anthropologists, like everyone else, are the product of the culture in which they are raised. In North America, homosexuality has been frowned upon and in many instances legally banned; therefore, American anthropologists have tended to avoid the subject.[1] According to Murray (1997: 2), most early anthropological studies of sexuality

---

1 Anthropological journals contained nothing about contemporary gay men until the 1990s, and as of 1997, there were no articles on the global nature of homosexuality in anthropological journals (Murray 1997).

briefly noted **gender variant roles** and then categorized the behaviour within notions of hermaphrodites.[2]

Most anthropological studies of homosexuality in North American aboriginal groups have acknowledged gender variant roles, with little investigation of sexual behaviour or desires. Indeed, Murray (1997) feels that new terminology, such as "Two-Spirits" replacing *berdache*,[3] is an attempt to de-sexualize alternative gender roles. There are exceptions, of course, such as the extensive research of Alfred Kroeber (1925) in a survey of the *berdache* in California aboriginal groups. Interestingly, Kroeber called his fellow anthropologists to task for not studying the *berdache* because of its association with homosexuality (Gay Bears 2002).

Outside of the Western world, there is some information on homosexual behaviour. James Peacock (1968) investigated Javanese theatrical troupes in his book *Rites of Modernization*, and Unni Wikan (1978) wrote one of the few articles on the Omani Xanith, introducing the concept of a third gender (Murray 1997). Unfortunately, anthropologists neglected to study pederasty,[4] the predominant form of male homosexuality in Muslim societies; therefore, we have little information on this practice.

Today, some anthropologists, such as Bruce Knauft (2005: 70), openly report evidence of homosexuality among their study groups:

> At first, I wasn't sure if Gebusi males engaged each other sexually.... I suspected that male trysts took place near the outhouse at night during séances and festive dances ... [but] ... I didn't want to 'project' sex between men onto the Gebusi if it wasn't documented.... At several feasts, I ultimately did see pairs of males slip out toward the outhouse, cavort with each other in the night shadows, and return a few minutes later.... [These trysts] tended to be between a teenage boy and a young initiated man.

As is evident in this narrative, the intensely personal and sensitive nature of sexual behaviour, and in particular homosexual behaviour, can have an impact on whether anthropologists are able to evaluate the true extent of homosexual behaviour in a cultural group. Only through prolonged fieldwork, such as that conducted by Knauft, will the whole story be told. Like Knauft, Wood and Lewin (2006) found that homosexual behaviour had been channelled into normative social behaviour and given ritual significance in many small-scale Melanesian cultures. They suggest (2006: 135) that when homosexual relations "are subject to cultural elaboration they almost always fit into a pattern of initiation into secrets, male exclusivity, and a low status for women."

Contemporary anthropologists are now turning their attention to homosexuality and same-sex marriages, backed by their cultural knowledge of marriage, family, and

---

2 Term used to describe people with ambiguous genitalia or biological sex.

3 A North American aboriginal man who in traditional times assumed the gender identity and roles of a woman.

4 Sexual relations between an adolescent boy and an older man.

households. When the debate regarding same-sex marriage heated up and legislation such as former president Bush's constitutional amendment to ban gay marriages was considered, the American Anthropological Association (AAA) felt compelled to issue a strongly worded statement:

> The results of more than a century of anthropological research on house-holds, kinship relationships, and families, across cultures and through time, provide no support whatsoever for the view that either civilization or viable social orders depend on marriage as an exclusively heterosexual institution. Rather, anthropological research supports the conclusion that a vast array of family types, including families built upon same-sex partnerships, can contribute to stable and humane societies. The Executive Board of the American Anthropological Association strongly opposes a constitutional amendment limiting marriage to heterosexual couples. (AAA 2004: n.p.)

THE NATURE OF MARRIAGE

From an anthropological perspective, marriage is a universal pattern of behaviour, though many forms of marriage are practised. Anthropological studies indicate that marriage means different things to different people, based on economic, ecological, historical, and demographic processes (Stone 2004). Therefore, developing an inclusive definition of marriage remains a challenge; to date, a definition that represents global marriage practices has not been produced by anthropologists or any other scholars. Haviland, Fedorak, and Lee (2009: 189) define marriage as "a relationship between one or more men (male or female) and one or more women (female or male) who are recognized by the group as having a continuing claim to the right of sexual access to each other." This rather convoluted definition recognizes that, globally, there are many forms of mar-riage, including same-sex marriage. It is also important to recognize that marriage is a cultural construct designed to meet the needs of a group of people, unlike mating, which is a biological behaviour.

"Our voices need to be heard in the current debate, not only to challenge unfounded claims by demagogues about the universality of any particular marital configuration, but to support the rights of lesbians and gay men to build their lives as full citizens." Anthropologist Ellen Levin, quoted in Wood and Lewin (2006: 140)

Marriage in most societies is heterosexual, yet even this is not a universal pattern of human behaviour. Among the Nandi pastoralist and farming communities of western Kenya, woman-woman marriage is recognized as a way for a barren woman to ac-quire sons through a female wife. The men own both the land and the herds, which they share equally with their wives. The wives hold this wealth in trust for their sons (Oboler 1980). A woman past child-bearing age who has not borne any sons is in a difficult situation—she does not have sons to inherit a share of her husband's property. To deal with this problem, the woman may marry a younger woman who can then provide her with sons through sexual liaisons with other men. The older woman, now known as a female husband, is expected to assume the **gender identity**, dress, and behaviour of a man. By doing so, she raises her status in the community to that of a man. Sexual activity between the two women is strictly forbidden; indeed, the female husband is expected to give up sex, including with her male husband. Readers may wonder why a young woman would enter into such an arrangement. Often she has given birth to an illegitimate child and can no longer make a good marriage, or her family may not have any status in the community. By marrying a female husband her status is raised, and any children she produces are ensured of a secure future.

ROLES OF MARRIAGE

An important role of marriage is to establish families in which to create and raise children; marriage confers legitimacy or birthright status on children produced in the union (Stone 2004). There are exceptions, of course, such as the Navajo, who recognize children as legitimate regardless of whether their mother is married. Parentage has also changed with advances in technology, such as surrogacy. Indeed, Stone (2004) identifies three types of "mothers": birth, genetic, and legal, and with DNA testing, the notion of paternity has become more certain. Despite these changes, marriage still acknowledges the relationship between a set of parents and their children (Baskerville 2006): "Kinship laws still establish married men's paternity through marriage, not through their biological relationship with children.... By this means, women are equated with nature and their relationship to children is biological, whereas men's relationship to children is established politically through the law of marriage" (Josephson 2005, quoted in Baskerville 2006: 65). Thus, legal systems around the world recognize fathers through marriage, not sperm.

For same-sex married couples, marriage confers social and legal benefits that assist in parenting. In Green's (2010) study the respondents felt that being legally married in the eyes of the law and society provided a stronger sense of stability and socio-legal support, and enabled them to parent with more confidence. Family formation and parenting, then, are viewed as part of their marital relationship, which is consistent with the attitudes of heterosexual married couples. Marriage, socially and symbolically, legitimizes same-sex couples and family. This stance fits with lesbian and gay assimilationists, who support same-sex marriage for the benefits and rights that same-sex married couples would enjoy if legally married—inheritance, health benefits, taxation, and childcare (Walters 2001).

A second major role of marriage is to constrain or provide guidelines for sexual behaviour. According to some social conservatives, marriage exists to "civilize" men, to control their sexual behaviour (Baskerville 2006), and to channel sexual desire into reproduction within marriage. Social conservatives do not believe that marriage will "tame" the libido of homosexuals because sexual desire in traditional marriage is channelled into reproduction, whereas same-sex marriage has no such goal (Green 2010).

Same-sex liaisons, then, eliminate paternity (Green 2010) and, in the eyes of social conservatives, may influence the next generation of children to redefine marriage to exclude childrearing (Baskerville 2006). Green (2010) found that the same-sex married couples he interviewed deviated from so-called marital norms when it came to fidelity. Secure in their marriages and committed to their partners and children, many felt that if they chose to, seeking sexual partners outside their marriage was acceptable.

Marriage creates the most basic of economic units: the household. From the household flows a great deal of economic activity, such as tilling the land, raising the livestock in traditional societies, and in more recent times earning wages and establishing businesses. The third role of marriage, then, is to define the roles and responsibilities or **division of labour** of each spouse. For example, in a foraging band, women gather the wild vegetables while men hunt wild animals and fish. In this way each spouse complements the other in economic duties. Despite the social conservative view that marriage creates division-of-labour guidelines, this is no longer the reality in most modern countries. When men and women work outside the home, division of labour is often dictated by choice—personal preferences and abilities—rather than by gender. This far more egalitarian system is a product of today's wage economy and the economic independence of women. Green (2010) found that this is also the case among same-sex married couples, who divide housework and other family responsibilities according to preference, skills, and abilities.

Westerners consider marriage a joining of two people, but in most cultures marriage is the joining of two families to create an economic and political support network. In North American society, marriage brings respectability that also creates social networks. Gays and lesbians have found that their relationships gain legitimacy when they marry; family, friends, and coworkers pay them more social respect, and they now enjoy the same support and standing that heterosexual couples enjoy (Green 2010).

In sum, marriage, both heterosexual and homosexual, curtails and regulates human sexuality, defines gender roles (whatever they may be), and provides a stable environment for procreating and raising children. Marriage also creates social, economic, and political networks between families, creating an expanded kinship network, and commands increased status and respect.

SAME-SEX MARRIAGE IN TRADITIONAL SOCIETIES

Same-sex relationships and marriage have a long history and wide geographical distribution (Lahey & Alderson 2004). In the southern Fujian province of China during the Yuan and Ming dynasties (1264–1644 CE), men married male youths in elaborate ceremonies (McGough 2004). When the marriage came to an end, the older man in the relationship paid a brideprice to acquire a wife for the younger man. In a similar vein, Japanese Samurai warriors entered battle with their apprentice warrior-lovers at their side. A formal exchange of written and spoken vows legitimized the relationship, which was based on romantic love and loyalty. Besides the sexual aspects of these relationships, the samurai provided "social backing, emotional support, and a model of manliness for the apprentice" (Eskridge 1996: 3). The apprentice, in turn, was expected to become a good student of samurai manhood. In medieval Europe, same-sex relationships were recognized, even celebrated, in several societies. Records of ancient Rome and Greece show evidence of homosexual unions. In the Classical period, Greek men (*erastes*) and youths (*eromenoi*) entered into same-sex marriages. These marriages required the father of the youth to give his consent to the union (Pickett 2002).

North American aboriginal groups, such as the Ojibwa, Lakota, Yuma, and Winnebago, also recognized and accepted unions between Two-Spirit individuals (Williams 1986). Two-Spirit marriages have also been recorded in the West Indies and among the Aztec, Maya, and Inca civilizations (Eskridge 1996). Two-Spirits are androgynous males or females who take on the roles, dress, and behaviour of the opposite sex. They gain social prestige for their spiritual and intellectual qualities, and they often possess shamanic or special ceremonial powers, such as burial and mourning rituals (Bonvillain 1998).

Same-sex marriages among the Mohave of the southwestern United States were institutionalized and socially accepted. A young man at the age of 10 participated in a ritual dance where he was proclaimed a Two-Spirit (*alyha*). The boy was ritually bathed, and given a woman's skirt to wear, along with a female name. According to Williams (1986), the Two-Spirit marriage closely emulated "regular" marriage in that it served to divide duties based on gender—the man took on the roles of a male and the Two-Spirit took on the roles of a woman. Two-Spirits never married other Two-Spirits. In some groups, such as the Lakota and Zapotec, the Two-Spirit was likely a second or third wife, while the husband had a female wife to produce children.

The main reason for Two-Spirit marriages appears to be economic—Two-Spirits could take on the roles of both a man and a woman and in the process enhance the social status of a group. By the late nineteenth and early twentieth centuries, Two-Spirits had almost disappeared, after Europeans settled in North America and refused to accept the existence of more than two genders, declaring homosexuality a violation of natural and divine laws (Bonvillain 1998).

As with the Nandi of Kenya mentioned above, woman-woman marriage was also a common practice in northern Nigeria, among the Yoruba, Yagba, Akoko, Nuper, and Gana-Gana cultures (Herskovits 2004). Sometimes a barren woman married a young girl who then mated with the barren woman's husband to produce children. In other cases, a wealthy older woman (female husband) married a young woman. Traditional marriage rituals, including offering a brideprice to the father of the girl, were observed in these marriages. The young woman mated with a man to produce children for the female husband. These marriages were viewed with favour.

One of the most extensively documented types of same-sex relationship was found among the Azande of Sudan (Evans-Pritchard 1974). Military men took "boy wives" as their marriage partners. A brideprice was paid to the parents of a boy and brideservice was performed. This marriage was both sexual and economic, in that the boy performed household and sexual duties. Some men had both female wives and boy wives—they took the boy wives into war with them to take care of the camp, while the female wife remained at home and cared for the children. This type of marriage was legally and culturally sanctioned by the Azande.

SAME-SEX MARRIAGE IN MODERN SOCIETIES

Canada is not the only modern state to recognize same-sex marriages; some European countries have also granted rights to same-sex couples. In 1989, Denmark became the first country to offer same-sex couples rights on par with heterosexual married couples, although they could not marry in a church. In 1996, Norway, Sweden, and Iceland passed similar legislation, followed by Finland in 2002. The Netherlands granted full civil-marriage rights, including the right to adopt, to gay couples in 2001, becoming the first country to do so. Belgium followed suit in 2003. On July 2, 2005, Spain legalized same-sex marriages and the right of same-sex couples to adopt, becoming the third country to legalize same-sex marriages (Robinson 2012).

FIGURE 8.1 TWO WOMEN CELEBRATE THEIR MARRIAGE

Other European countries have enacted legislation that grants gay and lesbian couples certain rights: Germany allows same-sex couples to register for life partnerships; France allows a civil contract called the Pacs; Luxembourg recognizes civil partnerships; and Britain passed legislation on December 21, 2005, that gave registered same-sex couples the same pension, joint property, and social security rights accorded to married couples (Demian 2005). In other parts of the world, New Zealand has passed a law recognizing civil unions between same-sex couples. With the exception of South Australia and Victoria, Australia recognizes same-sex partnerships. However, former prime minister John Howard amended the marriage laws in 2004 to ban same-sex marriages and same-sex couples from adopting.

In the United States, the struggle for same-sex marriage rights and equality is reminiscent of the anti-miscegenation laws that prohibited African Americans from state-sanctioned marriage until the early nineteenth century, and prohibited whites from marrying non-whites until 1967 (Green 2010: 402). Legislation in the United

States defines marriage as between a man and a woman, and many states have banned same-sex marriages. However, several Supreme Courts have struck down these bans for violating equal protection rights for gays and lesbians (Gullo 2012), most recently in California (although, at the time of writing, opponents of gay marriages are planning an appeal). On the other hand, Vermont has granted same-sex couples the same legal status as civil marriages, and on May 17, 2004, Massachusetts gave same-sex couples the right to civil marriage (Burns 2005). New Hampshire, Iowa, Connecticut, and the District of Columbia also grant same-sex marriage licences (Green 2010). More recently, New York has begun to recognize same-sex marriages (Layng 2009), and Maryland passed a law legitimizing same-sex marriage in February 2012 (Cathcart 2012).

Around the world, the struggle for equal rights is exemplified in gays and lesbians seeking the right to legally marry. Argentina was the first Latin American country to legalize same-sex marriage in July 2010 (Sina English 2010). Gay rights have strong support in Argentina, although there is also a strong anti-gay sentiment in this predominantly Catholic country. Despite heavy lobbying by the Catholic Church, the bill passed, spurring activists in other countries, such as Chile and Paraguay, to lobby for similar rights. Mexico City legalized gay marriages and has gone so far as to designate the city as a tourist destination for gay marriages (CNN World 2009).

> Anthropologist Ellen Lewin applauds legalization of same-sex marriages: "Commitment ceremonies, weddings, and other ritual occasions that seek to celebrate lesbian and gay relationships are in many ways very diverse.... But what they all attempt is to situate a relationship within a broader community context, to proclaim the authenticity of the relationship in a public manner." Wood and Lewin (2006: 139)

In most African countries, however, same-sex marriage is taboo. In Nigeria, Senate President David Mark rejected same-sex marriage, stating, "It is offensive to our culture and tradition" (Awom & Ukaibe 2011). The taboo has resulted in gay and lesbian Nigerians living in "fake" marriages, because in order to be respected in Nigeria, one must be married. So strong are the anti-gay sentiments in Nigeria that a bill is before parliament to criminalize same-sex marriage (Coward 2012). Uganda enacted a ban on same-sex marriage in 2005 and an anti-homosexuality law is before the legislature, further criminalizing homosexual acts, though the proposed death penalty is no longer part of the law (Smith 2012). On the other hand, same-sex marriage has been legalized in South Africa, the first and only African country to do so.

In Asia, attempts to legalize same-sex marriage in Taiwan, China, the Philippines, and Cambodia have so far been stymied by opponents in the legislature, although some politicians and even monarchs support legislation. In China, there have been small achievements. In 1997, the law that outlawed sodomy was repealed, in 2001 homosexuality was no longer classified as a mental illness (Li 2010), and four unsuccessful attempts to amend the marriage laws have been proposed. Discrimination continues, as most gays and lesbians must keep their sexual orientation a secret; societal and familial pressures usually force them into a straight marriage. The consequences of this systemic discrimination include rising rates of HIV/AIDS infection, psychological trauma and increasing suicide attempts, and a plethora of unhappy "straight" marriages that end in divorce.

THE DEBATE ON SAME-SEX MARRIAGE

The debate circling same-sex marriage contains little fact and a great deal of speculation on the part of both critics and activists as they contemplate social and cultural consequences if same-sex marriage is legally and socially sanctioned (Green 2010). To many, the continued quest to legalize same-sex marriages in the Western world is seen as a threat to the foundations of civilization—the honourable institution of marriage, the biological need to reproduce, and the social condition of parenting (Weeks, Heaphy, & Donovan 2001). It is important to note that the debate around same-sex marriage is a manifestation of our difficulty with defining the place of homosexuals in Western societies.

The debate centres on the discourse of three separate but often overlapping groups: social conservatives and the religious right, and feminist/queer critics, both of whom oppose same-sex marriage, though for different reasons; and lesbian and gay assimilationists, who support same-sex marriage (Green 2010). Social conservatives believe that same-sex marriage will erode gender-role differentiation and nuclear families, increase infidelity, and decrease family stability. In other words, legalizing same-sex marriage would jeopardize modern society. The religious right views same-sex marriages as a violation of the teachings of a supernatural being (e.g., God), and believes that allowing same-sex marriage sanctifies deviant and immoral acts that go against religious teachings. If same-sex marriages were legalized, then this would bestow societal approval on a way of life long maligned. The harshest criticism suggests that legalizing same-sex marriages opens the door to other forms of deviant marriage, such as polygyny, incestuous marriages, and marriages with animals. For the latter two, obviously these objections are based on fear and ignorance, while polygyny, when a man takes more than one wife at a time, has been a successful form of marriage the world over, except in Western countries.

Feminists/queer critics, though also opposed to same-sex marriage, see the result quite differently than social conservatives do. For feminist and queer critics, if gays and lesbians fall into a pattern of marriage, they will be bolstering the traditional social order of gender inequality, sexism, and patriarchy (Green 2010). They are afraid that marriage will "colonize" gays and lesbians, reducing unique queer culture to a mirror of heterosexual marriage, creating a form of homonormativity (Duggan 2002: 176). Their criticism of same-sex marriage is directly linked to their long-held criticisms of the institution of marriage, as a source of women's oppression and disempowerment. From the perspective of feminist/queer critics, then, same-sex marriage is a sell-out (Baird & Rosenbaum 1997: 11).

Gay and lesbian assimilationists support same-sex marriage and believe that legalizing these unions will strengthen same-sex families, give them some social respectability, and ultimately promote monogamy. Assimilationists make the case that this is a human rights issue, and that same-sex families deserve equal rights (Queers United 2008).

Adam I. Green (2010) attempted to determine whether same-sex married couples would prove or disprove the positions of these schools of thought. Green conducted in-depth interviews with 30 legally married same-sex couples in Toronto. He found that marriage for the same-sex couples gave them social legitimacy, reaffirmed commitment to spouse and family, facilitated parenting, and created a social support network of family, friends, and co-workers, just as it did for heterosexual couples. These findings support the stance of assimilationists and, to some degree, the feminist/queer critics who fear that same-sex marriage will "tame" homosexuals. On the other hand, Green also found that same-sex married couples are not as tied to traditional norms, such as monogamy and gendered division of labour, as heterosexual couples are, although it is important to point out that we are referring to idealistic norms of monogamy and gendered division of labour in traditional heterosexual marriages, not the new realities. These findings support the fears of social conservatives; however, these deviations from marital norms are not that different from those found within heterosexual marriages.

Green (2010: 399–400) believes that this opposition between conformity and nonconformity among same-sex couples is not surprising, given that gays and lesbians are socialized in two worlds—that of heterosexual tradition, which valorizes marriage and kinship, and that of queer tradition, which promotes sexual freedom and non-traditional gender roles. Green's (2010) study suggests that same-sex marriage both supports and subverts "traditional" marriage norms.

> "[I]t is not at all clear that, say, same-sex marriages will present a fundamental challenge to the institution of marriage or that gay parents will construct truly new ways of raising children.... These are, as we social scientists like to say, empirical questions." Walters (2001: 353), quoted in Green (2010: 400)

Those who support the right of same-sex couples to marry reject religious dogma influencing legal institutions such as marriage, and feel that granting same-sex couples the right to marry is a matter of equality. They also suggest that being able to make long-term commitments in a marriage encourages stability and monogamy. Proponents believe that banning same-sex marriages is a form of discrimination against an identifiable group that has been marginalized for too long.

SAME-SEX MARRIAGES AND FAMILY STRUCTURE

Social conservatives worry that family structure is jeopardized by same-sex unions and that a traditional nuclear family is the best environment in which to raise healthy, moral children, which in turn leads to a moral society (Josephson 2005). Is this true? How do we define family? Is it a nuclear unit composed of a mother (female), father (male), and 2.2 children? Or is it a young unmarried woman with a newborn baby and a 10-year-old basset hound? Is it a middle-aged Chinese man with his wife, their daughter, his wife's parents and her brothers and sisters, spouses, and children? Is it a woman and her children married to a polygynous husband who has three other wives and many children? Or is it two men raising their three children from previous heterosexual relationships? As with marriage, a family can mean many things to many people.

Social conservative concerns about the disintegration of family are somewhat justified. The traditional institution of family is in a constant state of flux, sometimes known as a "crisis of the family." What this means is that nuclear families, the preferred form in the West, are being challenged, and the definition of family now encompasses alternative family structures—what Weeks, Heaphy, and Donovan (2001: 9) call "families of choice." Indeed, in some areas of the United States, single-parent families outnumber nuclear families. Blended families, the result of divorce and remarriage of adults with children from previous marriages, have also become common. The fastest growing demographic in Canada is the common-law family, which now has legal recognition. These and other forms of family illustrate the ability of the so-called family institution to adapt and change its structure as society changes. This expansion of the concept of family has caused a great deal of concern and confusion among people with a firmly entrenched idea of what should comprise a family; however, it has freed families, including same-sex families, from the previous narrow interpretation.

Regardless, opponents of same-sex marriages express concerns about the well-being of children in same-sex families. They raise the issues of gender identity and sexual orientation. Questions concerning the "fitness" of gay and lesbian parents have also been broached, yet studies by Flaks et al. (1989) found that lesbian mothers seemed more concerned with good mothering than did heterosexual mothers. Research into the development of gender identity in Western states has found that children living in same-sex marriages experience little confusion about their gender identity, and they appear happy and comfortable with their gender. Behavioural studies found no difference in behaviours, such as toy preference, favourite television shows and characters, activities, interests, and choice of future career, among children regardless of whether their mothers were lesbian or heterosexual. According to studies on sexual orientation, most children identified themselves as heterosexual, and no evidence of an increase in the number of gay and lesbian children coming from same-sex families has been found. Peer relationships also appear normal among children of same-sex parents; they develop close friendships with same-sex peers, as do children from heterosexual homes. Proponents of legalizing same-sex marriages therefore argue that same-sex couples can and do provide the same nurturing atmosphere as heterosexual couples.

CONCLUSION

Culture change is an inevitable part of human society. Technology is the most obvious change, but our beliefs and patterns of behaviour also change, albeit more slowly. The process of expanding the definition of marriage is an example of culture change at work. It is also an example of the most difficult and, some would say, most painful type of culture change, where people slowly alter their ideas of what is right and wrong.

Has marriage changed? Despite the protestations of traditionalists, marriage has changed considerably, even within the last century (Sullivan 2004), evidenced by the dramatic rise in divorce rates since the 1960s that has created single-parent families and, if the adults re-marry, blended families that include a parent, step-parent, siblings, and step-siblings. Furthermore, in the West, marriage has shifted from an androcentric institution to one that is now much more egalitarian.

To remain culturally relativistic while examining such a sensitive subject as same-sex marriage is extremely difficult for many people, including anthropologists. Marriage speaks to the heart of our society: it is more than a civil, social, political, or religious union; it is central to our sense of well-being and existence. This is why the debate over same-sex marriages elicits such a passionate response, both from those who oppose any change in the definition of marriage, and from those who seek greater recognition of their identity through the right to marry. In Western countries, heterosexual relationships are predicated on love and commitment, as are same-sex marriages. Gay and lesbian couples simply want the same rights and respect as heterosexual couples.

Will legally recognized same-sex marriages ever become a full reality in the Western world? Perhaps, since it has already happened in Canada and several European countries, and none of the disastrous predictions of social conservatives have come to pass. As people become more aware of different ways of life, through the efforts of anthropologists and others, they also become more accepting. As well, the gay rights movement has been gaining strength and becoming a powerful political voice since the 1960s. Gays and lesbians are no longer willing to remain marginalized on the edge of society.

Yet homosexuality and same-sex marriages are far from being universally accepted. Moral and religious issues still factor heavily in the debate, despite the recognition of civil rights, and likely will for some time to come. Even if we step outside the civil and religious arguments, many of which are valid, there is still the matter of deep-seated sentiments attached to marriage that tend to be fairly rigid and difficult to change. As Sullivan (2004: xxx) expresses it: "In this culture war, profound and powerful arguments about human equality and integrity have clashed with deep convictions about an ancient institution."

Marriage is an evolving system; indeed, it always has been. Today, many countries are experiencing a transformation in marriage, family, and kinship that is predicated on choice as well as biology. The legalization and acceptance of same-sex marriage as a legitimate form of marriage are merely the most recent steps in this evolution.

QUESTIONS FOR CONSIDERATION AND CLASSROOM ACTIVITIES

1. Why do you think there is always a battle between liberal and conservative elements in society? Does this conflict promote healthy dialogue or does it divide society? How have the opposing views stymied and advanced the rights of gays and lesbians?

2. In your opinion, what constitutes a family? How does your definition fit with the diverse family structures of the twenty-first century in your country? Develop an inclusive definition of family. Does your definition offer the possibility of same-sex families?

3. Politicians and religious leaders worry about the breakdown of both the family unit and society. Do you think allowing gays and lesbians to marry will result in the breakdown of family and society? Why or why not? Now research the reality in Canada or a European country where same-sex marriage is legal. What has happened?

4. Like female circumcision, polygyny has often been used as an example of gender oppression and exploitation. Research this practice in an African culture. Based on your findings, do you agree or disagree with the Western opinion?

5. "Obviously, any examination of marriage requires an element of cultural relativism or it will simply degenerate into a judgment of the superiority of one marriage form to another." Comment on this statement.

6. Culture change is an inevitable part of human society. As you know, changing one system of culture often has an impact on the other systems of a culture. Identify some of the changes in our economic, social, political, and religious institutions that may arise if same-sex marriages are legitimatized.

7. Research the North American Two-Spirit. Are there any groups that still recognize and welcome Two-Spirits? Is their disappearance an example of culture change or cultural imperialism?

8. Do you believe same-sex marriages should be legalized? Give reasons for your answer.

SUGGESTED READINGS

Knauft, B. (2005). *The Gebusi: Lives transformed in a rainforest world.* Toronto: McGraw-Hill.

A forthright and clearly written ethnography that does not shy away from issues of human sexuality among the Gebusi.

Sullivan, A. (Ed.). (2004). *Same-sex marriage: Pro and con.* New York: Vintage Books.

A comprehensive reader that presents solid arguments for and against same-sex marriages from an anthropological perspective.

Chapter 9

WHAT IS THE ROLE OF SOCIAL MEDIA IN SOCIO-POLITICAL REVOLUTION?

Key Terms: blogosphere, civic media, cyberanthropology, cyberculture, enculturative force, flashmobs, globalization, human rights, media anthropology, media ecology, media epidemiography, netizens, participatory media, participatory politics, popular culture, smart mobs, social change, social media, social networking, technosociality

---

INTRODUCTION

A remarkable and unprecedented showing of people power took place in Cairo, Egypt on January 25, 2011. Hundreds of thousands of Egyptians, from all walks of life and political spectrums, joined together to demand a change in government and a chance for a better life. **Social media** platforms, in particular Facebook and Twitter, have been credited with spearheading the political protests and facilitating their success. Wael Ghonim, an Egyptian activist and Google marketing manager, became a symbol of these protests when he created an anti-Mubarak Facebook page that emboldened Egyptians to take to the streets and demand that President Hosni Mubarak step down. The spectacular events in Egypt, and earlier in Tunisia, have raised some important questions regarding the role of social media and the Internet in the mobilization of contemporary socio-political reform.

"This revolution started online. This revolution started on Facebook. Everything was done by the people [for] the people, and that's the power of the Internet." Wael Ghonim, Egyptian protest leader, quoted in interview on CNN (Cohen 2011: n.p.)

The debate regarding the power of the Internet began long before Facebook or Twitter existed, and long before the Egyptian and Tunisian protests. Anthropologists and other scholars have raised questions concerning the Internet's role in socio-cultural change—does it have an impact on social, political, economic, or religious systems within societies? Howard Rheingold (2003) suggests that with the advent of the Internet, people were able to act together in what he calls **smart mobs** that facilitate cooperation and group action. An early example of a smart mob was the *No Mas* FARC protest, where a young Colombian activist mobilized 13 million people to denounce the FARC guerrilla army[1] (Etling, Faris, & Palfrey 2010), and more recently smart mobs have

---

1 The FARC guerrilla army is accused of financing its political and military battle against the government with kidnappings, extortion, and drug trafficking (In Sight 2011).

been used to report election fraud (Rheingold 2008). Today, academic debate on the topic, although still in its infancy, is questioning whether social media has the power to topple governments or if it is only one factor in a much broader context.

Studies have found that greater participation in the political landscape is influenced by access to information, and this would include social media broadcasts (Etling, Faris, & Palfrey 2010). Indeed, Michael Hauben identified a new form of citizenship emerging from widespread use of the Internet. Hauben coined the term **netizens**, and he considered them crucial for building a more democratic human society. These individuals are empowered through the Internet and use it to solve socio-political problems and to explore ways of improving the world (Hauben 2011b: 19–20).

"Welcome to the 21st Century. You are a Netizen (Net Citizen), and you exist as a citizen of the world thanks to the global connectivity that the Net gives you. You consider everyone as your compatriot. You physically live in one country but you are in contact with much of the world via the global computer network. Virtually you live next door to every other single netizen in the world. Geographical separation is replaced by existence in the same virtual space." Michael Hauben, quoted in *The Amateur Computerist* (2011: 2).

In this chapter we will explore several questions, beginning with whether social media is as powerful as activists suggest or whether it is simply an effective communication tool. Television has been an **enculturative force** for 50 years; is social media now assuming the place of television by influencing and shaping its users' perceptions, or is it merely a reflection of ongoing social change? Given recent events, have social-media platforms empowered people to bring about socio-political change, and have they changed the way people react to socio-political repression? Alarms have been raised about the negative aspects of uncontrolled communications networks, so what are some of the inherent dangers and limitations of social media? Is the role of broadcast media,[2] such as *Al Jazeera*, changing in light of social media's success, or are they mutually beneficial types of media? Studies of media and technology are, by necessity, inter- and multidisciplinary and can be found in sociology, human geography, culture studies, communications and media studies, philosophy, and economics, to name but a few. Alongside these disciplines, the role of media anthropology in the study of social media will also be examined.

ANTHROPOLOGISTS AND SOCIAL MEDIA

The increasing use of social media in "people movements" may have far-reaching implications that have only begun to be addressed in academia. In the 1990s, anthropologists such as Debra Spitulnik and Faye Ginsburg bemoaned the lack of attention to media—it seemed a taboo topic for serious anthropologists (Ginsburg, Abu-Lughod, & Larkin 2003: 3). Yet some anthropologists have come to recognize that if they are to understand

---

2 Also known as mass media.

social phenomena in human experience, then media and technology, as socially constructed phenomena, must be studied through an anthropological lens.

The developing field of **media anthropology** examines how culture is shaped and transmitted through media and how media is produced and consumed by its audience. Media anthropologists have studied a wide range of Internet-related topics, including "telework, online religion, nation-building, ethnic conflict, free software, virtual materiality, digital fan films, the digital divide and Internet activism" (Postill 2009: 1). In its earliest form, **cyberanthropology**, the study of **cyberculture**, examined computer and information technologies—their construction, implementation, and utilization within societies, and the **technosociality** that these technologies create (Escobar 1994: 211). Anthropologists Daniel Miller and Don Slater (2000) conducted a ground-breaking ethnographic study of the Internet in 2000 (Budka & Kremser 2004). In their study, they analysed how Internet users in Trinidad became comfortable with the Internet and the social implications of becoming connected to the global community. They found that Internet technology held distinctive meanings and a distinctive place in the users' lives (Budka 2011). This type of ethnographic study deals with how technology is constructed and implemented in society and culture.

> "In anthropology it's very clear that the environment that you create influences people and how they behave." Joel Spolsky, quoted in Davis (2009: n.p.)

Social media provides most of the criteria laid out by anthropologist Debra Spitulnik (1993: 293) for how anthropologists should approach the study of media: as a communicative practice, a cultural product, a social activity, and an historical development. In addition, the methodology of anthropology, including ethnography, empirical diachronic and synchronic research, historical research, and theoretical perspectives on association and forms of sociality, can provide excellent resources for studying social media. Yet social media is not only produced and consumed; it is action-oriented, participatory, and a forum for socio-cultural change as well. This is where ethnographic, qualitative research of social mobilization via social media would benefit our understanding of technological transformations in societies. Media anthropologist John Postill (2011: 1) coined the phrase **media epidemiography**—a compilation of epidemiology and ethnography—to explain how anthropologists need to study "ethnographically the media epidemiology of popular protests that 'go viral' and morph into new social movements."

> "The study of human life can happen anywhere—there are opportunities for anthropological observation available all around us, all the time." *Anthropology in Practice* (2011)

One of the difficulties with studying social media using anthropological methods is its immediacy and speed. To properly study social media, anthropologists must become active participants, and this has been slow to develop, although some anthropologists have used blogs to communicate their thoughts regarding social media. Blogs are a more immediate medium for addressing issues than journal articles and create academic discourse between anthropologists and other interested scholars. Blogs also bring the discussion into the public domain—something anthropologists have been slow to do with any topic, which has made anthropology appear irrelevant to the real world.

According to Postill (2009: 1), "there is still no social media anthropology," although some recent research on indigenous activism (Budka 2004), anti-globalization activism (Juris 2008), and local-level activism (Postill 2008) is somewhat relevant to media anthropology. Pink (2011) has found that the study of media is essential in understanding **social change**, as media is continually interpreted and re-interpreted by producers and consumers. The processes of **globalization** and their implications for culture are of growing importance in anthropology; therefore, social media, as a symbol and product of globalization, should be an integral subfield within media anthropology. Also, since online domains (a.k.a. social media) are part of everyday social and cultural life, they should not be separated into online/offline lives (Miller & Slater 2000). In fact, social media has become a component of **popular culture**—the culture of our everyday lives (Fedorak 2009: 1). Thus, social media must be considered a fundamental component of contemporary culture and an essential field of study within anthropology.

> "It should be clear by now that the interactions and uses by which people make meaning, act, or build societies is as inextricably linked to software, networks, computers, devices, and infrastructures as we insist it is to kinship or social organization." Anthropologist Christopher Kelty (2010)

THE NATURE OF SOCIAL MEDIA

Social media can motivate and mobilize participants, organize actions such as protests, recruit new participants to a cause, give voice to the marginalized, and capture broadcast media's attention and captivate worldwide audiences. Social media has gathered local and international support, exerted political influence on governments, circumvented media censorship, and created global awareness of important issues. Social media is most commonly used by youth, who are also the largest demographic in developing countries, and the most likely to demand change in their socio-cultural environment. Thus, the socio-political impact of social media is enormous. Astute politicians and leaders are beginning to realize this; for example, President Obama used social networks to reach millions of people during his 2008 election campaign.

> "Humans [have] been empowered with the ability to engage and understand social networks in a profoundly different way to ever before." Shah (2009: n.p.)

Historically, Arab Spring activists were not the first to use Internet technology to revolutionize their society. In 1991, Russia's leader, Boris Yeltsin, foiled a coup d'état because of the fledgling Soviet email system known as RelCom (Zaks 2011). The coup plotters shut down newspapers, radio, and television, but they knew nothing of the forerunner to the Internet, hidden in the secretive Kurchatov Institute. RelCom fed its news, via email, to a pre-Internet global forum known as UseNet, sending tens

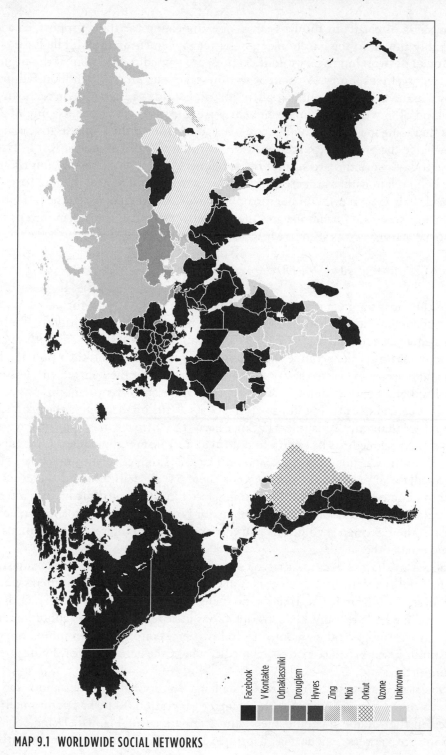

MAP 9.1 WORLDWIDE SOCIAL NETWORKS

of thousands of emails to the Russian people appealing for their support, in a move remarkably similar to the Facebook and Twitter movement in the Middle East.

Social networking to exert political pressure gained momentum at the beginning of the twenty-first century. A chain of text messages encouraged a million Filipinos to occupy a highway and demand President Joseph Estrada's resignation in 2001. In a different kind of movement, Chinese citizens were informed via text messaging of a dangerous flu raging in Guangzhou in 2003. This action forced the Chinese government to acknowledge the problem (Suárez 2011). According to anthropologist Robin Dunbar, because today's societies are so mobile, social networking is extremely important for maintaining relationships and creating large networks of associates that are forever expanding (Shah 2009: n.p.). Dunbar's prophetic words also recognized the potential for social media to create **flashmobs** and the herd effect that can transform into powerful joint social action, as was seen in Moscow in 1991.

THE VALUE OF SOCIAL MEDIA

One of the most significant benefits of social media is the ability for people to evade media censorship, so common in authoritarian regimes and within tightly controlled media systems. Social media, through its anonymity, provides netizens with opportunities to enter political discourse and to criticize governments and their policies. Social media and networking is also a way for new voices to enter the debate, with less fear of reprisal and more opportunities to learn about an issue and offer their opinions. Citizen journalists can take control of information and its diffusion, becoming the producers of media rather than only consumers (Etling, Faris, & Palfrey 2010). One of the greatest benefits of social media is its ability to upload almost instant global news. Tyrants have little ammunition against this speed and outreach, making cover-ups much less simple. Social media also provides an ongoing commentary on daily life and the events that matter to people and continues to do so long after conventional media lose interest in a particular story, such as happened when major North American broadcast media lost interest in the Egyptian revolution. Thus, it serves to keep interested individuals more informed than other media.

Social media has become the voice of the people, giving previously invisible or marginalized groups a means to communicate. An Iranian female student who suffered horrendous brutality during the post-election crackdown by Iranian authorities used social media to recount her suffering (Tomlin 2011a). She spoke about her experiences and encouraged other women to follow her example. A 28-minute segment of her testimony was broadcast on social media, where she gathered worldwide attention and support.

Social media is also being used to challenge traditional attitudes about the treatment of women, especially among the younger generation. Rape has traditionally been silenced in the Middle East and the victim stigmatized or blamed. Using social media to inform viewers of what has happened is changing deeply entrenched attitudes about women and sexual abuse. Hadi Ghaemi, executive director of New York-based International Campaign for Human Rights in Iran, sees social media as a vital communication tool in this regard. Social media opens up discussion about abuse, and even fuelled a campaign to persuade the United Nations to hold President Mahmoud Ahmadinejad accountable for **human rights** abuses in Iran. In an impressive display of **participatory media**, 160,000 Twitter users turned their profile photos green as a sign of solidarity during post-election protests in Iran (Zuckerman 2011).

In Egypt, women are using social media to hold authorities accountable for atrocities during the revolution, and to challenge attitudes that keep women silent if they have been sexually harassed.[3] YouTube postings by women such as Salwa-Al-Housiny Gouda, who was arrested, tortured, and subjected to "virginity" tests by police during the revolution, have brought sexual harassment problems in Egypt to the world's attention (Tomlin 2011b). Partly because of social media, on December 27, 2011, an Egyptian court ruled that virginity tests on women in military custody are illegal (Afify 2011). The fact that these images went "viral" on social networking sites likely provided the political pressure that led to this court's findings. *Harassmap* is a social media site that allows women to report sexual harassment by sending text messages, thereby bringing the problem into the mainstream media spotlight. One of the goals is to end victim-blaming by shifting the responsibility onto the perpetrator (Tomlin 2011b).

In Mexico, where violence between drug cartels has claimed some innocent victims, Twitter is used to report gun battles and road blockades[4] (Cave 2011). Victim's names and how they died, as well as photographs and videos of the dead, are posted to alert the public. Thus, social media can and is playing a valuable role in denouncing violence in Mexico, and has become one of the loudest voices where traditional media has been largely silenced or compromised by corruption. On the other hand, the drug cartels are using their own websites to threaten anyone posting information (Shoichet 2011).

Saudi women have harnessed social media in their campaign for the right to drive (Zuckerman 2011). Najla Hariri, a mother living in Jeddah, Saudi Arabia, drove her children to school and then tweeted about her experience. She received a flood of support in the Gulf nations via Twitter. A week later a computer security consultant, Marial Al-Sharif, drove her car, with her brother, son, and a Saudi women's rights activist along for the ride. She videoed the drive and posted it on YouTube. Saudi authorities arrested Al-Sharif and she was charged with violating public order. Her arrest garnered global attention and the support of Amnesty International. More protests by Saudi women followed, and a Facebook group was formed, rallying for a protest on June 17, 2011. The small-scale protest[5] was muted and went off with little incident. It did, however,

---

3   The degree of sexual harassment of women in Egypt is astonishing. Most women, myself included, seldom pass a day without experiencing some form of sexual harassment from Egyptian men in the streets. Authorities are of little help; indeed, police on the streets are among the most common perpetrators of sexual harassment.

4   The vast majority of violent deaths in Mexico are among drug cartel members, not the general public, despite North American broadcast media sensationalism.

5   Only those with driver's licences from other countries could participate.

FIGURE 9.1 NAJLA HARIRI DEFIED A BAN ON WOMEN DRIVING IN SAUDI ARABIA AND THEN ANNOUNCED HER DEFIANCE USING SOCIAL MEDIA

gain a great deal of attention from Western politicians, who tweeted their support, and viewers launched participatory responses. Social media gave the campaign momentum and advertised the struggle to a global audience. This is an example of **civic media**, where communities create and share actionable information using media (Zuckerman 2011).

Egypt's protests have been called a "Facebook revolution" that opened the way for other groups to utilize social media in their socio-political campaigns. Ahmed Mahir, one of the founders of the April 6 Youth Movement in the Egyptian revolution, was instrumental in showing Egyptians that social networks could be powerful political organizational tools (Ackerman 2011). Other organizations have also realized the power of social media; for example, Russian bloggers instigated the Facebook rally, where thousands took to the streets to protest elections they claimed were fraudulent. Social media circumvented the state-controlled media, which did not air the protests. According to journalist Sergei Parkhomenko, "Nothing like this has ever happened before. This all started with a few posts on Facebook and (blogging platform) LiveJournal" (*The Times of India* 2011: n.p.). Facebook, with its capability to allow users to share videos of police brutality, express political anger, and announce protests on its dissident pages, helped build the momentum and set the stage for the "it was now or never" action in Egypt. This is why Tufekci (2011) believes that social media, or what she calls new **media ecology**, is a game changer, and a potent tool for socio-political change as it alters collective-action dynamics.

CRITICISMS OF SOCIAL MEDIA

"There's a current fascination with the idea popular movements can be created using virtual tools. While there's good reason to suspect that the role of Facebook has been overstated in the Arab Spring, there's also good reason to believe that the role was real and significant, especially as it came to documentation." Media researcher Ethan Zuckerman (2011: n.p.)

Peterson (2011) calls social media a vehicle for social change. Yet a few so-called media experts dismiss the power of social media. Journalist Malcolm Gladwell suggests that social media is not successful at "providing the discipline, strategy, hierarchy, and strong social bonds that successful movements require" (Gladwell 2010: n.p.), even though a great deal of organization and planning among various protest leaders has taken place through social media. Ramesh Srinivasan, a professor of information studies, counters Gladwell, suggesting that using social media facilitated the organization of Middle Eastern revolutions, but that people in charge of organizing the masses created and sustained the revolution. This, too, took place over social media (Srinivasan 2011).

One novel way of examining the power of social media is to ask the question, how did Hosni Mubarak in Egypt and Zine Ben Ali in Tunisia hold on to power for so long? What are the mechanisms that maintain authoritarian regimes? According to Tufekci (2011), the answer lies in a "collective action problem," or a society-level collective problem, where the cooperation of many people is required to solve a problem, but there are serious repercussions and disincentives for any one individual to participate, and the means for organizing dissent is quickly stifled through torture and lengthy prison sentences. Dissent is repressed through censorship and isolation—key mechanisms for a regime to survive. Twenty years ago the Jordanian bread revolution, fuelled by high unemployment and increased costs for bread and oil, created a popular uprising that barely registered on the global media radar (Dahdal 2011). Why? The protestors lacked an effective communication tool, such as *Al Jazeera*, that could sidestep the heavily censored Jordanian media, and they lacked social media and its power to mobilize protestors.

Rheingold (2003), however, warns that authoritarian regimes can also use social media to control citizens or discredit opposition, as the Iranian regime did in 2009 (Suárez 2011). Leaders of authoritarian regimes can use the Internet to spy on dissidents and may use social media to control ideas. The popularity of social media in revolution can also backfire—some authoritarian governments such as China have blocked Facebook and Twitter (Evangelista 2011). Other authoritarian regimes have resorted to filters, surveillance, and cyberattacks to stop activists from using the Internet (Etling, Faris, & Palfrey 2010).

The reliability of social media is also open to question. Could Facebook be used to spread false information? Could Twitter become a gossip column? Does social media provide a complete picture of the situation? In the case of Egypt, many of the leaders of the Muslim Brotherhood were thrown in jail shortly before the protests. Tweeters complained that their leaders were invisible, without investigating why. Social media may be used for nefarious deeds as well. In 2007, text messages incited attacks against minorities in Kenya (Etling, Faris, & Palfrey 2010). In December, 2011, images of a young Egyptian female protestor being beaten, stripped of her *hijab* and *abaya*, and then dragged through the streets by soldiers roused worldwide horror. However, the legitimacy of these images has been called into question by some Egyptians. Adel Abdul Sadek, head of the Arab Center for Cyberspace Research, warns that images or videos may be fabricated to promote particular ideas or motivate a particular response.[6]

> "People protested and brought down governments before Facebook was invented. They did it before the Internet came along."
> Malcolm Gladwell, quoted in Ingram (2011: n.p.)

---

6 Adel Abdul Sadek's comments should in no way be construed as confirming that this incident did not happen. The video in question was taken by a Reuters photographer and then distributed over social media as well as broadcast media.

"Citizens or public audiences of today are no longer mere audiences, but part of the media revolution that is shaping the world today." Joyce Barnathan, President of the International Center for Journalism, quoted in Garcia (2011: n.p.)

He also points out that this particular video only showed the girl being stripped, not the soldier who covered her up and protected her, therefore making the "story" biased and incomplete (Suleiman 2011).

THE EGYPTIAN REVOLUTION[7]

What caused the Egyptian revolution? Analysts have identified numerous factors that led to an inevitable explosion of anger: decades of government corruption and dictatorship; grinding poverty; high unemployment, especially among youth; police brutality; and an arrogant, wealthy elite. All of these factors were catalysts for the Egyptian revolution and the earlier Tunisian revolution. Social media served as the mobilizing force, the tool through which activists called the people to rise up and demand change. Estimates vary from three to six million Facebook users in Egypt, many of whom used these platforms to organize the protests and share information and videos of the demonstrations in Tahrir Square. Their images captivated audiences around the world.

When the Egyptian government shut down the Internet in an attempt to stem the flow of information, engineers from Twitter and Google developed a "Speak-to-Tweet" service, a way to send voice messages through designated numbers that were automatically translated into type and sent on as tweets (Suárez 2011). Twitter provided police locations, meeting places for protestors, and updates on media coverage, all within seconds. Twitter was also used to rally new recruits to the protest and broadcast the goals of the protestors to the world at large. Thus, Twitter became the "eyes, ears, and voice of the day to day life of the protest" (Watkins 2011: 1).

Although the Egyptian uprising may have appeared spontaneous to outsiders, an unprecedented political alliance of disparate factions, including the secular leftists and Muslim Brotherhood, quietly worked toward the overthrow of the Mubarak regime long before 2011 (Hauben 2011a). The Kifaya movement—*kifaya* meaning change—emerged in 2004–05, bringing together Islamists, communists, liberals, and secular-leftists in a common goal—the ouster of Mubarak. Activists in the Kifaya movement used the **blogosphere** to create a new political language free from terms of secularization or fundamentalism. An alliance between Egypt's workforce and online netizens spread information and encouraged online discourse. These blogs were used to report police abuse, while videos were used to incite the people to action. Indeed, by 2008, blogs had become the surrogate news media, easily and quickly circumventing Egypt's censorship

"Sometimes decades pass and nothing happens, and then sometimes weeks pass and decades happen." Vladimir Lenin, quoted in Sreberny (2011: n.p.)

---

7 Not everyone agrees that a true political revolution took place in Egypt. The military rulers now in power are former henchmen of Mubarak, and they apply the same brutal tactics for suppressing opposition. Nevertheless, a mental/intellectual revolution is indisputable—Egyptians have never risen up against their dictators *en masse*; thus the events of January and February 2011 changed the victim mentality and the apathy so common in Egypt.

FIGURE 9.2 EGYPTIAN MAN USING CELL PHONE TO TWEET NEWS FROM TAHRIR SQUARE IN CAIRO DURING THE EARLY DAYS OF THE JANUARY 2011 REVOLUTION

laws (Mahmood 2011). These early movements heralded the organizing potential of social media. Anthropologist Charles Hirschkind (2011) believes that these online discussions coalesced diverse political ideas into a common political goal that finally erupted on January 25, 2011, the Day of Anger. On that day, protestors used social media to gather information, support, and news, and to send videos and photos across the network. In turn, mainstream media, particularly opposition newspapers, relied on bloggers for stories that journalists could not write without facing prosecution.

Egyptians made use of a wide range of media during the revolution, ranging from email and mobile phones, to leaflets and other print media. Mahir Marc Lynch, director of the Institute for Middle East Studies, warns that although social media such as Twitter and Facebook played a significant role in the Tunisian revolution, the full impact was not felt until their images made it onto broadcast media. Broadcast news, particularly opposition media in Egypt, and later international television, relied on Twitter and other social media to receive instant news. In Egypt, the Day of Anger protest in Tahrir Square was coordinated via Facebook

"This is a revolution in the making sparked by youth who are determined to alter the dominant paradigm of politics and power that precludes the central idea which undergrids democracy—citizenship under a social contract." Hovesepian (2011: n.p.)

and Twitter, using the hashtag #jan25 to post news as it happened. Mainstream media then re-broadcast the images worldwide. *Al Jazeera*, the international television news network based in Qatar, played a pivotal role in getting the message out.[8] Nevertheless, when expediency is paramount, e.g., during a natural disaster or the early moments of a revolution (Zuckerman 2011), social media has proven far more effective than broadcast media. Social media offers alternative viewpoints and analysis; for example, during the Libyan civil war, broadcast media reported only the views of Libyan defectors from the military and the opposition (Hauben 2011a). However, as seen in the Egyptian revolution, broadcast media and social media can work together to provide different, but effective news.

Imagery has always been a powerful tool/weapon in campaigns against injustice. Images of Khaled Said, who was beaten to death by security police when they arrested him at a cybercafé in Cairo, became an icon of the revolution when his brother posted post-mortem pictures on Facebook (*Technology Review* 2011). A Facebook group called "We are all Khaled Said" addressed police corruption and brutality and is considered instrumental in organizing Egyptian protesters (Martin 2011). Some of the most profound images coming from Tahrir Square depicted the bonding of Egyptians from disparate walks of life in a common cause, from protecting each other during prayers, to cleaning up the trash in the square. Thousands of Egyptian protesters took on the responsibility of streaming photos and updates, and tweeting to the world. These protestors became the producers of news, giving new meaning to the term **participatory politics** (Watkins 2011).

CONCLUSION

In the early 1990s, the late Michael Hauben recognized that the Internet would bring about "new social consciousness and identity" (*The Amateur Computerist* 2011). His prophetic words ring true in light of the events in 2011. Facebook and Twitter have become major conduits for news, information, and commentary, uniting grassroots movements for socio-political change (Evangelista 2011). Freedom on the Internet to express an opinion has had a significant impact on political processes.

In this chapter, social media is considered a communication tool rather than a catalyst. The value of social media such as Facebook lies in its ability to provide "a space where silence and fear are broken and trust can be built, where social networks can turn political, and where home and Diaspora can come together" (Sreberny 2011: n.p.). Social media has the power to influence and shape viewers' perceptions, beliefs, and behaviours while also empowering people by giving them a forum to participate in political action (Suárez 2011).

---

8 For people living in Egypt at the time of the protests, myself included, *Al Jazeera* International was a vital link to the happenings in downtown Cairo.

Would the Tunisian and Egyptian revolutions have happened without social media? Perhaps, but social media brought these revolutionary movements to the attention of the world, and this may have had a great deal to do with their success, in the sense that "the world was watching." Postill (2011) believes online activism is part of a broader twenty-first-century cultural revolution, and a global shift in power and knowledge. Indeed, ultimately, these revolutions were about people power; social media was merely one of the tools that facilitated, albeit in a significant way, their success. Social media did not bring down the Egyptian government; people did. Social media is not the reason revolutions occur but it has changed the very nature of social activism in ways that media experts, political pundits, and academics have only begun to analyse.

> "If you want to liberate a society, just give them the Internet." Wael Ghonim, quoted in "Internet: Road to Democracy ... or elsewhere?" (NPR 2011).

The power of social media and social networking is not always predictable, but there is little doubt that it is transforming how people communicate, become informed, and advocate. The Egyptian activist leaders have been quite vocal in their estimation of the power of social media: without it, their revolution would not have succeeded. Having personally witnessed and experienced the dramatic flow of instantaneous information and the incredible organizational feats during the revolution, I tend to agree. Our world has changed; the public now has the power, and the private will never again be able to coerce, force, or bully without everyone knowing.

Although slow to embrace the study of social media, anthropologists have the opportunity and the obligation to join the discourse on the role of social media in culture change and transformation. They will bring strong ethnographic and qualitative research traditions to the study of political and social mobilization via social media, along with unique perspectives on the implications of gender, socio-economic class, and ethnicity on using social media. In the future, the anthropology of social media will become an integral subfield of the discipline in its ongoing attempts to remain academically and socially relevant.

QUESTIONS FOR CONSIDERATION AND CLASSROOM ACTIVITIES

1. In this chapter, social media is classified as a communication tool, not a catalyst for change. Do you agree with this assessment? Why or why not? How much influence does social media have on your world views? Are you involved in any activism platforms? Explain.
2. Smart mobs are defined as people using the Internet to act together to facilitate cooperation and group action. Find three or more examples of smarts mobs and their activism.
3. Are you a netizen? Why or why not?
4. Create a chart of media used for communications. Identify the type of media best suited for activism, promotion, propaganda, news, education, etc.

5. Research project: How has social media been used in indigenous activism, anti-globalization protests, and local-level activism?
6. Social media has been used to circumvent censorship in many parts of the world. Provide three examples of current socio-political action using social media.
7. Marginalized women are using social media to tell their story. What other examples of marginalized groups are using social media?
8. In your opinion, is the role of social media over-exaggerated?

SUGGESTED READINGS

Campbell, D.G. (2011). *Egypt unshackled: Using social media to @#:) the system.* Portland, OR: Cambria Books.

This timely book describes how social media can reshape history by using the riveting "tweeting history" of the last days of the revolution. Must-read book.

Katz, J.E. (Ed.). (2008). *Handbook of mobile communication studies. E-book.* Cambridge, MA: The MIT Press.

This book is full of expert analysis of the impact of social media on everyday life and culture, from around the world.

Chapter 10

WHAT ARE THE SOCIO-ECONOMIC AND POLITICAL IMPACTS OF HUMAN MIGRATION?

Key Terms: discrimination, emigration, ethnic enclaves, globalization, human trafficking, immigrants, immigration, migration, modern-day slavery, multiculturalism, systemic racism, transnational communities, xenophobia

---

INTRODUCTION

Large-scale human migration, although not a new phenomenon, is a process of **globalization** with unprecedented implications for both source and destination nations. Indeed, Moses (2006: n.p.) describes international migration as "globalization's last frontier." The term **migration** means **emigration** *from* a place and **immigration** *to* another place (Fitzgerald 2006); internal migration can be from one locality to another within the same country, while international migration means crossing borders.

Immigrants are loosely categorized as political or economic immigrants, family-sponsored immigrants, refugees, sojourners (temporary residents, such as students or seasonal workers), and, increasingly, environmental refugees or immigrants who are forced to leave a locality because of environmental disaster or degradation. Another category, not usually included in a discussion of immigration, is the victims of human trafficking. The United States State Department defines **human trafficking** as "modern day slavery involving victims who are forced, defrauded or coerced into labour or sexual exploitation" (CIA World Factbook 2009: n.p.).

Dramatic "push-pull" factors trigger immigration patterns. Push factors in countries of origin are often driven by economic considerations. Limited economic opportunities, including low wages or unemployment, poor investment opportunities, and inadequate access to credit to start businesses (Rosenblum & Brick 2011) may drive people to emigrate. Corrupt and authoritarian governments, war

> "... large scale movements of people arise from the accelerating process of global integration ... migrations are not an isolated phenomenon: movements of commodities and capital almost always give rise to movements of people."
> Castles and Miller (2003: 4)

and ethnic conflict, and natural disasters that uproot families are other push factors. Immigrants also respond to pull factors in the destination countries, such as secure employment, legal equality, political stability and safety, and limited government interference. Social networks of friends and family already in the destination country also encourage immigration.

Immigration may cause unpredictable socio-economic changes in destination countries (Castles 2000), which are considered threats to national sovereignty, security, and identity. As a result, in the last half of the twentieth century many governments established restrictions on immigration, including country-of-origin quotas and favouring immigrants with financial and investment means or credentials in preferred professions. These closed-door policies hamper low-skilled, visible-minority populations from legally entering countries, leading to increased irregular (or illegal) immigration and human trafficking (Wickramasekara 2008). Resentment and fear of these influxes of irregular immigrants has caused discrimination and social disparity in some destination countries.

In this chapter we will situate international migration within the context of globalization. The multidimensional reasons for immigration flows, as well as the challenges facing immigrants and the source and destination countries will be addressed. Immigration policies in developed countries have changed as their labour and investment needs have changed. We will briefly examine immigration policies in Canada and the United States, two of the main destination countries in the world. The challenges faced by destination countries have led to an increase in discrimination against immigrants, and to a global trend toward social exclusion and economic inequality (Munck 2010). In particular, the increase in discriminatory practices against African immigrants and global human trafficking for sexual exploitation or forced labour will be featured in this chapter.

International migration is a characteristic of the worldwide interconnectedness (globalization) of finance, trade, ideas, media, and technology (Castles 2000). Therefore, any discussion of immigration must be multidisciplinary; the analysis of human migration in the twenty-first century will be informed through sociology, political economy, immigration law, history, culture studies, human geography, and of course anthropology.

ANTHROPOLOGISTS AND HUMAN MIGRATION

Anthropologists have a long-standing interest in human migration; however, globalization has caused a shift away from studying specific cultures living in clearly defined areas to examining the flow of people from one locality to another and the corresponding disruptions in cultural systems (Fitzgerald 2006). To do this, anthropologists must conduct multi-sited ethnographic fieldwork, following immigrants between source and destination countries. Participant observation, although somewhat transformed, provides a means for anthropologists to follow immigrants to multiple sites. Archival and historical literature, intensive interviewing, and surveys are also employed more frequently than in the study of a single, stationary population. Fitzgerald (2006) believes that exploring the connections between ethnographic sites may rejuvenate comparative ethnography to understand how different source and destination localities affect and are affected by immigrant experiences.

Anthropologists analyse population movements, the relationships between populations, and the continuity or discontinuity between the "home" culture and the adopted culture (Eriksen 2003). One advantage of twenty-first-century human migration is that communication and transportation systems enable immigrants to maintain familial and cultural connections with their ancestral homeland, creating **transnational communities**. Smith (2005) studied such transnational communities among immigrants from a Mexican town who moved to New York City. This study demonstrated how the migrants integrated into the New York culture while still maintaining strong political, economic, and cultural ties with their home culture (Fitzgerald 2006).

> "What anthropology has to bring to globalisation studies is the recognition that social and cultural worlds, which are constituted from diverse materials of various origins, are always expressed through meaningful relationships."
>
> Eriksen (2003: 15)

Anthropologists are particularly interested in the inter-relationships between new immigrants and citizens of destination countries, in the social disparities that immigrants must deal with, and in the relationships between immigrant communities and the outside world (Eriksen 2003). For example, Karen Fog Olwig studied the sense of community among Caribbean immigrants in North America. Using family narratives, Olwig focused on migratory family networks and the way in which these networks and interpersonal relationships created and maintained an awareness of being "Caribbean," regardless of where they now lived. Of particular note, she changed her conceptual framework of culture to a process, rather than a thing, that bridges time and geographical dispersal (Olwig 2007).

Collaboration, increasingly important in all avenues of anthropological research, has taken on an added importance in migration studies. A collaborative study by Orellana and colleagues (2001) of children from Yemen, Korea, Mexico, and Central America who had immigrated to Los Angeles and Oakland led to the concept of "transnational childhoods" (Fitzgerald 2006). Thus, ethnographic research in the twenty-first century requires a willingness to move beyond the "field" as a specific location and into a conceptual space. In the words of anthropologist Arjun Appadurai (1991), "The task of ethnography now becomes the unraveling of a conundrum: what is the nature of locality, as a lived experience, in a globalized, deterritorialized world?" (Fitzgerald 2006: 10).

THE NATURE OF HUMAN MIGRATION

Human migration is the new world order, and with it comes increasingly complex, multidimensional issues. Many immigrants are fleeing war-torn, politically unstable countries and seeking a safe environment for their families. Canada has become a destination of choice because of its relative political stability, low crime rate, and a global reputation for embracing **multiculturalism**. The major reason why immigrants leave their homelands is for new economic opportunities. Immigrants are enticed to countries like Canada by higher wages and job security, and credit and capital for entrepreneurial plans.

Furthermore, virtually all Western countries are experiencing declining birth rates. These countries encourage immigration to replenish their populations and, more specifically, to replenish their aging workforces (Halli & Driedger 1999).[1] This is also true in European countries, where an aging population and increasing labour shortages persist. Humanitarian reasons also play a role; countries such as Canada have been inundated with requests to accommodate refugees and asylum seekers. The need for foreign investment may also determine government immigration targets. During the 1980s and 1990s, Hong Kong entrepreneurs and investors were encouraged to immigrate to Canada. In return, they created economic boons for major urban centres.

For the source countries, emigration alleviates population pressures and unemployment, creates diaspora networks, and leads to human capital accumulation (e.g., education and skills) if the migrant returns home. Immigrants send wealth to their home country through remittances to families, creating what Glick Schiller (2008) calls a social field of networks that connect people across borders.

Immigrants choose the destination country for various reasons. One common factor is prior links to countries through colonialism, political influence, trade, cultural ties, or reciprocal investment (Castles 2000). Migrants from the Caribbean tend to choose former colonial powers (e.g., Jamaicans immigrate to Britain) as their preferred destination (Castles 2000). Similarly, Koreans and Vietnamese choose the United States due to past military involvement in their countries. African migrants have preferred Europe largely because of its geographic and language proximity, colonial ties, and more favourable economic conditions (Katseli, Lucas, & Xemogiani 2006).

SOCIO-ECONOMIC AND POLITICAL CHALLENGES

Human migration presents some interesting challenges for both governments and residents in destination countries, as well as for the immigrants themselves. Immigrants may hold different traditions, beliefs, and political views than residents of the host country. They often speak different languages, may look visibly different, and can overwhelm a region's infrastructure (e.g., transportation, education). Consequently, some citizens in destination countries may react negatively to an influx of immigrants who threaten the illusion of homogeneity.

Differing perspectives on multiculturalism may also create disharmony in destination countries. On the one hand, ethno-nationalists champion a homogeneous,

---

1 In 2005, *Maclean's* reported that, according to then-foreign affairs minister Pierre Pettigrew, Canada needs 40 million people to offset the aging baby boomers heading for retirement (*Maclean's* 2005).

unilingual, and unicultural nation and claim that multiculturalism dilutes nationalism. In Europe, some fear that cultural diversity will destroy national symbols and icons and replace them with "foreign" cultural components. On the other hand, multiculturalists believe that ethnic, cultural, religious, and social diversity enhances the quality and variety of life. Multiculturalism is a mechanism designed to peacefully manage a nation founded on ethnic diversity. However, as will become clear, the degree to which this multiculturalism is welcomed and facilitated varies from one society to another.

Anti-immigrants also fear that immigrants will jeopardize their standard of living and the social cohesion of their society (Castles 2000). Immigrants are often made scapegoats for unemployment and crime, the growing disparity between rich and poor, the shrinking of the middle class, the reduction in the availability and quality of education, and the rising costs of housing and health care (Glick Schiller 2009). Illegal immigration bears the brunt of most of this fear and anger. Some regions and nation-states have responded to public pressure by deporting illegal immigrants (e.g., Libya), building walls (e.g., Arizona, Israel), corporal punishment (e.g., Singapore), and sanctions against employers who hire illegal immigrants (e.g., South Africa). These attempts to stop illegal immigration tend to fail, however, as the push-pull factors override the danger. Still, in Europe anti-immigrant campaigns are gaining power, and this politicalization of immigration often leads to social conflict.

Immigrating to a new country is a daunting experience. To maintain some semblance of familiarity, they may settle in urban centres where there are well-established populations from the same source regions. These areas are known as **ethnic enclaves**. Balakrishnan and Hou (1999) found that residential segregation helps maintain cultural identity but also prolongs the sense of separateness from mainstream society and the process of integration. Yet most immigrants try to fit into their new society while also preserving parts of their culture. For example, Chinese immigrants to Canada have a cultural identity that is neither discretely Canadian nor Chinese, but Chinese Canadian (Chow 1996). This dual identity enables them to maintain their Chinese cultural heritage while adopting Canadian cultural elements. Multiculturalism has aided in preserving and celebrating Chinese heritage while encouraging the Chinese to adapt to Canadian society (Ng 1999). Even in the United States, which has always touted a melting-pot philosophy, immigrants have maintained their ethnic identity, and in reality the United States is as pluralistic as Canada (Soria 2005).

Neuwirth (1999) warns that integration of new immigrants is a two-way commitment. Immigrants, for their part, must learn the official language, obey the laws of the land, find employment, and become involved in the community. The host country must ensure meaningful employment is available, and share the basic values, ideology, and traditions of the country with new immigrants. If immigrants are excluded from economic and social institutions, they will not adopt the host country's practices and norms, and will, out of a sense of preservation, try to maintain their traditional culture.

Despite attempts to become part of their new country, visible minorities may still experience barriers that prevent them from accessing economic opportunities in destination countries—what Li (1988) calls **systemic racism**—much more commonly than "white" immigrants. Because of physical and behavioural differences (e.g., darker skin, religious beliefs), they have been kept on the margins of society. Refugees are particularly vulnerable because of the political turmoil and hardships they have escaped, and because it is likely that they fled with few employable skills or economic resources. Anti-immigration discourse ignores the contributions that even low-skilled immigrants make to society: they provide important labour and services, and they support other services—the food industry, housing, education and training, transportation, and so on (Glick Schiller 2009). Immigrants improve neighbourhoods previously considered undesirable, create new businesses and industries, and restructure the social fabric of a region.

"Migrant workers can make their best contribution to economic and social development in host and source countries when they enjoy decent working conditions, and when their fundamental human and labour rights are respected." Statement by the Director-General of the ILO, Roundtable 3 on globalisation and labour migration, 2006 ECOSOC High-Level Segment, Geneva, 5 July 2006 quoted in Alsvik (2009: n.p.)

The common misconception that immigrants take jobs away from native-born citizens is refuted by economists. In the United States, for example, those states with high immigration rates enjoy lower unemployment rates and job creation because of increasing demands for goods and services (Soria 2005). A second misconception is that immigrants put pressure on an economy without giving anything back. However, immigrants "pay taxes, pay into Social Security and boost the economy with their added consumption" (Soria 2005: 301). The same holds true for Canada, where immigration results in a net increase in jobs (Kymlicka 2003: 205). The tendency to accuse immigrants of hurting the economy becomes particularly evident during times of economic recession, when immigrants are blamed for the economic woes of native-born citizens (Spencer 2003). Above all, immigrants need to be viewed as an asset, not a liability (Soria 2005), and attitudes toward immigrants will often determine how successfully they integrate into the new society.

HISTORY OF GLOBAL MIGRATION

Human migration in response to economic need, political instability, religious persecution, or climate change has a long history. Indeed, migrations of early humans spread across the continents in search of abundant food resources, open spaces, and milder climates. In the fifteenth century, migration became more structured in response to colonization and industrialization processes (Castles 2000). Soldiers, traders, farmers, and administrators moved to the colonies, and 15 million African slaves were captured and taken to the colonies between the fifteenth and nineteenth centuries. European industrialization created dislocation and poverty, encouraging people to leave for the Americas, where economic growth and nation building welcomed newcomers.

In the early twentieth century, economic stagnation slowed immigration, and public attitudes toward immigrants, especially those from Eastern Europe, turned negative—they were considered unassimilable and a threat to American values, leading to the establishment of the first quota system. In Europe, France continued to recruit Italian, Polish, and Spanish workers until the Great Depression, when many were deported (Cross 1983). Nazi Germany also recruited, by force, to replace conscripted Germans. Prior to World War II, American immigration excluded "undesirables" such as Asians. This exclusion list was periodically added to, including such people as the mentally challenged. By the 1920s, quotas based on nation of origin were legislated, and this trend continued well into the 1960s.

Following World War II, immigration gained momentum; people from every socio-economic and cultural background immigrated to Western Europe, North America, and Oceania. The American Bracero Program brought in large numbers of temporary workers, mainly for agriculture. In a more humane approach, and likely a product of the civil rights movements, asylum seekers were admitted. Most of these immigrants originated in the Caribbean, Central and South America, and Europe (Simmons 1999). Rather than a points system, family sponsorship appears to have played a larger role in the United States than in Canada in the early years.

In the 1960s, Canada changed its earlier policy of drawing immigrants from England and Northern Europe for lower-paying jobs and began admitting qualified immigrants from all parts of the world. Immigrants from Asia (particularly Southeast Asia), Africa, and Latin America, who had historically been refused entry, now made up the bulk of immigration to Canada. Refugees and asylum seekers were also regularly accepted. Both of these policies reflected an easing of restrictions against visible minorities and recognition of the need to expand Canada's population and economy. In the 1980s and 1990s, immigrant entrepreneurs, investors, and professionals were most often accepted (Simmons 1999).

Canadian immigration policy has changed once again, from accepting those with money to encouraging educated and skilled foreigners to choose Canada as their new home, and thereby reduce the country's looming skilled-labour shortage. Indeed, the Canadian government encourages immigrants with trade skills, such as pipe fitters and truck drivers, and graduate students already here to choose Canada as their permanent home (United Press International 2005). In 2012, Canada's immigration policy is predicated on an ever-shrinking list of occupations, such as dentists and chefs. Other avenues for immigration have been closed off; a two-year moratorium has been imposed on sponsoring parents and grandparents of immigrants. Yet the government still recognizes that with Canada's aging population and gaps in skilled labour, immigrants are needed (Canadavisa.com 2012).

For the last four decades, migration rates from Mexico, El Salvador, Guatemala, and Honduras have accelerated. Approximately 14 million immigrants from these four countries now live in the United States (Rosenblum & Brick 2011). Although typically immigrants from Mexico originated in the central part of the country and looked mainly for agricultural jobs in the American Southwest, today they come from several districts and possess a broader occupational profile, working in construction, maintenance, food service, and manufacturing. Nonetheless, most of these immigrants do not have resident status, and illegal immigration from Central American countries has emerged as a major concern. American immigration policy is focused on curtailing this illegal immigration.

In the mid-1970s, immigration to southern Europe, the Gulf oil countries, Latin America, Africa, and Asia expanded. However, since 9/11, visible minorities from the Middle East have been targeted as potential terrorists. This has made life more difficult for immigrants, especially in the United States and Europe, where immigration policy has shifted to security control (Spencer 2003). In Canada a 2005 survey suggested that two-thirds of Canadians fear that immigrant groups will bring their ethnic conflicts to Canada with them (Innovative Research Group 2005). They call for tough screening of potential immigrants in order to weed out terrorists. On a more positive note, 63 per cent of Canadians polled worry that concerns over terrorism could lead to a decline in civil rights for Canadians from Arabic or Islamic countries (Butler 2005).

International migration from developing countries to developed countries grew rapidly in the 1990s but now faces severe restrictions. Some European Union countries view foreigners, rather than permanent residents, as solutions to short-term labour shortages (Simmons 1999). Indeed, today some European countries are trying to drastically curtail or even eliminate immigration from non-European countries. In September 2005, European Union ministers from Spain, Germany, Italy, and Belgium met to discuss "the immigration problem" (de Francisco 2005), where Spain proposed a plan to develop a joint European–Mediterranean police and judicial network to stop irregular immigration, drug smuggling, and terrorism. This selective immigration policy is predicated on racism and **xenophobia**, which is on the rise throughout Europe and America. One dramatic example of this xenophobia, and its ensuing discriminatory practices, is France.

DISCRIMINATION AGAINST IMMIGRANTS IN FRANCE

Migration policies and integration strategies, as well as managing cultural diversity, have always been a challenge for France. Despite France's immigration policies supposedly being designed to prevent **discrimination** while promoting integration of new arrivals into French society, the country's history is fraught with discriminatory practices against immigrants. For one, multiculturalism is taboo in France, echoing a recent comment by Germany's Chancellor Angela Merkel that multiculturalism is dead. France views retention of ethnic identity as a deterrent to integration. To become a French citizen, no ethnic or cultural differences are allowed. As a consequence, France is raising a generation of dispossessed people who often become scapegoats for France's ills. In a human rights survey, three-quarters of the respondents blamed immigrants for increasing unemployment and crime in France and for decreasing educational standards. Forty per cent of the respondents agreed with forcible repatriation of the unemployed, and 22 per cent wanted forcible repatriation of all immigrants. The 2000

Eurobarometer found that only 31 per cent of French respondents supported laws outlawing discrimination against minorities (Randall 2008). These alarming statistics indicate a growing resentment toward immigrants.

Theoretically, everyone is equal in France: religion, colour, and other similar factors are all supposed to be irrelevant. However, in reality France's immigration policy perpetuates an exclusionary attitude, especially toward Muslims, and exacerbates anti-immigrant vigilantism and discrimination. For example, there are no Muslim state schools, no Muslim chaplains in the army, and employment ads often clearly state "whites only," "no coloureds," or "French nationals only." Paradoxically, France is home to the largest Muslim community in Europe (Hamilton, Simon, & Veniard 2004), imported in the 1970s to meet labour-market needs. When French women began entering the job market in the 1970s, France no longer needed as many immigrant workers, and so restrictive immigration policies were put in place: foreign graduates of French schools could not accept employment in France; waiting periods for family reunification doubled; spouses who were illegal before their marriage to a French citizen were denied residence; and asylum appeals were limited. These restrictive immigration policies created resentment, discontent, and strife, especially among visible-minority youth.[2]

> "We're French but we're not considered as real French people." Chrisafis (2010: n.p.)

In a detailed study of employment discrimination, Decreuse et al. (2010) found a distinct correlation between employment inequality among African immigrants and residence patterns. In those areas where there was a large base of prejudiced customers, and where jobs required close contact with the customers, African immigrants faced poorer job prospects. Decreuse et al. (2010) conclude that regional variation in population demographics plays a role in employment inequality, which has had an impact on living standards: 48 per cent of African immigrants live in social housing, compared to 15 per cent of French natives.

Xenophobia in France has even been exploited by politicians for political gain. In February 2004, the government passed a bill banning religious symbols in public schools. Although the bill did not specifically target Muslim veiling, the intent was clear. This bill is one of many actions taken against immigrants in an effort to keep France secular (Hamilton, Simon, & Veniard 2004). Some, however, accuse the French government of being anti-Islamic rather than pro-secularist, and say that they are indirectly legitimizing anti-Arab stereotypes and fostering racism. Others view the bill as the right step since it may provide an option for girls who do not want to wear the veil.[3]

France's discriminatory policies, both nationally and locally, have created a culture of tension. In October 2004, this tension boiled over into suburban riots (Chrisafis 2010). The catalyst was two young boys who were electrocuted while hiding from police in a power substation. The root cause was the hopelessness of a generation of

---

2 The term visible-minority youth is used here because many of the people experiencing serious economic, social, and religious discrimination in France are fourth- or fifth-generation French citizens, but the colour of their skin still sets them apart.

3 This is predicated on the assumption that Muslim women are forced to veil, which is far from true.

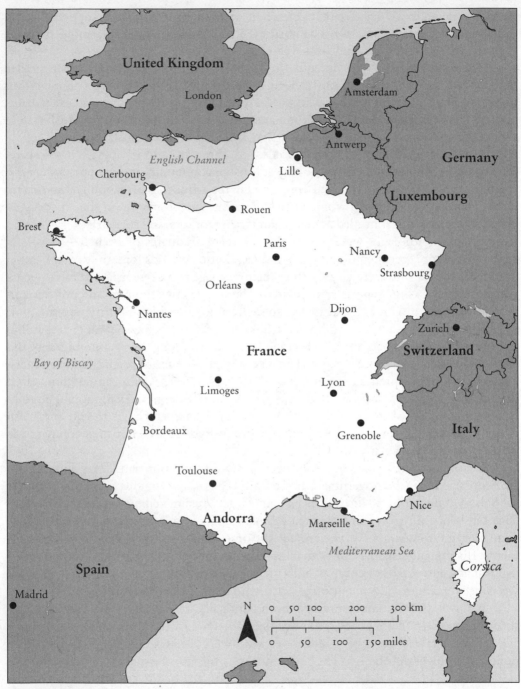

MAP 10.1 FRANCE

youth, ghettoized, marginalized, and unemployed, and the racist policies against Muslims, even those who are native-born
French citizens (Kamber & Lacey 2005).

Former president Nicolas Sarkozy won the French
election in 2007 on a right-wing, anti-immigrant platform,
attracting votes from the extreme right Front National party.
Once elected, Sarkozy ordered the expulsion of 25,000 irregular immigrants. The police roundups of Roma, Muslims, and
other minorities took place outside schools, metro stations,
and businesses, and created a backlash of protest from many
French citizens. Some even hid children of illegal immigrants
in their homes. The round-ups eerily resembled the time when
the French collaborationist government deported 75,000 French citizens and Jewish
refugees to Nazi concentration camps during World War II (Chrisafis 2010).

"Sarkozy's constant talk of
immigration and national identity
chips away at you, but worse is
the perpetual police stops and
searches. Cops insult us, saying
'Get back to your own country,
you're not welcome.' That's
pretty hard to stomach when
you're French." Fariz Allili, 21,
son of an Algerian café owner,
quoted in Chrisafis (2010: n.p.)

HUMAN TRAFFICKING

Former United Nations secretary-general Kofi Annan has warned that forced labour
and exploitation are among "the most gregarious [organized] violations of human
rights" (UNODC 2000). Human trafficking for forced labour now surpasses drugs
and arms trafficking in incidence, cost to human well-being, and profitability to the
criminal traffickers (Schauer & Wheaton 2006). Worldwide, more people now live in
slavery than during the slave-trade era (Perrin 2010). Trafficking, then, has become
a global problem, and it is a form of transnational organized crime (Chu 2011) that
flourishes because of the demand for "free labour, sexual services, child soldiers and
human organs" (Oosterman 2010: n.p.). Restrictive immigration policies in destination
countries are credited with channelling low-skilled immigrants into irregular (illegal)
migration.

According to the United Nations International Labour Organization, globally an
estimated 12.3 million people are in forced labour or sexual exploitation (EFC 2009).
These victims are coerced, threatened with harm to their families, have their passports
confiscated, and are locked up in inhumane conditions. The consumers are employers
of trafficked labour (e.g., "johns" or home owners who employ household staff), and
the products are human beings (e.g., prostitutes, domestics). Traffickers are the intermediaries between vulnerable victims and unscrupulous employers (Wheaton, Schauer,
& Galli 2010).

Profit is the driving force behind trafficking and is a response to poverty, war,
and conflict, dislocation from homeland, social and cultural exclusion, and limited access to education or employment in source countries (UNODC 2008: 75). Women are
most often sexually exploited, while men are sold into bonded labour, and children
are forced to beg or enter the sex trade. Others work in agriculture, domestic service,
factories and workshops, mining, land clearance, and selling in a market (Bales 2005).

Most victims of **modern-day slavery** are low skilled—traffickers prey on those who cannot immigrate legally. Some are kidnapped, others misled about opportunities, and still others—children—sold by their desperate families. Victims of slavery suffer physical injury from beatings and abuse, and psychological trauma, including post-traumatic stress disorder, anxiety, depression, and alienation.

"Looking in a victim's eye and telling her that the Police will do everything they can, but it is now up to the law and the court system to make sure that these guys will never hurt her again can be really scary to rely on." Timea Nagy, survivor of trafficking, now educator and advocate, in an email message to Canadian Members of Parliament, Sept. 30, 2009, quoted in Oosterman (2010: n.p.)

Canada and the United States are often viewed as the lands of dreams, but an illegal economy that plunges vulnerable people, mostly women and children, into a nightmare of slavery and exploitation thrives beneath the surface. Slavery has been illegal in Canada since 1807 and in the United States since 1865, yet people continue to be bought and sold in both countries. Thousands of Canadian citizens are trafficked to other countries for forced labour and sexual exploitation; others, usually illegal immigrants, are trafficked through Canada into the United States; a third group, foreigners, are trafficked into Canada every year (Stirk 2009). Internally, traffickers recruit Canadian girls for the sex trade by using coercion, deception, and force. These traffickers use both Craigslist's erotic service section and Facebook to buy and sell sexual services. Internationally trafficked victims are shipped into Canada from Asia and Africa, and then they are forced to pay off inflated "debts" by selling their bodies or forced labour. This modern-day slavery is a thriving business in Canada—one victim can earn as much as $280,000 for their "owner" in a year (Online Press Conference 2010).

"Human trafficking is a form of modern-day slavery and a priority of the RCMP.... Public awareness is the first step towards putting an end to this horrific crime that robs one person's freedom to benefit another." Inspector Steve Martin, RCMP, news release, quoted in Byrne (2010: n.p.)

What can be done to prevent trafficking or to rescue victims? The United Nations has adopted a common-sense approach to dealing with human trafficking: 1) prevent trafficking; 2) prosecute traffickers; and 3) protect victims. The United Nations Protocol (General Assembly 2004) established strategies, including media campaigns in source regions, to inform people of the dangers inherent in agreeing to be smuggled[4] into another country, and improving economic opportunities for people in their own countries. Most experts suggest that diminishing demand (e.g., from sex consumers) is the most effective way to stop trafficking. In Sweden, for example, the purchase of sexual services is now penalized as "male sexual violence against women and children" (Oosterman 2010: n.p.). Consequently, the rate of trafficked victims has dropped dramatically. Prompt prosecution of traffickers may also slow trafficking. Proponents also advocate changing the definition of *victim* to include sex workers as victims of trafficking.

---

4 Smuggling is different from trafficking and means illegally crossing a border; however, smuggled individuals may then find themselves trafficked—forced into indentured servitude to pay off inflated debts.

In Canada, human trafficking has become an offence under the Criminal Code, and advocacy against this underground illegal economy is being promoted in the media, creating more public awareness. In his book *Invisible Chains* (2010), Benjamin Perrin brought to light sexual exploitation in Canada. He recounts how a Canadian teenager, only 14 years old, was auctioned over the Internet for men to purchase by the hour; how slave traders took a young woman from an African war zone and brought her to Edmonton to exploit her as a prostitute; and how a Quebec gang lured teenagers with false promises of job opportunities, and then sold them for sex to high-profile men in the community. Perrin believes that Canada needs a national action plan to end human trafficking. "While traffickers have 'playbooks' to teach each other tactics to exploit victims, there's no such government plan," says Perrin. "Canada needs to protect and provide services for victims, and ensure that the perpetrators of these crimes are brought to justice" (Online Press Conference 2010: n.p.).

"Police are no longer willing to look at these cases as simply prostitution cases, which is historically how they have been dealt with and often dismissed by many people.... Now they're being recognized for what they are, which is serious allegations of child sex trafficking." UBC law professor Ben Perrin, interviewed on CTV News (2011)

Elsewhere in the world, particularly in Asia, the situation is dire. In Thailand, for example, trafficking of children into the sex trade is a continuing problem, although the demographics have changed somewhat (Arnold & Bertone 2002). As the economy has improved, there has been a gradual decline in the number of Thai women entering the sex trade, but an increase in girls and women trafficked into the country or from the hill tribes of northern Thailand. The sex industry in Thailand is directly linked to the sex tourism industry: men from Europe, North America, and Japan travel to Thailand to engage in sex with children. Although some prostitution in Bangkok is "voluntary," others are trafficked within and into Thailand for the sex trade. Many of the young women come from Myanmar; they have agreed to work as prostitutes in Thailand in the hope of a better life than the violence, rape by military personnel, and poverty they face in Myanmar. Once in Thailand, however, they are physically or psychologically forced and coerced to work in conditions they did not expect. Girls from Yunan province in China are sent to southern Thailand, where demand for light-skinned girls is high. Girls from Myanmar are sent to northern Thailand, while those from Laos and Cambodia go to Bangkok and northeast Thailand.

The police, government, and NGOs in Thailand are working to stop the sex trade. Social movements against trafficking, prostitution, and sex tourism are well established and organized, and the under-classes, who usually do not have a political voice, are participating in these movements. Campaigns have been launched to prosecute foreigners who have sex with children; however, if a child between the ages of 12 and 15 is paid for sex, it is considered consensual in Thailand. Foreigners are granted bail, after which they leave the country. Therefore, a great deal of work needs to be done to end sex tourism in Thailand. Again, stopping the demand would end the sex trade (Arnold & Bertone 2002).

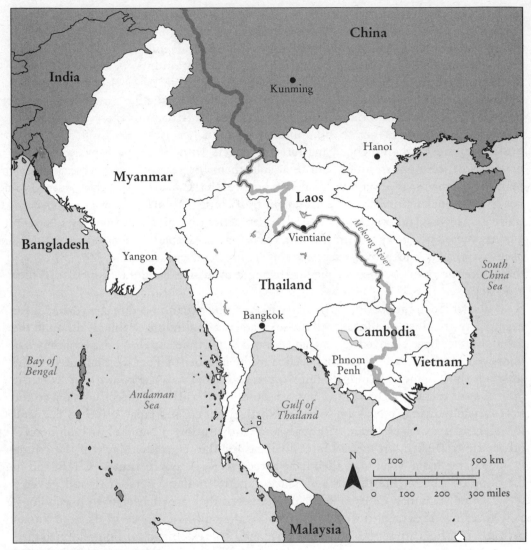

MAP 10.2 MEKONG RIVER BASIN

 Can human trafficking be stopped? According to Bales (2005) if poverty, corruption, population explosions, environmental destruction, conflict, and international debt are eradicated and laws and legislation are enforced, then yes. But these are lofty goals, so obviously we need to find other solutions, such as reducing demand and prosecuting those who traffic in human beings.

CONCLUSION

The future belongs to those nations that recognize migration as a global reality. Until immigrants are granted social, economic, religious, and political equality, social discord is likely to continue in destination countries. Leaders must work creatively with the key players to find equitable solutions to prevent racism and conflict that could destroy the social fabric of their societies instead of transforming them into multicultural, collaborative, and inclusive societies.

Economic and political change is an integral component of globalization and is closely tied to people movements. Attempts to regulate immigration have met with limited success, and short-sighted immigration policies have created an environment for illegal immigration that encourages exploitation and human rights abuses of the most vulnerable—women and children, and low-skilled workers. According to Wickramasekara (2008: 1247), "there is an imperative need for fresh approaches and bold initiatives to promote international labour mobility for the welfare of the global community."

Anthropologists, as Perrin has shown, have important roles to play in disseminating information on the many issues attached to global migration, including the inequalities and inhumane treatment that our most vulnerable global populations sometimes endure. Anthropologists are also equipped to keep the human aspects of immigration in the forefront of discussions and policy decisions. Rather than presenting impersonal statistics and quotas, anthropologists, through their study of social networks, can make known the life experiences of real people who happen to be immigrants.

Although most of the misconceptions and ignorance at the root of discrimination have given way to a growing social maturity and acceptance among citizens, we would be naive to assume that intolerance and bigotry have disappeared from Western countries, a case in point being France, where attitudes toward immigrants appear to be regressing. Exclusionary rhetoric portrays immigrants as unskilled, threatening, and disruptive invaders, thereby dehumanizing people when they are at their most vulnerable. In the twenty-first century, a major challenge for the international community will be to build bridges, not fences, and to embrace a global labour market that does not trample on the human rights of people in search of a better life.

QUESTIONS FOR CONSIDERATION AND CLASSROOM ACTIVITIES

1. Put yourself in the shoes of a new immigrant. You are in a foreign country, unable to speak the language, with only a limited supply of money, and you must quickly find a place to live, a job, and necessities, such as food and water. Outline your strategy for surviving, and then becoming comfortable in your new surroundings. What assistance would you welcome from the locals?
2. Here's a second scenario. You are in a foreign country. The people stop and stare at you because you look different (e.g., skin colour, height), they make fun of and

laugh at you, and when you approach someone for help, they walk away with an impatient shrug at your feeble attempt to speak their language. Analyse why they are responding to you this way. How would these responses make you feel?

3. If you moved to another country, would you try to hold on to your cultural practices and values or would you adopt (assimilate to) your new country's culture? Depending on your answer to this question, how can you expect any more from people immigrating to your country?

4. Investigate how Canadian immigration policies have restricted the ability of immigrants to settle comfortably into Canadian society. Choose an immigrant group and discuss how they have coped with the restrictions placed on them. What could the government and the people of Canada do to help them integrate into Canadian society?

5. Examine immigration policies in a country not discussed in this chapter. Identify some of the strengths and weaknesses in this policy.

6. Develop a definition of multiculturalism, and then create a class debate on the positive and negative aspects of this policy. Why do you think some Europeans are rejecting multiculturalism? What is the alternative? How would life be different for immigrants if multicultural policies were changed?

7. Interview a newly arrived immigrant student using prepared questions in order to write a personal narrative about his/her experiences with discrimination in your country. Read this narrative to the class.

8. In groups of three or four, search for job ads on the Internet that possess discriminatory and/or inflammatory information in them. Now "clean up" the ads using inclusive, culturally sensitive language.

SUGGESTED READINGS

Cameron, E. (Ed.). (2004). *Multiculturalism and immigration in Canada. An introductory reader.* Toronto: Canadian Scholars' Press.

A comprehensive collection of essays on the historical, social, and cultural issues of immigrating to Canada. This book deals with many of the issues presented in this chapter.

Perrin, B. (2010). *Irresistible chains: Canada's underground world of human trafficking.* Toronto: Viking Canada.

An engaging examination of the underground economy flourishing in Canada and providing either sex services or forced labour. This book offers an insightful introduction to the sex trade in Canada and the actions needed to stop sex exploitation.

Chapter 11

WHAT BENEFITS DO NGOs PROVIDE DEVELOPING COUNTRIES, AND HOW CAN THEIR PRESENCE GENERATE NEW CHALLENGES?

Key Terms: applied anthropology, civil society, cultural imperialism, cultural sensitivity, development, engaged anthropology, human rights, missionism, modernization, NGOs

---

INTRODUCTION

When a massive earthquake struck Port-au-Prince, Haiti, on January 12, 2010, more than 220,000[1] people were killed, 300,000 injured, and millions displaced (People in Need Partnership 2012). Hundreds of buildings were reduced to rubble, essential services such as hospitals and schools were destroyed, communication systems went down, and roads were covered with debris, preventing relief workers and the military from reaching people. Donations of food, medicine, equipment, and search and rescue teams poured in from the international community, and humanitarian relief agencies provided food, water, and tents for some of the victims, but in the early days, confusion about who was in control prevented any major organization.

An immediate crisis was body collection; government trucks roamed the navigable streets collecting thousands of bodies and burying then in mass graves or burning them right on the streets. Medical supplies ran out and violence erupted as people fought over limited food supplies or looted abandoned stores. More than a million and a half Haitians moved into make-shift tent cities set up in the parks and streets. Later, cholera struck and thousands more died or became ill from contaminated water.

Haiti is the home of countless non-government organizations (NGOs). **NGOs** are non-governmental, not-for-profit organizations that provide emergency humanitarian services and development aid to those in need. Their mandates vary, covering conflict

---

1 Estimates vary widely.

resolution, educational programming, environmental protection, missionism, and human rights advocacy. Many NGOs focus on **development**, such as agricultural projects. Yet NGOs in Haiti have been criticized for their lack of tangible results, the speed and efficiency of their service delivery, and their hidden political and economic agendas that have created more problems than they have solved. Indeed, the term "NGO industry" is used to implicate the self-serving ambitions of these organizations. For years now, people—some in positions of power—have raised questions concerning the purpose, power, and usefulness of NGOs. NGOs are criticized for their lack of accountability and their questionable connections with donors and sponsors. Indeed, democratization and creating "civil societies" is almost always at the root of NGO mandates, regardless of what other services they provide (Stephenson 2005).

Anthropologists have a difficult relationship with NGOs, with some being openly hostile to the interference of NGOs in local communities and others supporting NGOs that have the welfare of people and the protection of fragile, small-scale cultures in mind. Still other anthropologists have taken it upon themselves to study NGOs and their role in development. Certainly, the ongoing question of the relevance of anthropology in the modern world can be partly answered through **applied anthropologists** working in social development projects and project evaluation (Lewis 2005). This type of work, whether research-based or applied, removes anthropology from the exotic "other" and places the discipline within cultural issues of modern societies (Marcus & Fischer 1986).

In this chapter we will explore the roles of NGOs, their successes and failures, and the challenges that can arise from NGO involvement in developing nations. We will review various types of NGOs and their projects, including emergency humanitarian efforts in Pakistan and cultural sensitivity; missionism and cultural imperialism; medical assistance and grassroots health NGOs; and, human rights and politicizing of family. Our case study is Haiti, a country that currently has more NGO involvement than any other nation in the world, yet it has very little to show for it. Expertise from sociology, psychology, law, and development studies, as well as anthropology, will be drawn on to present a critical analysis of the impact of NGOs on developing countries.

ANTHROPOLOGISTS AND NGOs

According to Lewis (2005), anthropologists view development from three different perspectives: as antagonistic observers, as reluctant participants, and as engaged activists, the latter combining research and action anthropology. Antagonistic observers view the motives behind development projects with suspicion and maintain a critical distance, while anthropologists who become involved in development do so either to earn a living or to apply their research knowledge to support and assist marginalized groups with whom they are interacting on a local level.

Part of the difficulty anthropologists have with NGOs and development schemes lies in NGOs' attempts to change the way people live. The ethnographic study of NGOs enables anthropologists to understand how knowledge and information is produced, and the danger of imposing Western ideals and programs on other countries without understanding or respecting the local culture (Ishkanian 2004). NGOs often create more problems than they can solve, and they eventually abandon projects because of local resistance. Consequently, anthropologists who find themselves involved in development projects do so because of their "long-standing concerns with the social and cultural effects of economic change in the less developed areas of the world" (Lewis 2005: n.p.). They become **engaged anthropologists**, working with activists, policy-makers, and professionals within the field of development. For example, Valentin and Meinert (2009) examined the role of NGOs as "civilizing" institutions through the growing field of children's rights. Anthropology's culturally relativistic perspective highlighted the problems with a narrow, Northern (Western) definition of children's rights and a "proper childhood" that politicizes family within the guise of universal **human rights**. Anthropologists ask probing questions such as "To what extent can and should existing social and cultural practices be respected while still insisting on a set of universally valid rights?" and "Should/can aid be unconditional?" (Valentin & Meinert 2009: 24).

Anthropologists have also conducted ethnographic studies of the internal workings of NGOs and, ultimately, the reasons why they fail. This is particularly relevant given the criticisms of NGOs for not producing tangible results. Anthropologists have been instrumental in investigating and disseminating information on the activities of NGOs and the impact of their infiltration into cultural systems. Daniel J. Smith (2010) of Brown University ethnographically investigated corruption in Nigeria's NGO sector, while Jacqueline Solway (2009) studied the Ju/'hoansi of Botswana, who went to court to regain lands confiscated by diamond miners and NGOs.

Anthropologists employ ethnographic methods that identify the most efficient, culturally sensitive ways of delivering programs that are compatible with the local cultural norms, and that are sustainable and practical. Anthropologist Armine Ishkanian (2004: n.p.) conducted ethnographic research on NGOs to better "understand the multiple perspectives, discourses and strategies of various actors, the relationships between these actors, and how the foreign aid has affected the development of civil society and democracy in Armenia." This type of research has become significant as donors or sponsors of NGOs have adopted the "civil society" mantra. Smith (2010: 244) defines **civil society** as "occupying the political space between the individual or household and the state." The concept suggests broad societal participation in the organization of a state from many walks of life, not just official government. Proponents of civil society believe it is a necessary ingredient of a democratic nation (Stephenson 2005).

Applied anthropologists involved in development work use participant observation in open-ended, long-term field work (Lewis 2005). For example, Lewis, Wood, and Gregory (1996) identified a range of unknown intermediaries within local fish-production and marketing networks in Bangladesh. Their findings contributed to the

ODA aquaculture project refocusing its efforts on rural poverty reduction rather than only on production (Lewis 2005). In addition, Valentin and Meinert (2009) conducted ethnographic research on education, health, and child/youth issues in Uganda, Nepal, and Vietnam. They collected data using participant observation and interviews with children and their families, who had been targeted by NGOs because their lifestyles contradicted the notion of a normal or "proper childhood." Applied anthropologists have also promoted indigenous knowledge to development agencies. For example, Loomis (2000) used his research in Māori communities in New Zealand to highlight the local concepts of resource conservation that would be sustainable.

Although it may appear that anthropologists do not approve of development aid and the projects established by various NGOs, this is not entirely true. Some anthropologists have become valuable consultants within NGO communities in recent years. Indeed, Minorities Rights Group, Cultural Survival, and International Working Group for Indigenous Affairs are NGOs formed by academic anthropologists (Tishkov 2005) to work with, rather than change, indigenous populations. The mandate of Cultural Survival is to protect vulnerable communities and their way of life when threatened by developers (Lewis 2005).

THE NATURE OF NGOs

The concept of development and aid emerged following World War II, when organizations and government agencies wanted to provide assistance to developing nations to hasten modernization. However, anthropologists view **modernization** cautiously, because it generally means making other nations over in the Western image. This is what most development projects set out to do, although their goals are often couched in terminology such as "building civil society" and "sustainable development" (Lewis 2005). Development agencies also concentrate on economic growth through programs to reduce inequality, and on support for human rights and social welfare (Lewis 2005).

NGOs gained recognition in the 1990s since they worked closer to the ground than state or intergovernmental organizations, delivering aid more economically. Humanitarian assistance alongside peacekeeping missions became one of their primary roles. As consultants in the United Nations, NGOs have pushed for resolutions on disarmament and human rights. For example, the International Campaign to Ban Landmines NGO successfully lobbied governments and mobilized states and other NGOs for the Ottawa Convention that was signed in December 1997, and continues to monitor compliance among the 143 states that signed the treaty. NGOs continue to bring issues before the United Nations, including women's and children's rights, and were involved in the formation of the International Criminal Court (Stephenson 2005).

CULTURAL SENSITIVITY

One issue of great concern to anthropologists is **cultural sensitivity** toward the local culture. When an earthquake devastated northern Pakistan and Kashmir in October 2004, Pakistani and international aid workers rushed to the region (Wilder & Morris 2008). Once the initial trauma was over, accusations of cultural insensitivity and reports of national and international aid workers not respecting the cultural norms of behaviour began. One source of conflict was the difference between the standards of behaviour held by the people of northern Pakistan and Kashmir and those of national (Pakistani) relief workers. Indeed, the international staff earned the locals' respect for dressing and behaving appropriately, the only exception being the Cuban medical workers who wore shorts and T-shirts, tried to procure alcohol, and had men and women sharing tents. The Pakistani aid workers, especially the women, were criticized for interacting with men (talking to them, playing sports) and not wearing appropriate (concealing) clothing. It appears, then, that the national staff was judged under a stricter set of standards than the international staff, and that the national female staff were expected to follow stricter standards of conduct than the national male staff. There was also some concern that exposure to liberal Pakistanis and international aid workers' behaviour would influence the local Kashmiri women (Wilder & Morris 2008).

These problems could be summed up as ignorance about local customs, a general lack of cultural sensitivity on the part of aid workers, and the inability of aid agencies to properly train their staff. However, the World Health Organization actually provided an advice checklist to their staff that suggested that these types of disaster provided Western agencies with a "window of opportunity for challenging gender inequality" (Wilder & Morris 2008: 2), leading to the suspicion that some of this behaviour was a deliberate attempt to show the northern Pakistani and Kashmiri women how Western men and women interact. Questions of how aid agencies should respond to this concern, and whether local norms can be respected without compromising aid workers' rights to self-expression and cultural freedom, should be addressed with anthropological input.

POLITICIZING OF NGO ADVOCACY: CHILDREN'S RIGHTS

Advocacy for children's rights is not a new phenomenon. In 1924 the League of Nations adopted the World Child Welfare Charter's key principles: children have the right "to material, moral and spiritual development, to special help in case of hunger, illness, disability and orphan status, to relief in situations of distress, to protection against economic exploitation, and to an upbringing towards societal responsibility" (Black 1996, quoted in Valentin & Meinert 2009: 24). The right to be protected against discrimination on the basis of race, colour, gender, and language, and the right to name and nationality, were added in 1959.

During the 1990s, the legally binding United Nations Convention on the Rights of the Child (CRC) was almost universally ratified (Boyden 1997). The fact that the

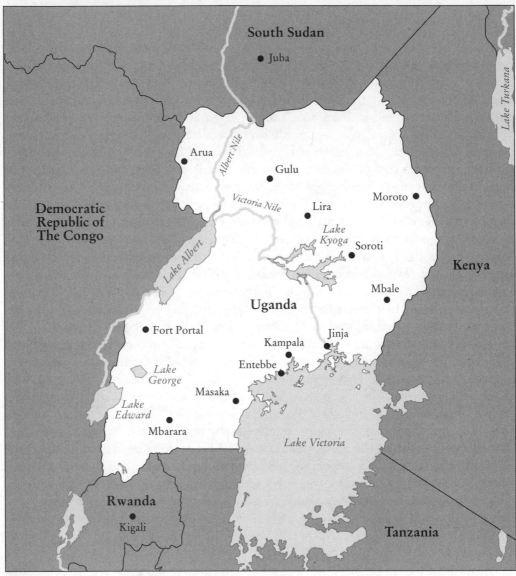

MAP 11.1 UGANDA

CRC is legally binding gives states the right to intervene in another state's affairs if children's rights are being violated. Children's rights became institutionalized, and morality and policy became intertwined. However, as with other aid and development agencies, the CRC is also a political tool that provides Western donors with a legitimate rationale to set conditions for receiving aid (Valentin & Meinert 2009).

Children's rights are of great interest to anthropologists, partly because of Western NGOs' assumptions about what constitutes a proper childhood and proper parenting, and because of their attempts to legitimize Western views through universal rights. This returns us to a fundamental question that has been addressed in several chapters in this book: "To what extent can and should existing social and cultural practices be respected while still insisting on a set of universally valid rights?" (Valentin & Meinert 2009: 24). Doubtless the goal is to improve the lives of children; however, the Westernized concept of a good childhood, and the attempt to cultivate "proper" (Western-style) children and parents, have created conflict and resistance.

Suggesting that parents and entire nations do not know how to take care of their own children is culturally insensitive (Valentin & Meinert 2009) and fails to recognize that socio-economic conditions in many states prevent children from enjoying so-called universal (Western) rights, including the right to education and leisure time. The individualistic, egalitarian view of children in the Convention contradicts generational hierarchies and social structures within many nations that do not separate child from family. In response, for instance, Vietnamese authorities passed the Child Protection, Care and Education law in 1991, which states that children must show their parents affection and respect and obey them (Burr 2006).

Uganda provides an example of how standards and ideals from the international community can have an impact on issues such as children's rights (Valentin & Meinert 2009). The Ugandan government has been in conflict with the Lord's Resistance Army in the north for 25 years. People live in internally displaced camps, having lost their land, homes, and livelihood. NGOs have criticized the rebel army for turning innocent children into soldiers or sex slaves, and the Ugandan government for not protecting children, and took the Ugandan government to the International Criminal Court. Although their response to the situation may seem positive, NGOs were offering aid and then commenting on social practices. Essentially, NGOs became the moral watch-dogs for the state. NGOs, then, appear to play a crucial role in civilizing, enlightening, and socializing children in the "Western way." As a further illustration of this point, anthropologist Lotte Meinert became involved in a Child Rights Education program organized by the Save the Child Denmark NGO. Workers indoctrinated children, teachers, and parents into children's rights, and then had to act as mediators in the conflict between children and their parents and teachers when the children demanded their right to leisure time but the parents needed them to work for the survival of the family (Valentin & Meinert 2009).

Children endure hardships all over the world due to economic, political, and religious persecution. NGOs have done much to ameliorate these harsh conditions, especially in health care. However, at times children have been turned into contested objects for political motives (Pupavac 2000, quoted in Valentin & Meinert 2009), which is patronizing and reminiscent of early Christian missionism.

MISSIONISM AND NGOs

The subject of religious conversion is controversial; many people, including most anthropologists, decry the destruction of traditional beliefs and the ensuing cultural disruptions. The aim of early **missionism** was to assimilate non-Western cultures into Western ideology and practices (Cudd 2005). Indeed, missionism has been accused of being an agent of **cultural imperialism**—the imposition of one culture over all others, ultimately destroying or significantly changing a traditional culture. For example, at Fiske Seminary in Persia, early missionaries encouraged Nestorian women to renounce Islamic female-seclusion practices. These changes to their cultural traditions caused friction between Nestorians and the dominant Muslim culture and led to the persecution and eventual decline of the Nestorians (Tomasek 1999).

Medical missionism has given missionaries a great deal of power over people suffering from diseases, but even in the early twentieth century debates raged over the ethics of conversion under the guise of offering medical aid. Some medical missionaries have viewed medical work as merely "a tool for evangelization" (Macola 2005). The proselytizing can undermine social, cultural, and political authority in the community. On the other hand, there is little doubt that Christian-based organizations have provided desperately needed services to areas of the world stricken with devastating diseases. An excellent example of humanitarian work is that of John Tucker, with the US-based Catholic Markoll Missioners, who has worked in Cambodia since 2001 providing shelters and medical care to children with HIV and AIDS (Fraser 2005).

Missionaries provide international aid, especially after major ecological or natural disasters. In some instances, however, this aid has come with conditions. Following the Indonesian tsunami, American evangelist agencies travelled to India, Indonesia, and Sri Lanka purportedly to offer humanitarian aid but also distributed Christian literature, prompting the US National Council of Churches to protest their behaviour (Baldauf 2005). This tactic, known as "conversion for aid," is at best coercive. Proselytizing to traumatized people angered local Christian groups, who feared a backlash in Sri Lanka, which already suffers from serious religious tensions (Rohde 2005).

Most missionaries and their sponsoring churches have come to terms with their colonial past. By the mid-twentieth century, development-oriented missionary work—establishing local infrastructures (e.g., building roads and hospitals, digging wells) and providing medical and educational services—became a common strategy, still with the goal of converting the locals to Christianity, but with a more humanitarian focus. Indigenous peoples are more likely to listen to missionaries if the messages are offered along with building schools and clinics (Marx 2005). Today, missionary NGOs assist people in their struggles against repressive regimes and work tirelessly to improve the standard of living of indigenous peoples.

CHALLENGES FOR NGOs

NGOs face many challenges, some economic, others political or cultural. Funding is an ongoing concern: they have to solicit funding in an increasingly competitive field, and often their sponsors have agendas attached to their funding. At times NGOs are created "to order," in other words, to carry out a specific mission, often politically motivated (Tishkov 2005). In Armenia, for example, NGOs established in the 1990s were shaped by donor initiatives and funding strategies rather than the needs and concerns of the local people (Ishkanian 2004). One project dealt with domestic violence, even though Armenians consider this a private family matter and have no desire to make it public or risk government intervention. Nevertheless, funding poured in and hotlines and crisis shelters were established at the bequest of sponsors. To suggest that a private family matter should be made public alarmed Armenians, especially the women, who saw it as inviting surveillance and humiliation, and as challenging the sacredness of family. Furthermore, the hotline was not a feasible idea because phone lines do not work properly in Armenia, using them is expensive, and the poorest and most vulnerable women do not have phones in their homes. Shelters were also a failure, because according to Armenian law if a woman leaves her home, she loses her access to health care, any kind of financial support, and subsidized housing. Plans to train the police force to deal with domestic violence were ill-conceived, since calling the corrupt police would open a family to abuse and extortion (Ishkanian 2004). This study exemplifies the failure of Western NGOs who do not become familiar with the local culture but instead attempt to impose Western methods and beliefs in countries and cultures where they simply do not work.

NGOs, particularly from the United States and Europe, have a pro-democracy directive. This type of work carries with it many challenges and even dangers. A current example is the problems that NGOs have encountered in post-revolutionary Egypt. In February 2012, 43 NGO staff from several countries were arrested and charged with encouraging unrest and fostering political unrest. They were also accused of being spies for foreign governments. The National Democratic Institute and the International Republican Institute, two NGOs with close links to the American Congress, promote democracy in Egypt. Foreign interference such as this would never be tolerated in the United States, yet it is often part of NGO policies in other countries. The Egyptian authorities accused these NGOs of spying and inciting unrest. This case is a prime example of a major criticism of many NGOs: that they cross the line from providing development aid and step into political interference, and that they are really instruments of American foreign policy (Spoerri 2012). Swedish anthropologist Steven Sampson, who analysed NGO activities in the Balkans, suggests that despite some successes, "the most suitable term for Western intervention in the Balkans would be benevolent colonialism" (Sampson 2002). Thus, the tendency to view local organizations that operate outside the Western NGO model as worthless has created a great deal of tension between locals and NGOs workers who are known as "project elites" (Tishkov 2005).

THE CRISIS IN HAITI

Haiti is the poorest country in the Western hemisphere, with the highest rates of infant and maternal mortality, extremely poor nutrition, and the worst AIDS epidemic in the Americas (Partners in Health 2009–2012). When the earthquake struck in 2010, thousands of NGOs already stationed in Haiti, and many more that would soon arrive, sprang into action. Yet, over two years later, Haiti and its people are still in dire straits. Nearly half a million people still live in tent refugee camps that do little to protect them from the elements, and many are without toilets or potable water. Even those not in the camps are living in badly damaged houses that should be torn down. One of the questions being asked is this: Why have the tremendous amounts of aid and the numerous NGOs sent to Haiti not benefitted the people?

The crisis in Haiti exemplifies the problems and ultimately the failures of NGOs. Zanotti (2010) argues that the lack of democracy, the political unrest, the earthquake, and other excuses are not the reasons for Haiti's problems; rather, NGOs are the root cause. Essentially, international strategies have "promoted NGOs as substitutes for the [Haitian] state" (Zanotti 2010: 20). The constant presence of thousands of NGOs, international peacekeeping units, and multilateral and bilateral aid has eroded the ability of existing state institutions to provide for their citizens, and the country is sinking deeper into dependency on foreign aid. Joseph G. Bock (2010), of the Kroc Institute for International Peace Studies at the University of Notre Dame, believes the greatest danger from the aid industry lies in fostering a state of dependency rather than enabling Haitians to help themselves.

Many of the problems with NGOs addressed in this chapter are also evident in Haiti. Indeed, these problems appear to be endemic to the aid industry: 1) poor coordination between agencies, leading to ineffective delivery of services; 2) donor/sponsor influence that channels aid into specific economic or political agendas; 3) lack of accountability and exclusion of Haitians from the decision-making process; 4) destruction of local economies; and 5) corruption and misuse of funds (Zanotti 2010). So entrenched are these impediments that the Organization of American States' (OAS) special representative to Haiti, Ricardo Seitenfus, was removed from his position for denouncing the United Nations' "imposed occupation" that is "transforming Haitians into prisoners on their own island" (Doucet 2011: n.p.).

> According to Ruth Derilus, a Haitian aid worker, "There might be a camp with 3,000 families and they're trying to distribute 200 items. Of course there are going to be fights.... Some camps have four or five organizations helping them, and none of them seem to be working together. Other camps have received nothing." Lindsay (2010: 20)

John Holmes, United Nations official in charge of humanitarian aid, has attributed many of the problems with distribution of much-needed resources to "a lack of coordination among international organizations" (Lindsay 2010: 20). This poor coordination resulted in the neglect of some regions desperate for relief, while other regions were overwhelmed with redundant NGOs. The aid agencies ignored camp committees and refused to distribute food unless

American or United Nations troops were present. The food distribution often turned into a melee because people were desperate, although many families refused to attend these distributions, unwilling to fight for food despite their hunger (Lindsay 2010).

Other critics point to corporate and business influence that searches for ways to make a profit from the aid industry, or forces NGOs to develop projects because of their profit potential. Indeed, 84 cents of every dollar spent in Haiti is returned to the United States through salaries (Zanotti 2010: 760). Other donations are spent on foreign experts, hotel bills, car rentals, and hotel conferences rather than on the people in need. A recent investigation found that most reconstruction contracts are awarded to American companies, who are getting rich off the reconstruction business. Thus, Haiti's reconstruction has been "privatized, outsourced, or taken over by foreign NGOs" (Doucet 2011: n.p.).

"Of all the money they send here, only 10 percent actually makes it to the ground." Ruth Derilus, a Haitian aid worker, quoted in Lindsay (2010: 20)

Foreign political institutions with hidden agendas have manipulated aid to support various regimes, and bankrolled and endorsed the recent election that most Haitians consider illegitimate. Indeed, the most popular political party in Haiti, led by exiled former president Jean-Bertrand Aristide, was excluded from the election. A weak government in Haiti ensures that NGOs and other interested parties can continue to profit from Haiti's crisis (Doucet 2011). Thus, NGOs have taken political processes out of the hands of the Haitian people and their leaders (Zanotti 2010).

Haitians have also been excluded from the decision-making process. Local Haitians are banned from meetings where international aid groups discuss strategies for distributing aid. The 12 Haitian members of the Interim Haiti Reconstruction Commission (IHRC), which determines where to use donations, protested to co-chairman Bill Clinton that they are being "completely disconnected from the activities of the IHRC" (Doucet 2011: n.p.). Indeed, the large aid organizations do not reach out to local, community-based organizations at all.

One of the issues repeatedly denounced by Haitians is the destruction of the agricultural industry. Thirty years ago Haitians produced most of their food and enjoyed a diverse diet of "manioc, breadfruit, yams, sweet potatoes, plantains, millet, corn and rice" (Doucet 2011: 21). In 1986, a military junta, backed by Washington, flooded the market with cheap imported rice subsidized by the United States government. These American imports and the ongoing food donations have decimated the Haitian agricultural sector. Farmers need assistance in refrigeration and storage technology; instead, NGOs donate more food that continues to impede the sustainability of Haitian agriculture. Farmers are now unable to feed the population, and Haiti has become dependent on imported rice from the United States. The 2010 earthquake has increased this dependency on such imports.

According to Lindsay (2010), in the days following the 2010 quake, most NGOs, United Nations peacekeepers, and Haitian police were absent from the streets. Survivors formed security brigades to ward off looters and other criminals, and set up camps, while local doctors and nurses established community clinics. Camp committees were

FIGURE 11.1 HAITIAN TENT CAMP

organized to locate the missing NGOs and procure emergency aid (Lindsay 2010). Delivery of aid was hampered because the Port-au-Prince airport was blockaded by the United States government; only troop deployments and delivery of military equipment were allowed to land. Inside the camps, families worked together to earn enough money to survive. Some pooled money to buy a gas-powered generator and then started a cell-phone recharging business, young boys cleaned car windows for tips, and others removed rubble for a pittance (Bock 2010).

"Giving food aid from day to day is fine, but they should help us develop our natural resources for the long term." Anse Rouge, community leader, quoted in Lindsay (2010: 21)

Despite the many criticisms of NGOs, most of them justified, there are some NGOs that have been able to effectively provide assistance to the Haitians. These NGOs are locally accountable, internationally connected, and financially independent. They provide services and create economic sustainability without eroding the capacity of the state to provide for Haitians in the future (Zanotti 2010). One example of a successful NGO in Haiti is Partners in Health (PIH). PIH grew from a small clinic in 1985 into one of the largest NGO health-care providers in Haiti, with facilities that include an infectious-disease centre and a women's health clinic. In 2009, PIH launched the first neonatal intensive care unit (NICU) in Central Haiti and established a Red Cross blood bank and a dozen schools (Partners in Health 2012).

Partners in Health operates in a similar fashion to other successful NGOs. It encourages accountability to the community and is connected to diverse international networks of support. It remains independent, however, since no one agenda is dominant. PIH ensures the transfer of economic resources and knowledge directly to the community and focuses on the needs of the poor. This holistic model combines academic research with social activism, operating under five principles: access to primary health care; free health care and education for the poor; community partnerships; addressing both social and economic needs; and serving the poor through the public sector (Zanotti 2010: 763). For example, the staff will provide primary health care and medications for the sick, but also food to reduce malnutrition, and money for the family to continue care. PIH also provides access to clean water and agricultural programs to feed the poor.

> "We're going to fight against the way in which they are giving aid.... These meetings of the big foreigners are the ones that will decide our future. We can't be afraid of what they think of us. We need to speak when we're not in agreement." Ruth Derilus, quoted in Lindsay (2010: 21)

In summary, PIH decisions regarding allocation of services are needs-driven and based on community requests; therefore, the NGO is accountable to the local population and its mandate is not defined by donors or sponsors. For 20 years, PIH has provided free health-care services, advanced sustainable life by paying its workers, promoted local food production, created social capital by promoting literacy and professional skills, and encouraged a spirit of solidarity in the community.

CONCLUSION

As we have seen throughout this chapter, the actual roles and purposes of non-governmental organizations (NGOs) are being questioned. This concern centres on the accountability of NGOs and whether their mandates are really to assist those in need or whether they are a new form of colonial imperialism. Anthropologists have long questioned the legitimacy of development and aid agencies, especially their role as agents of change. In Haiti, and elsewhere, some NGOs have lost their way and no longer fulfill their original mandate.

Ultimately, NGOs create a Catch-22 situation in developing countries. As seen in Haiti, the population desperately needs assistance from large, financially established NGOs; however, development agencies are often charged with promoting Western-style democracy, with little regard for the culture, customs, or economic realities of the nations they "occupy." For some NGOs, the not-for-profit label is little more than a veneer for hiding the enormous financial profits earned by sponsors.

Although there is little doubt that some NGOs have successfully launched and completed highly beneficial projects, such as the landmine ban, in most cases their interference and very presence create challenges, not the least of which is increasing dependence on foreign aid. Other issues, such as cultural sensitivity, meddling in private family affairs, destruction of local economies and state institutions, and proselytizing for aid, all suggest that NGOs cause more harm than good. To regain their reputations and legitimacy, NGOs will have to return to their original directive—emergency humanitarian aid—and leave other matters to state institutions, grassroots organizations, and local governments.

Haiti is a prime example of a nation that is more victim than beneficiary of NGO "aid." More than two years after the quake in Haiti, reconstruction has barely begun. Most of the rubble has not been cleared, streets are still impassable, and half a million people are living in decrepit, dangerous tent camps. Information on what happened to the 2.1 billion dollars raised is conflicting; some say it is almost all spent, while others suggest that much of the money never made it to the streets or to the Haitians.

The NGO featured in this chapter, Partners in Health (PIH), has learned that community-based, accountable, needs-driven organizations can create positive, sustainable results for the local community. PIH has provided many positive changes, but only because their holistic, community-based vision takes the NGO back to grassroots organization—and ultimately this is the reason they have been successful when so many others have failed.

QUESTIONS FOR CONSIDERATION AND CLASSROOM ACTIVITIES

1. In your opinion, is missionism unethical?
2. Put yourself in the position of Ugandan parents: authorities from another state have accused your leaders of neglecting the rights of children. NGOs move into your community and begin "educating" you and your parents, as well as teachers and local leaders, on what a "proper childhood" means. This advice runs counter to the life you have known. How would you and others in your community react to this interference? What if your leaders have no choice but to obey the new conditions?
3. Choose an NGO and research its work in Haiti. Has it been successful? What challenges and obstacles has this NGO faced when delivering aid to Haitians? Who or what do you think is most responsible for the debacle in Haiti?
4. When Hurricane Katrina struck New Orleans, the United States was overwhelmed with the magnitude of the disaster. Where were the NGOs?
5. The Red Cross is an NGO, and yet very few criticisms are levelled at this organization. Why?
6. Define civil society. Is your country a civil society? Why or why not?
7. Design an ethnographic study of a local NGO. Conduct the study with a partner, spending at least seven days in the organization during the term. What limitations are there in this type of "quick and dirty" ethnographic research?
8. If NGOs cause so much harm, why don't the leaders of nations like Haiti "kick them out"?

9. Devise a plan for clearing the streets of rubble in one suburb of Port-au-Prince, and then create a budget and timeline for completing the project.

SUGGESTED READINGS

Apale, A., & Stam, V. (2011). *Generation NGO*. Toronto: Between the Lines.

This is a must-read book for anyone contemplating international aid as a career. It provides personal accounts of Canadian young people working in international development, dealing with issues such as inequality, abject poverty, stereotyping, and injustice.

Vachon, M., Bugingo, F., & Phillips, C. (2008). *Rebel without borders*. Toronto: ECW Press.

This is a sharply critical, but fascinating, examination of global humanitarian aid through the lens of Doctors Without Borders. This is a behind-the-scenes look at the burgeoning business of aid.

Chapter 12

IS THE PRACTICE OF *PURDAH* AND WEARING *HIJAB* OPPRESSIVE TO WOMEN OR AN EXPRESSION OF THEIR IDENTITY?

Key Terms: cultural identity, discrimination, emic perspective, gender stratification, *hijab*, patriarchal society, *purdah*

INTRODUCTION

The image of an Afghan woman hurrying through the streets draped from head to toe in voluminous folds of thick blue cloth, with not even her eyes visible, resonates among Westerners. These women are wearing *hijab*, a full body covering, and observing the ancient custom of *purdah* or female seclusion. To Westerners, *purdah* and *hijab* are symbols of female subjugation and oppression, tangible evidence that women in Muslim societies are treated like second-class citizens, forever submissive and secluded from the public eye. But is this an accurate assessment, or a remnant of colonialist perceptions of all things non-Western? Do women who follow *purdah* and wear *hijab* consider themselves oppressed, and what, if any, differences are there in the way the practices of *purdah* and *hijab* are viewed and applied from one culture to another?

In this chapter we will address gender stratification through the age-old practices of *purdah* and *hijab*, or what is commonly called veiling.[1] *Purdah* and *hijab* will be examined from an historical, religious, socio-cultural, and economic perspective. Since *purdah* is both religious and cultural, the degree of *purdah* and *hijab* practised, and the meaning(s) attached to the practice often vary, depending on differing internal and external factors, including religious piety, socio-economic class, familial expectations, political agendas, and cultural mores. For this reason we will take a cross-cultural perspective, examining the practice in Palestine, Iran, and Afghanistan, as well as more briefly in countries such as Egypt. As people from Muslim states migrate to other countries, the issue of human rights and *purdah*, and the meaning of *choice* itself, become

---

1   Veiling is the term Muslims use when referring to wearing a head scarf.

more complex. We will consider the challenges faced by people who wish to continue *purdah* and *hijab* while those around them disapprove.

Anthropologists have grown increasingly conscious of a new voice in the study of humankind—that of the people being studied. In this case, the thoughts of women who follow *purdah* and wear various forms of *hijab* will be heard, as it is their interpretation that is most relevant. Internet sources are drawn upon extensively, since it is here, rather than in academic papers, that Muslim women have found a timely forum for expressing their views on the experience and meaning of *purdah* and *hijab*. Finally, this chapter not only considers whether *purdah* and *hijab* are oppressive, but it also examines the *perception* of oppression that many Westerners hold.

ANTHROPOLOGY AND GENDER STRATIFICATION

Anthropologists study gender stratification and its impact on the socio-economic, political, and religious structures of cultural systems. Just as gender is a cultural construct, so is gender stratification culturally defined. **Gender stratification** reflects inequality between males and females, based on the access to wealth and resources, power and self-determination, and prestige and status afforded to men and women. Anthropologists measure the social and political positions that women hold in a culture, the economic independence they are able to achieve, and the decision-making power they have over their lives and bodies. Using these measurements, anthropologists have found that some degree of female gender stratification exists in all modern-day societies. The question here is whether *purdah* exemplifies a form of gender stratification.

Anthropologists from the culture being studied provide an insider's or **emic perspective** on veiling. Homa Hoodfar is a Canadian anthropologist of Iranian descent who has focused her research on the experience of veiled Muslim women. She draws on historical accounts and anthropological data, as well as her personal perspective as a Muslim. Hoodfar (1993: 5) argues that "in Muslim cultures the veil's functions and social significance have varied tremendously, particularly during times of a rapid social change." Therefore, *hijab* is a dynamic practice. To that end, the discussion in this chapter will consider the changing perceptions and practice of *purdah* and *hijab*.

THE NATURE OF *PURDAH* AND *HIJAB*

The Persian word **purdah** means curtain (Khan 1999); it can also mean screen or veil (Arnett 2001). Most people associate *purdah* with clothing that covers a woman; this is really veiling or *hijab*, while *purdah* is a more general term for the seclusion of women, whether beneath concealing clothing or through isolation in their homes. To Muslims, following *purdah* symbolizes the importance of feminine modesty and purity, and reflects positively on her family. The Qur'an (24: 30–31) states: "And say to the believing women that they should lower their gaze and guard their modesty; and that they should not display their beauty and ornaments except what must ordinarily appear thereof; that they should draw their veils over their bosoms and not display their beauty except to their husbands."

The modest covering of a woman's head and body is known as **hijab** or veiling. *Hijab* comes from the Arabic word *hajaba*, meaning to hide or conceal from view (Ali n.d.). If a woman does not wear her veil in the presence of a man, then she considers him kin (MacLeod 1992). Besides modestly covering a woman's body, the clothing must be loose and shapeless, and opaque so as not to draw attention.[2] To many women, *hijab* is the truest expression of being Muslim.

Many cultural groups practise *hijab*, although the form of *hijab* adopted varies considerably. Azerbaijani women wear a head scarf to cover their hair, while women of the Rashaayda Bedouin wear a married woman's mask. There are many other expressions of *hijab*, such as the Indian *sari*, Sudanese *tobah*, Iraqi *abbayah*, Turkish *yashmak*, North African *djellabah* and *haik*, and Egyptian *milaya* (Fernea & Fernea 2000; Hoodfar 2003). These coverings are tangible expressions of cultural practices that hold deeply rooted meanings in each of these societies.

The practice of veiling is not unknown in Western society—witness the white veil covering a bride during a Christian wedding ceremony. This veil symbolizes chastity and purity. Until the 1960s, Catholic women were required to cover their heads when in church. Many cultural groups have traditionally worn head scarves, including Hutterites, Amish, and Canadian Doukhobors. Catholic nuns also wear habits that exemplify a form of *purdah* and *hijab*.

So why do some Muslim women wear *hijab*? According to Hoodfar (1993: 3), "veiling is a lived experience." Hence, the reasons for *purdah* and wearing *hijab* are myriad, complex, and at times contradictory, although usually associated with religious beliefs, cultural expectations, and social status (de Souza 2004). Wearing *hijab* or even a head scarf identifies a woman as a socially active Muslim, shows her solidarity with other Muslims, and publicly proclaims her identity as Muslim. *Hijab* is a form of expression of spirituality, personal dignity, and sexual integrity. *Hijab* has also become a symbol of Muslim women's struggles for gender and ethnic equality when they publicly proclaim their Muslim identity in countries such as the United States. For some, wearing *hijab* empowers them and enables them to challenge stereotypes about Muslims. According to Islamic scholar Wadud Ahmed,

"Women from Pakistan ... [wore] comfortable *salwar kameez*—silky tunics drifting low over billowing pants with long shawls of matching fabric tossed loosely over their heads. Saudi women trod carefully behind their husbands, peering from behind gauzy face veils and 360-degree black cloaks that made them look, as Guy de Maupassant once wrote, 'like death out for a walk.' Afghan women also wore 360-degree coverings, called *chadris*—colorful crinkly shrouds with an oblong of embroidered lattice work over the eyes. Women from Dubai wore stiff, birdlike masks of black and gold that beaked over the nose." Eyewitness account by journalist Geraldine Brooks (1994: 21) at the Cairo airport

---

2 In Cairo, young women wear form-fitting tunics that are colour-coordinated with their *hijab*. They wear tight blue jeans beneath the tunics. This dress appears more of a fashion statement than a religious symbol.

American Muslim women are able to integrate Islam with American social and political activism by wearing *hijab* (Paulsell 2011).

Muslim clergy believe that good Muslim women should wear *hijab* to protect their virtue and help men control their sexual appetites. Ensuring that females remain sexually pure until marriage—and faithful to their husbands after marriage—is the most common reason cited for *purdah* (Khan 1999). In Egypt, women cover their bodies to ward off sexual harassment in the streets (Martin 2010). In Afghanistan, the *chaadaree* veil completely covers a woman's head, thereby protecting men from distraction as they go about their religious and social duties (Hughes 2007). Furthermore, many Muslim women living in the West feel that wearing *hijab* isolates them from the Western tendency to objectify women. Observing *purdah* is also a symbol of the Muslim world's rejection of Western morals and political ideology; *hijab* has become a political statement, announcing the inherent differences between Islamic states and the West. Indeed, women in Egypt have worn the *hijab* to express their Muslim identity, but also to reject Mubarak's ties with the West, in particular the United States (Hughes 2007).

> "When a woman is covered, men cannot judge her by her appearance but are forced to evaluate her by her personality, character, and morals. 'The *hijab* is not a responsibility, it's a right given to me by my Creator who knows us best. It's a benefit to me, so why not? It's something every woman should strive to get and should want.'" A North American woman who chooses to veil, quoted in Barr, Clark, and Marsh (n.d.)

From a religious perspective, the Qur'an appears to sanction female seclusion: "And when you ask his wives for anything, ask it of them from behind a curtain (*hejjab*). That is purer for your hearts and their hearts." According to the Qur'an, then, *purdah* is considered a code of behaviour that sustains a woman's privacy, protects her reputation, and prevents sexual exploitation (Geissinger 2000). Many Muslim women see the *hijab* as a submission to their God and faith, not to men (Bullock 2001). Fernea and Fernea (2000: 239) call the *hijab* "portable seclusion" that enables a woman to affect an aura of respectability and religious piety, thereby bringing honour to her family. Despite the religious link to *hijab* and *purdah*, however, the Qur'an does not specifically recommend veiling or seclusion (Mernissi 1991).

Purdah helps in the maintenance of control over wealth and property (de Souza 2004). Women are the mothers of sons who will inherit property and wealth from the patriarch; the paternity of these sons must therefore be ensured. Consequently, veiling has strong socio-economic implications, since "the more economic rights women have had, the more their sexuality has been subject to control through the development of complex social institutions" (Hoodfar 2003: 6). Thus, in some states, *purdah* is deemed more important for the wealthy upper classes that have property to protect than for the poorer lower classes. *Purdah*, then, becomes a symbol of status—only wealthy women can afford to practise it, while women who must work to help support their families find it difficult to practise.[3]

---

3 In Egypt, working women wear their *hijab* at work, or if they are domestics, they change into "working clothes" once in their employer's residence.

FIGURES 12.1A AND 12.1B   WOMEN WEARING THE *HIJAB*

Although *purdah* requires women to wear concealing clothing when they leave the house, it also refers to female seclusion, or what Young (1996) calls segregation of the sexes. This segregation is practised among the Rashaayda Bedouin, who recognize private domestic spaces for women and open public spaces for men. In some cases, *purdah* has been used to keep women from participating in socio-economic and political life. Among the Yusufzai Pakhtun of the Swat Valley in northeast Pakistan, women remain secluded inside domestic compounds, leaving only to attend weddings, funerals, and circumcision rituals. If they do leave their homes, they must be accompanied by other women or a male family member (Lindholm & Lindholm 2000). This practice ensures that women spend most of their lives within the domestic sphere and are unable to obtain employment or an education, or participate in other activities within their community.

THE HISTORY OF *PURDAH* AND *HIJAB*

The origin of *purdah* remains unclear, although it may have developed in ancient Persia. Regardless of its origin, *purdah* was practised long before Islam (Nashat 1988). In fact, *purdah* did not spread to the Middle East until the Arab conquest of the region in the seventh century. Ancient Babylonian women were masked and chaperoned by a male relative when they left the house. They were also segregated in a separate part of the household. Similarly, respectable Assyrian women were hidden behind screens in their houses (Arnett 2001), while prostitutes were forbidden from veiling (Keddie & Baron 1991). Evidence of *purdah* and *hijab* has also been found in classical Greece, Byzantium, Persia, and India among the Rajput caste (Women in World History Curriculum 2011). In Assyrian, Greco-Roman, and Byzantine cultures, and in the pre-Islamic empire in Persia, *purdah* was a mark of prestige and status, and in India, *purdah* was practised as early as 100 BCE to protect royal women from unwanted gazes (Khan 1999). Records suggest that the practice of *hijab* began in Islamic society after Mohammad's wives were insulted (Fernea & Fernea 2000).

"... although Egyptian women of low income classes never veiled their faces and wore more dresses which did not prevent movement, they nevertheless regarded the upper-class veil as an ideal. It was not ideology which prevented them from taking 'the veil'; rather it was the lack of economic possibilities."
Hoodfar (1989: 21)

By the eighth century CE, female seclusion was well entrenched in Persia and the Eastern Mediterranean among the upper classes (Khan 1999), but not until the reign of the Safavids (1501–1722) did the veil emerge as a symbol of status among Muslim ruling classes and elite in Persia and the Ottoman Empire (1357–1924) (Hoodfar 2003). In India, *purdah* was followed even during colonial rule. Indeed, most of the negative perceptions that Westerners have regarding the veil originated during colonial periods, when veiling was cited as an example of Muslim "backwardness" (Hoodfar 1993). This supposed subjugation of women within a patriarchal society in turn justified colonialism. However, colonialism did not better the position of Muslim women. In India, they lost their right to inherit property and wealth, and to maintain control over income they earned, bringing the economic rights of Muslim women more in line with Hindu and British women of the time. In essence, colonial rule destroyed the matrilineal societies of southern India (Khan 1999).

In the late nineteenth and early twentieth centuries, liberals and intellectuals pushed for an end to *hijab* and *purdah*. Following the 1923 international feminist meeting in Rome, Islamic feminists in Egypt publicly de-veiled (Hoodfar 1993). Despite Islamic feminism labelling the veil a symbol of oppression in the early twentieth century, especially in Egypt, Iran, and Turkey, by the latter half of the century this ideology was revisited. As the twentieth century progressed, *hijab* enjoyed a revival, especially in areas where people felt that Islam was being threatened by Western influence. *Hijab* became a symbol of religious piety, **cultural identity**, and feminine virtue.

Today, *hijab* is compulsory in Saudi Arabia and Iran, and expected in countries such as Egypt, Algeria, Kuwait, and Palestine. In other Muslim countries, conditions remain volatile, with some segments advocating *hijab* while others have rejected the custom. Women find themselves at the centre of this debate, often enduring harassment and discrimination whether they wear *hijab* or not, depending on the current political and ideological atmosphere.

PURDAH AND *HIJAB* AS OPPRESSION

Those outside the Muslim world often have the perception that Muslim women occupy a subordinate position in Middle Eastern countries (Cohen & Peery 2006), and *hijab* is a symbol of this supposed oppression. However, we should question whether oppression and subjugation are a reality for Muslim women. Indeed, a recent resurgence of the *hijab* has been noted among educated Muslim women who wish to announce their faith and traditions: "Young Muslim women are reclaiming the *hijab*, reinterpreting it in light of its original purpose—to give back to women ultimate control of their own bodies" (Mustafa n.d.: 1).

Read and Bartkowski (2000) conducted a study of two dozen Muslim women living in Austin, Texas. Half of these women wore the veil and the other half were unveiled. They found that the unveiled women viewed *hijab* as a mechanism for the **patriarchal** domination of women: "The veil is used to control women" (408). Both groups felt that *hijab* was directly related to men's sexuality and lack of control: "Men can't control themselves, so they make women veil" (408). Many of the unveiled respondents sought to weaken the link between *hijab* and religion: "Women are made to believe that the veil is religious. In reality, it's all political" (408). But some narratives from veiled women indicate that they do wear *hijab* for religious reasons: "I wear the *hijab* because the Qur'an says it's better" (403). Another woman believed that "the veil represents submission to god" (403). *Hijab* can also be a cultural marker—a statement of a Muslim's ethnic and cultural distinctiveness: "The veil differentiates Muslim women from other women. When you see a woman in *hijab*, you know she's Muslim" (404). Even the unveiled women considered *hijab* an important cultural marker: "Some Muslim women need the veil to identify them with the Muslim culture" (409).

> "Women who wear the hijab are not excluded from society. They are freer to move around in society because of it." A North American Muslim woman, quoted in Read and Bartkowski (2000: 405)

Although the veiled women in this study did not explicitly discuss the idea that men's sexual activities must be controlled, they did allude to the problem: "If the veil did not exist, many evil things would happen. Boys would mix with girls, which will result in evil things" (404). The sense of female distinctiveness was articulated by one woman: "Women are like diamonds; they are so precious. They should not be revealed to everyone—just to their husbands and close kin" (404). Contrary to the Western perspective that *hijab* restricts women, the veiled women in Read and Bartkowski's (2000) study felt that the veil liberated them. To these women, *hijab* has overlapping religious, gendered, and ethnic significance.

Opponents see *purdah* as oppressive, depriving women of the right to education, economic independence, and participation in community life. They see it as a way to marginalize and subjugate women. Interestingly, some feminist writers on *purdah* suggest that women are veiled to mute their sexual desires and their potential danger to men (Bonvillain 1998), while women who wear *hijab* believe it is men's sexual desires that are controlled. Opponents also point out that *hijab* originated before Islam and outside the Middle East; using religious scripture to support wearing *hijab* is false reasoning, and interpretations of the scriptures and hadiths are highly questionable.

A common rationale for *hijab* is the sense of anonymity. "Wearing the *hijab* has given me freedom from constant attention to my physical self," says Canadian-born Muslim Naheed Mustafa (n.d.: n.p.) who began wearing a head scarf at the age of 21. While others tend to see her as a terrorist or an oppressed woman, she feels liberated—free from unwanted sexual advances and the body politics of Western "gender games." Empirical evidence suggests that men interact differently with women wearing a *hijab*. Supporters of *purdah* also suggest that seclusion can offer women protection and safe haven, a place where they can relax and enjoy their favourite activities.

> According to one female informant, "Women have been exploited so much, and men make such silly fools of themselves over women, that I really think it is a good thing for men, that women wear *hijab*." Bullock (2001: 2)

Although the discussion thus far has taken a rather positive perspective toward *purdah* and *hijab*, in the following cultural examples, you will see that they can also be used as a vehicle of control over women and children, as well as to fulfill political and military agendas.

PALESTINE

During the intifada[4] of the 1980s in Gaza, Hamas extremists attempted to impose *hijab* on Palestinian women (Hammami 1990). These women, who had enjoyed relative freedom to choose to wear *hijab*, and in what form, now found their dress code under increasing scrutiny and pressure to conform to the Hamas interpretation of *hijab*. Although *hijab* was common among older Palestinian peasant women, many educated urban women had given up wearing any form of *hijab* by the 1950s (Hammami 1990). Even those wearing *hijab* considered it a symbol of group identity, not a genderized restriction. For some, *hijab* was a symbol of resistance to Israeli occupation in Gaza. Regardless of how the *hijab* was viewed, most Palestinian women were against forced imposition of *hijab*. The Hamas, however, sought to "restore" *hijab* as part of a movement to return to a moral and social order closer to their interpretations of Islam and the way Muslims should live. Hamas considered *hijab* a reflection of traditional Islamic piety and political affiliation. Women who refused became targets for attacks by "religious" youths, who threw stones at them and shouted verbal abuse. The original religious and modesty aspects of *hijab* seemed lost, and *hijab* became a sign of a woman's political commitment to the intifada. As one woman said, "It [the *hijab*] is not an issue for me.... In my community [Abassan] it's natural to wear it. The problem is when little boys, including my son, feel they have the right to tell me to wear it" (Hammami 1990: 26).

In May 1988, hooligans, acting under the auspices of Hamas, broke into a school and demanded that the girls wear the *hijab*, and in September of that year a group of

---

4 Intifada symbolizes the Palestinian uprising against Israeli occupation of the lands.

males attacked girls at the Ahmad Shawqi school in Gaza City for not covering their heads (Hammami 1990). When the attacks on women spread to Jerusalem, the Unified National Leadership of the Uprising (UNLU) political leaders in Gaza finally came to the aid of Palestinian women. After a particularly ugly incident in which two women were harassed and accused of being collaborators, the UNLU condemned the attacks in a statement, and the attacks stopped for a time (Hammami 1990). Unfortunately, in 1990 Hamas resumed the *hijab* campaign with a vengeance, only now they were advocating full body coverage. Hamas also issued orders that women were to have a male relative with them when leaving the house. Hamas has even advocated for the imposition of Sharia law, with particular attention to Islamic dress code, and in February 2011, women's hairstyling by men was banned in Gaza (Cunningham 2010). Hammami (1990: 25) feels that, in this case, *hijab* is being used as an instrument of oppression, "a direct disciplining of women's bodies for political ends." Despite this resurgence, Palestinian women have continued to resist patriarchal domination in Gaza.

Palestinian women resisting the pressure to wear *hijab* are not against the practice as such, but they want the right to choose. They also resist the patriarchal control that Hamas has been trying to wield, and fear that *hijab* is only a first step in an offensive against Palestinian women's rights. In 2012, the majority of Palestinian women wear the *hijab*, but those who do not wear it experience social pressure to conform, and some women have even been arrested. As an example of how extreme this pressure can become, Al-Azhar University, although a far less conservative institution than some of the universities in Gaza, insists that female students wear the *hijab* to receive their graduation certificate (Saldanha 2010).

IRAN

The story of women and *hijab* in Iran has taken a convoluted path that differs dramatically depending on socio-economic class. The veil was banned by Reza Shah Pahlevi in 1936 (Talvi 2002) as part of the Women's Awakening and the Shah's plan to modernize Iran. For modern urban Iranian women, this project opened up educational and employment opportunities—if they gave up their veils (Amin 2002). Following the project's failure, urban women experienced a backlash from men; some unveiled women were even attacked by religious extremists. For lower- and middle-class Iranian women, banning the veil created scandal and great inconvenience. These women were socialized from birth to see the veil as the only respectable way to dress, and they did not want to appear in the streets "naked" (Hoodfar 1993: 10). Where they had previously shopped and built social support networks in the neighbourhood, they now stayed at home—too embarrassed to appear in public without their *hijab*. Since many of their husbands were away working, they were reduced to begging male relatives and neighbours to perform public tasks for them.

There were also economic implications. Moderate families no longer allowed their daughters to attend school if they could not wear *hijab*. Young women who used to attend carpet-making workshops to earn some independent income now stayed home. Some resorted to making carpets at home, but their male relatives had to sell them, thereby gaining control over the women's productive strategies and income. The women also lost their only avenue for socializing with neighbours. Thus, this new law created a culture of dependency among middle- and lower-class conservative women and led to further seclusion and isolation of women in Iranian society.

By the 1960s and 1970s, Iranian women under the rule of the Shah enjoyed a degree of independence. They obtained education and worked in traditionally male professions. However, this does not mean that Iranian women were free from oppression. Iranian women who veiled were arrested and their veils forcibly removed, at least until dress codes became more open and women were allowed to wear the veil if they so chose. In the 1970s, the political atmosphere changed and Iranian women began wearing the *chador* (black, loose-fitting robes).

"Some Western feminists have such strong opinions about the veil that they are totally incapable of seeing the women who wear them, much less their reasons for doing so." Hoodfar (1993: 14)

When the Shah was deposed in 1979 and the Islamic Revolution swept the country, the *chador* became compulsory, and women were once again punished—this time for not wearing *hijab* (Talvi 2002). Under the Ayatollah Khomeini, religious and cultural fundamentalism forced women to veil and take on more traditional female roles. Women were seen as pivotal to changing Iran's moral code, and those who resisted were mocked and called "unchaste painted dolls" (Women in World History Curriculum 2011). Witnesses recounted the terrors of executions by public stoning of women who broke the strict laws of Islamic appearance and conduct (Talvi 2002).

When Faegheh Shirazi visited her home country of Iran in 1997, graffiti slogans such as "Death to the improperly veiled woman" covered the walls of buildings, reminding her that *hijab* was not only a cultural and religious custom to Iranians, but an ideology that permeated every aspect of their lives as well. Propaganda on the virtues of the veil was everywhere: television programs, newspaper and magazine articles and ads, and even stamps had the word *hijab* inscribed on the lower left corner (Shirazi 2001).

Although wearing the *hijab* has been the custom in several periods of Iranian history, in modern Iran, choice is no longer an issue. This suggests that currently *hijab* is an instrument of gender oppression in Iran, and a symbol of the degradation of women's rights, along with the reinstatement of polygyny, the lowering of the legal age of puberty to seven, and changes to ownership, inheritance, divorce, and child-custody rights. However, we should not construe from the above that Iranian women are passive, powerless pawns in the regime. Women have ways of exerting power: for example, if a man outside the family argues with a woman, she may insult him by dropping her veil, indicating that she does not consider him a real man (Hoodfar 1991). Resistance against the veil is also common through small gestures, such as leaving strands of hair free. These acts of defiance "develop [women's] identities specifically for the reason that they are forbidden; and enables them to construct their identities against the torturous rituals governing what they are forced to wear, how they are expected to act, the gestures they have to control, the daily struggle against arbitrary rules and restrictions" (Shilandari 2010: n.p.).

AFGHANISTAN

The image of an Afghan woman scurrying through the streets, completely concealed beneath a *burqa*, is difficult for Westerners to reconcile with their sense of personal freedom and human rights. Afghan women under the control of the Taliban had to be concealed beneath a form of *burqa* called the *chadri* when they were in public spaces. Only close family members—husbands, children, fathers, and siblings—and other women were allowed to see a woman without her *chadri*. Afghan women were also forbidden to work outside the home or pursue an education. Indeed, many were under house arrest. Feminists liken the lives of Afghan women under the rule of the Taliban to "gender apartheid" (Geissinger 2000).

Resurgence of the *hijab* began in the 1970s; the Taliban simply made the custom a law. Since the overthrow of the Taliban, women have returned to school and university and have assumed professional positions. Yet their lives are far from peaceful or safe; warlords who have traditionally practised ethnically motivated rape are now in positions of power sanctioned by the United States. Thus, many Afghan women continue to wear the *chadri*, partly for safety, and partly because of the historical and cultural significance of *purdah*. Afghanistan remains a highly patriarchal society where women obey their husbands (Women in World History Curriculum 2011). To the men, women are socially immature and likely to behave irresponsibly, so to protect the family honour, strict regulation of *purdah* is necessary. Thus, social and familial pressures continue to perpetuate the practice of *purdah* among Afghan women.

The purpose of the *burqa* is ostensibly to silence or make women invisible. It has served to do both in Afghanistan; however, international development consultant Michelle Risinger (2012) sees a transformation of the *chadri* taking place, from a symbol of oppression to a means of resistance and empowerment. Afghani women, in their resistance to Taliban culture[5] and its proponents,[6] have learned to use the *chadri* for concealment and protection (Boone 2010). Women's resistance movements, including the Revolutionary Association of the Women of Afghanistan, run orphanages and women's literacy classes, and raise awareness of women's rights among Afghani women. They are also suspected of being the organizing force behind the public demonstration against a law that gave Shia males "the right to demand sex from their wives while denying them basic rights" (Boone 2010: n.p.) Thus, although self-determination for Afghani women is a distant dream, there are women within the country who are working toward that goal.

---

5 Although United States troops drove the Taliban out of Kabul, the cultural environment the Taliban created still exists.

6 Boone (2010) considers President Hamid Karzai, the warlords, the Taliban, and United States troops to be enemies of women.

WESTERN PERCEPTIONS OF *PURDAH* AND MUSLIM WOMEN

Since September 11, 2001, Muslims in North America have found themselves under a new and intense scrutiny—what Alan Lebleigez, an European Union parliament member, called Islamophobia (Bishr n.d.). **Discrimination** against, and harassment of, women dressed in *hijab* in "free" countries, such as Canada, has shocked the Muslim community and reiterated their status as that of the "Other." *Purdah* has become symbolic of this otherness. In response to this discrimination, Muslims are re-asserting their identity, including wearing *hijab*. However, *hijab* makes Westerners feel uncomfortable because women as people seem to become invisible, and a negative image of *purdah* and *hijab* is still evident in the West (Bullock 2001). Canada has also banned face veils at citizenship oath ceremonies and is considering banning veils in schools, hospitals, and government buildings (BBC News 2011).

"'Take those clothes off, you don't have to wear that. You're in Canada now,' shouted the elderly lady.... Normally I would have replied with something witty, but being in a state of shock, all I could come up with was, 'I know where I am.'

'Then take them off. You make me feel hot!'

'I'm wearing this by choice,' I replied.

'No you're not. You're being controlled. You're being controlled by males!'

Her striking words ... caught me off-guard. I felt certain that this woman was not just repeating an old stereotype. This was what she really believed!" Sara Zahedi (n.d.)

Muslim women have been accosted by other Canadians and accused of bringing "backwardness" to Canada. Even some Muslim women have decried the *hijab*, wanting Muslims to modernize. Forcing a woman to conform to Canadian ideals of dress (whatever that might be) and give up a symbol of her Muslim identity is a form of discrimination and is as oppressive as forcing a woman to wear *hijab*.

Readers might ask how something like this could happen in a multicultural country like Canada. The answer lies in the uneasy truce between religion and the secularization of Canadian institutions. Culturally, Westerners have not moved beyond the image of *hijab* as oppressive. They continue to express the concern that women who wear *hijab* must have been pressured or coerced into doing so by male relatives or religious leaders. Despite Canada's official multiculturalism policy, when it comes to *hijab* there is a sense that Muslims must comply with Western behaviour.

In March 2004, France banned conspicuous religious symbols and attire in schools—children were no longer allowed to wear Islamic head scarves, Christian crosses, Jewish skull caps, or Sikh turbans (IRNA 2005). Yet the target in France was Muslim veiling. According to the Stasis Commission, created by former French president Jacques Chirac to examine the principle of secularity, the veil is a rejection of *mixité*—co-education and the mixing of the sexes (Debré 2003, quoted in Scott 2005). Banning the veil in France meant that Muslim girls could no longer attend co-educational schools. Full face veils[7] were also banned in Belgium in 2010, setting off a firestorm of debate, especially since so few women actually wore face veils. Amnesty International has condemned the

---

7 Full face veils are very rare, reserved for the most conservative of Muslim sects.

Belgian law, calling it "an attack on religious freedom" (Hasan 2010: 22). Some states in Germany have passed similar legislation. Muslim women and their supporters protested this move, demanding their religious freedom and a right to express their beliefs. In fact, human rights activists and some European Union parliament members are demanding that EU countries respect the freedom of faith and dress (Islamonline.net).

In Turkey, where veiling is not encouraged, educated urban women are returning to *hijab*. This is a reflection of renewed interest in their religious and cultural identity, and a desire to publicly affirm their Muslim identity and physically announce resistance to Western domination. However, this return to traditional dress has been met with opposition, even in Muslim countries. In Turkey, scarves have been banned from educational institutions and state offices, and young women have been arrested for wearing a head scarf to class (Geissinger 2000). Women have also been expelled from government positions. In Uzbekistan men with beards and women with scarves have been harassed and arrested. In Cameroon, veils are banned in state-subsidized schools; this ban has been blamed for the establishment of private Islamic schools (van Santen 2010). These acts of discrimination have been justified on the basis that they are meant to stamp out fundamentalism and terrorism.

> "If I don't stand up for Muslim women's right to wear *hijab* when they want to, who's going to stand up for me when I'm attacked?" A non-Muslim supporter, quoted in Capeloto (2004: 1)

Debate among Islamic groups continues to rage today. Some groups, such as the Women's Action Forum (WAF) in Pakistan, actively reject attempts to impose *hijab* on women, while the women's mosque movement in Egypt aims to return the veil to a symbol of religious piety rather than religico-cultural identity (Mahmood 2003). According to Hajja Nur, a mosque teacher, Egyptian women "understand forms of bodily practice (such as veiling) to not simply express the self but also shape the self that they are supposed to signify" (Mahmood 2003: 843). European activists have demonstrated at state buildings to demand religious freedom of expression. And at a Wayne State University protest in the United States, scarves became a weapon against ignorance and a symbol of solidarity (Capeloto 2004). Non-Muslim women donned the scarves alongside Muslim women in defence of a growing worldwide campaign to show support for the right to wear *hijab*.

CONCLUSION

The practice of *purdah* is a complicated issue. *Hijab* represents three major tenets in a Muslim woman's life: religious faith and adherence to religious commandments; cultural and personal identity representing status, class, kinship, and culture membership; and political consciousness and activism. Although the custom is often symptomatic of a patriarchal society, it is also a way for women to affirm their religious beliefs and their respectability. In many ways, wearing *hijab* is a liberating practice—de-emphasizing the beauty and sexuality of a woman, and drawing attention to her self-worth.

Veiling is certainly a dynamic cultural practice with myriad meanings. Unfortunately, much of the literature takes a negative and rather limited stance on *purdah*, whether the history of the custom is being examined or contemporary practices discussed. It is only when we ask the women themselves what *purdah* means to them and why they choose to continue wearing *hijab* that we learn there are many facets to the issue. The changing meanings of *hijab* and *purdah* are above all symbolic of the way in which beliefs can transform through time and region.

Fernandez (2009) suggests that Western concern for Muslim women is merely a shield for anti-Muslim sentiment. She also warns that focusing on gender-equality issues such as veiling is facilitating the institutionalization of Islamophobia. Within the broader scope of geopolitics, the controversy surrounding Muslim women and the veil is coinciding with Europe's retreat from multiculturalism (Mullally 2011). As well, the language of multicultural accommodation is losing out to concepts such as civil integration of immigrant communities.

There is an enormous difference between voluntarily adopting *hijab* and being forced to wear it. Although shrouded in religious dogma, *purdah* and *hijab* are far more a political issue. The three cultural examples in this chapter exemplify this point: in Palestine, Iran, and Afghanistan, the political agendas of Hamas, the Iranian regime, and the Taliban exploit *purdah* as one of many forms of control. The *hijab* is just one symptom of a repressive society. The key here seems to be that of choice. If a woman chooses to wear *hijab*, then that is her will. However, if the practice is forced on her, either through insidious social pressure, familial demands, or overt threats of punishment, then it is oppressive, no matter the country. With regards to female seclusion, the issues are more clouded. It appears that women obey seclusionary rules in order to keep peace with parents, husbands, and religious leaders. Choice does not appear to play a significant role in the equation. Does this mean that secluded women are oppressed—victims of gender exclusion and inequality? Only these women can answer that, and they have not yet spoken.

The issue should not be whether women are wearing *hijab*, nor should they be stigmatized for so do. Rather, the issue should be whether they have access to the same resources and opportunities as men. Obviously, many women choose to wear the *hijab*. The reasons for this choice are numerous, and to a certain extent they may be connected to oppression, but not the oppression of the veil—rather, the oppression of societies that fail to offer women equal status and treatment. A woman who feels safer covered in folds of cloth so that men will not leer at her or make unwanted advances is being oppressed by men, not by the veil. A woman who feels she will be taken seriously as a human being with something to offer the community only if she is anonymously hidden behind concealing clothing is being oppressed by societal views, not by the veil. A woman who must hide behind the anonymity of a *burqa* in order to attend school or a women's rights rally is being oppressed by political factions, not by the veil. This type of oppression is worldwide, and is as serious an issue in the West (if not more so) than anywhere else in the world.

QUESTIONS FOR CONSIDERATION AND CLASSROOM ACTIVITIES

1. Do you consider it oppressive to force young Muslim women to remove their head scarves or other religious symbols? Why or why not? Are students free to wear religious symbols at your institution?
2. Research the meaning of *purdah* to Muslims, and then compare it to the meaning held by most Westerners. How are these views influenced by cultural environments, media, and body politics?
3. Why do you think wearing *hijab* has increased in some countries in recent years?
4. Ultimately, this chapter was about gender stratification, although readers should recognize that this oppression does not come from *purdah*, but rather that *purdah* is a symptom of global female oppression. Examine your own society. How are women limited in their opportunities, or "inconvenienced" by the attitudes of society?
5. Although this chapter focused on female *purdah*, in some cultures there are male *purdah* rules as well. Identify *purdah* requirements for men in Egypt, Pakistan, and Sudan.
6. Evaluate the three states examined in this chapter. Which systems of *purdah* seem oppressive and which do not? How has the system of *purdah* changed in the last decade in these states (or has it)?
7. Debate: Is *purdah* oppressive? Choose a country and argue your side based on the reality of that country.

SUGGESTED READINGS

Heath, J. (Ed.). (2008). *The veil: Women writers on its history, lore, and politics.* Berkeley: University of California Press.

A collection of 21 essays that provide valuable discourse on the multiple meanings of veiling, through the voices of women. These essays cross time, space, and culture. A must-read book for anyone interested in current women's and human issues. You will never look at veiling in the same way again.

Shirazi, F. (2001). *The veil unveiled: The hijab in modern culture.* Gainesville: University of Florida Press.

This book is an engrossing non-academic treatment of *purdah* and the *hijab* that actually examines *hijab* as part of everyday or popular culture. Shirazi attempts to dispel some stereotypes of Muslim women without resorting to theoretical perspectives, which makes this book a refreshing read for almost anyone.

CONCLUSION

The topics discussed in this volume were chosen to provide a glimpse into the world of anthropology and its relevance to contemporary society. The discussions are designed to answer the question: "Of what relevance are anthropological research, principles, and application in the everyday lives of humans?" In part, this question refers to our growing awareness that anthropology, like other disciplines, cannot remain on the periphery of society. Anthropologists recognize that they must apply their knowledge and insights to find solutions to, or at the very least to understand, the problems that confront human existence. In this concluding section of *Anthropology Matters* we will briefly examine the relevance of anthropology in our everyday lives, and in the larger context of our local and global communities.

THE VALUE OF ANTHROPOLOGY

Education brings awareness—awareness of the world around us, and the myriad ways in which people interact with other people in this world. Learning about other ways of life can stoke our imagination and challenge our sense of being. As an example, investigating female circumcision and *purdah* raises the question of whether these practices promote gender inequality or if this is merely a narrow Western perception. From an anthropological perspective, we are encouraged to view these issues through the eyes of the practitioners. The goal is not to change our opinion, but to recognize that these issues are not one-dimensional, and that not everyone agrees with the Western way of life. It is difficult to understand another point of view when it comes to sensitive topics like gender equality, but this is when the true value of anthropology becomes obvious. Anthropology challenges us to question our beliefs and practices—to ask if there are other ways of living as undeniable as our own.

Anthropology is also an examination of self—who we are, where we have come from, and where we are going. Our satisfaction with ourselves and the world around us begins with an understanding of our sense of place and identity. All of us have questions regarding identity; this struggle is particularly evident in the question of human sexuality and marriage practices, and for nations experiencing extensive immigration. In both discussions, the ambiguity and intolerance toward those who own a different identity is clearly evident. Even more relevant to the question of self is the concept of body image—why are humans, especially females, so obsessed with an "ideal" body?

THE ROLES OF ANTHROPOLOGY

Cultural diversity is a hallmark of human existence that has been equated with genetic variation: just as species are threatened with extinction if they lose their genetic diversity, the human species is also threatened if we lose our cultural diversity. Cultural diversity provides humanity with the ability to respond to varying environments and situations. Anthropologists involved in preserving endangered languages recognize the importance of linguistic diversity and the cultural knowledge reflected in these languages. In a world steeped in modernization and globalization processes, how do we protect cultural diversity and ensure our continued existence? Richard Lee (2003: 200) has this response: "As the world enters the new millennium, the two most pressing issues are first, how to rediscover 'democracy' and 'just' society, and second, how to find ways of living in balance with our finite resources. The lessons of Ju/'hoansi and other indigenous peoples offer insights into both these questions and challenge the current complacencies. Their new-found recognition is a cause for optimism. Let us take heart: ecological and cultural diversity may still have a place on this planet."

Anthropology helps us understand that each culture and each way of life is equally valid in its own right. Anthropologist Bruce Knauft (2005: 4) recognized this fundamental principle when studying the Gebusi people: "The Gebusi were not simply 'a society' or 'a culture'; they were an incredible group of unique individuals." This is why the goals of NGOs are so conflicting for anthropologists: we know that change in society is inevitable, but outside forces implementing these changes can have a profound effect on the well-being of societies.

Today, anthropologists study not only exotic indigenous peoples living in distant locales, but also people living in our own neighbourhoods. The "anthropology of shopping" highlights consumer behaviour and the importance of shopping as a social outlet. In a similar vein, social media has changed the way people mobilize for social, economic, or political activism, and likely will continue to have an impact on the sociopolitical stage for some time to come.

The world of anthropology has much to offer, both in knowledge and perspective. We owe a great deal to the anthropologists who have come before us, who have diligently tried to understand cultural diversity and share it with us. Their interpretations of culture are the building blocks of contemporary anthropological consciousness, ensuring that the field continues to be relevant.

THE GOALS OF ANTHROPOLOGY

The ultimate goal of anthropology is to teach people to *appreciate* cultural diversity, rather than only *tolerate* it. On an individual level, this change in attitude is particularly relevant when we live in a country where immigration from diverse parts of the world occurs. Appreciating cultural diversity makes us more comfortable when interacting with other people who look different, speak different languages, practise different customs, and hold different beliefs.

Many people live in cultural environments other than their own—it is one of the most valuable experiences an individual can undertake and for young people can become a rite of passage to adulthood. Appreciation of cultural diversity may enable these global nomads to better appreciate cultural diversity, reject narrow provincialism, and become global citizens. On a global level, we face numerous ethnic and religious conflicts; dealing with the inequalities and paradoxes in the world around us is a constant challenge, one that anthropology views from a holistic perspective.

As discussed in the Introduction, the sharing of knowledge and understanding of cultural diversity are central goals of applied anthropology, yet anthropologists also help preserve the memory of cultures that have undergone significant change. When asked what value he attached to his research on the Plains Cree, anthropologist David Mandelbaum (1979: 4) responded that his work provided, "for their descendants, some record of their forefathers and of a way of life that many of them would increasingly want to know about. Together with their own oral traditions it could provide that sense of personal and social roots that most people want to have."

Throughout this book, the importance of understanding someone else's point of view and acknowledging that there are many ways of living has been emphasized. This is what makes anthropology most relevant. Through the lens of anthropology we view other people and the way they live as deserving of the dignity and respect that we ourselves expect. Currently, anthropologists are lending their expertise to questions concerning NGOs and the possible exploitation of the poorest segments of human society. Although not the answer to all our difficulties, an anthropological perspective promotes understanding, acceptance, and appreciation of the amazing cultural diversity of our global community.

On a reflective note, although I continue to believe that anthropology matters, I was often tempted, while writing the second edition of this book, to suggest that anthropology *could* or *should* matter. This became increasingly obvious to me as I researched some of the more timely chapters in this book, for example, the chapter on social media. Although a few astute anthropologists quickly engaged in anthropological commentary using blogs, for the most part the discipline contributed little to the study of the amazing events taking place in Egypt in January of 2011. Where were the anthropologists? We have much work to do if we want to remain relevant in these times of rapid change.

GLOSSARY

androcentrism   Male-centredness.

anthropology   The study of humankind in all times and places. Sub-disciplines: biological anthropology, archaeology, linguistic anthropology, and socio-cultural anthropology.

anthropology of genocide   The study of the deliberate extermination of an ethnic group.

anthropology of suffering   The study of cultural systems that have broken down due to war and conflict, or economic or environmental collapse, and the impact this has on people.

applied anthropology   The practical application of the knowledge, expertise, and skills of anthropologists to help solve societal problems.

applied economic anthropology   Applying anthropological knowledge to consumer research and marketing projects.

applied linguistic anthropology   Providing solutions to linguistic issues, such as language revitalization programs.

biculturalism   A sense of belonging to more than one culture, usually after a person has lived in another culture.

blogosphere   A network of connected blogs, which are personal journals online.

body modification   Decoration (e.g., tattoos, jewellery, painting) or modification (piercings, cuttings, branding) of the human body.

body dissatisfaction   Feelings that one's body is imperfect in comparison to the ideal body in a society.

body image   A culturally defined image of beauty that influences the way people view their bodies.

business / corporate anthropology   Anthropologists working in private industry, applying anthropological concepts and methods to business-related issues.

civic media   The use of social media to garner attention and encourage action from a global audience.

civil society   A society where violence is relatively absent and people live in peace rather than fear of oppression. May also refer to those elements of society not associated with government or business.

class   A segment of society whose members share similar economic and educational status and lifestyles.

clitoridectomy   A female circumcision ritual, where part or all of the clitoris is removed, as well as part or all of the labia minora.

commercial anthropology   Anthropologists hired as consultants for private firms.

conspicuous consumption   Acquiring and displaying goods and services to acquire status.

consumer behaviour   The way consumers shop, the products they purchase, and the expectations they have for the shopping experience.

corporate anthropology / ethnography   Anthropologists working for corporations to improve productivity and marketability by employing ethnographic methods to study corporations or consumers.

cosmopolitanism   The ideology that all humans belong to the same global community and are of equal value. May also include the philosophy that no one way of living is more right than any other.

cross-cultural comparison   The comparison of a cultural trait (e.g., ritual) in many cultures to develop hypotheses about human behaviour.

cultural diversity   The distinct traditions, beliefs, and language of different cultures. Analogous with ethnic diversity.

cultural identity   The sense of belonging that an individual feels toward a particular culture, based on upbringing, residence, heritage, customs, and language.

cultural imperialism   Promoting a nation's values, beliefs, and behaviour above all others.

cultural relativism   The principle that each culture and its practices are unique and valid in their own right, and must be viewed within the context of that culture.

cultural sensitivity   Being respectful toward other ways of thinking, believing, and living.

culture   The shared ideals, values, and beliefs that people use to interpret, experience, and generate behaviour. Culture is shared, learned, based on symbols (e.g., language), and integrated.

culture-bound   Seeing the world only through one's own eyes; for example, using the Western term "government" to refer to all types of political organization.

culture change   The process of changing the behaviour, technology, or beliefs within a culture.

culture shock   A feeling of disorientation, confusion, and irritability that results from living in an unfamiliar foreign environment.

cyberanthropology   The study of emerging social phenomena in online communities and subcultures.

cyberculture   Online communities that exhibit cultural traits.

cyberpunks   Individuals who embed technology and science fiction into their lives.

development   Usually refers to assistance given to developing countries to create infrastructures (e.g., education, health care, business).

development and modernization approach   The theoretical perspective that change will come not from outside forces, but rather from large-scale social changes, for example, women becoming more empowered in their communities through access to education and employment.

discrimination   Differential attitudes toward people and access to resources and opportunities based on gender, age, sexual orientation, disabilities, or ethnic identity.

division of labour   A way of organizing duties. In households, may refer to differentiation of duties based on gender.

eating disorders   Severe disturbances in normal eating behaviour and attitudes toward food and body image.

economic anthropology   A specialization that focuses on production, distribution, and consumption in small-scale and industrial societies.

emergency anthropology   Collecting data from a cultural group that is in crisis.

emic perspective   To consider a culture from its members' (insider) point of view rather than the **etic perspective**—anthropologists' (outsider) point of view.

enculturation   The process of learning one's culture, usually through transmission from one generation to the next.

enculturative forces   Forces that serve to introduce children in particular to the customs or behaviour of their culture, e.g., parents, schools, government.

endangered language   Languages that have few speakers and are in imminent danger of disappearing.

engaged anthropology   Using anthropological knowledge and insights to participate in and contribute to public debate on cultural issues and to disseminate anthropological findings to a general audience (public anthropology).

ethics   The rules that anthropologists follow when conducting research. The primary rule is to "do no harm." Anthropologists have an obligation to protect the privacy of their study group, uphold the integrity of anthropology, and meet the needs of their funding agency, which may cause conflicting loyalties or an **ethical dilemma**.

ethnic boundary markers   The indicators or characteristics, e.g., dress, that identify individuals as belonging to a particular ethnic group.

ethnic cleansing   *See* genocide

ethnic conflict   A conflict between ethnic groups due to ethnic nationalism or economic and political power plays.

ethnic enclave   A locality, often a neighbourhood, where most of the members are of the same ethnic origin. For example, Chinatown.

ethnic group   A group of people with shared ancestry, cultural traditions and practices, and a sense of common history.

ethnic identity   The identity we possess based on our membership in an ethnic group.

ethnicity   The identity of a group of people based on their common place of origin, history, and sense of belonging.

ethnic stratification   Institutionalized inequality with differential access to wealth, power, and prestige based on ethnic identity.

ethnocentrism   The attitude that one's own culture is superior to all others.

ethnographic research   Anthropological fieldwork involving the collection of first-hand descriptive data on a culture by an **ethnographer**, who lives with the study group for an extended period. The end result is a written description of the people and their way of life known as an **ethnography**.

ethnoscapes   A landscape of group identity that is not limited by location.

expatriates / expats   People who live in a country other than the one in which they were born, but who retain citizenship in their natal country.

exploitation   In this context, it means using people for selfish purposes, and often causing harm in the process.

family   People who consider themselves related through kinship: nuclear, extended, single, blended.

female circumcision / female genital cutting   The removal of all or part of a female's external genitalia for religious, traditional, or socio-economic reasons. **Female genital mutilation** is the Western term used to exemplify disapproval of this procedure.

fieldwork   *See* ethnographic research

flashmobs   A group of people who gather quickly to perform a function, such as a political protest, and then disperse.

gender / gender identity   A cultural construct that gives us our social identity, status, and roles in society based on our sexual identity (e.g., male or female) and expected gender roles in society.

gender stratification   Unequal access to resources, opportunities, and prestige, usually for women, because of their gender.

gendered behaviour   Differences in behaviour that are based on gender identity and expectations.

gender-variant role   Exhibiting gender traits that are not typical for one's biological sex; for example, a boy who displays feminine traits and behaviour.

genocide / ethnic cleansing   The deliberate extermination of one cultural group by another, usually to gain economic and/or political control over a region.

globalization   Worldwide integration of economies, assisted by global transportation, communication, and information technology.

global nomads   People who live and work in countries other than their own.

heritage language   Languages that have a long history within a community.

hijab   A head covering for Muslim women.

holistic approach   Viewing the systems of a culture (e.g., economic, social, political, and religious) as an integrated whole, with each system influencing and being influenced by the other systems.

homosexuality   Sexual attraction between individuals of the same sex.

human migration   Movement of people, often in large numbers, from one locality to another. Often involves cross-border movement.

human rights   Principles that ensure the equal treatment of all people, regardless of gender, age, or ethnicity, including the right to health, safety, and security. Embodied in a set of guidelines adopted by the United Nations General Assembly in 1948.

human trafficking   The illegal selling or trading of people for sexual exploitation and forced labour, a form of modern-day slavery.

immigrants   People who have left their home country and moved to another country, usually for economic or political reasons.

immigration / emigration / migration   The movement of people from one place to another, be it to a new country, from rural regions to urban centres, or from one region to another. **Emigration** refers to movement out of a (source) country; **immigration** refers to movement into a (destination or host) country.

indigenous people   Members of cultures who self-identify as the original inhabitants of the land based on a long history of habitation.

inequality   Unequal access among individuals, usually to wealth, power, and status, but also on the basis of gender, class, etc.

infibulation   *See* pharaonic circumcision

key informant   A knowledgeable member of a culture who supplies information to an ethnographer.

language   A complex system of communication, using mutually understood sounds, words, and other meaningful symbols.

language isolate   A language that has no known relationship with any other languages.

language loss   The process by which a language becomes extinct.

language nests   Immersion programs that teach young children their heritage languages.

language retention / revitalization   Efforts to keep endangered languages alive by teaching them to the younger generation.

language shift   When a speech community changes to another language.

linguicism   Linguistic prejudice or discrimination.

linguistic anthropology   The study of how people use language to interact with each other and transmit culture.

linguistic diversity   The number of different languages spoken today, the linguistic version of biodiversity.

linguistic homogenization   The elimination of linguistic diversity and creation of one global language.

linguistics   The scientific study of language from a historical and descriptive perspective.

marriage   The joining of two or more people to form a conjugal bond.

media anthropology   The study of influences of media on culture.

media ecology   The study of modern communication systems and their influence on human interaction and experience.

media epidemiography   The study of the distribution and patterns of media use.

missionism   The process of converting people to another belief system.

modern-day slavery   *See* human trafficking

modernization   The process of making other societies over in the image of the West by changing their social, economic, political, and religious systems.

Modern Primitives   A countercultural movement that uses neo-tribal rituals and body modifications.

multiculturalism   The philosophy that people can maintain their distinctive cultural traditions, values, and beliefs while still participating in mainstream society.

nation   A cultural group that shares the same language, religion, history, territory, and ancestry, such as the Plains Cree; also refers to an independent state, such as Canada.

nationality   A sense of belonging to a particular nation, even if not living in that nation.

netizens   Members of a new form of citizenship that uses the Internet to solve socio-political problems.

NGOs   Non-government organizations involved in humanitarian aid and development.

norms   Expected and predictable behaviour within a given culture.

participant observation   A research method whereby an anthropologist lives with the study group, learns its language, and participate in its daily activities.

participatory media   Active participation by people in media, including creating content.

participatory politics   Participation by people in the political system, involving taking part in decision-making processes, and at times directing policy through social media and networking.

patriarchal society   A male-dominated society.

pharaonic circumcision   The removal of the clitoris, labia minora, and most or all of the labia majora. These cut edges are stitched together using thorns or other materials, leaving a small opening for urine and menstrual flow. This stitching is known as **infibulation**.

popular culture   The culture of our everyday lives, such as television, sports, arts and crafts, fiction, and music.

purdah   A Muslim tradition of secluding women, either within their homes or beneath concealing clothing.

qualitative research The use of interviews, documents, and participant-observation data, rather than statistics and other quantifiable data. This type of research is most often used to explain human social behaviour.

quantitative research The gathering of statistical and measurable data.

queer subculture A term sometimes used to refer to gay and lesbian subcultures.

race A misleading concept used to place individuals and populations into categories based on broad biological and/or behavioural traits that do not hold up to scientific scrutiny.

refugees Individuals seeking asylum in another country from political, economic, social, or religious strife in their home country.

relativism *See* cultural relativism

retail / consumer anthropology The study of people's shopping behaviour.

reverse culture shock Experiencing culture shock upon return to one's own country and home.

rite of passage Rituals that mark important stages in an individual's life, for example, puberty.

ritual Organized actions that have historical/traditional value.

same-sex marriage Legal union between individuals of the same sex.

sexuality One's sexual identity or orientation, the types of sexual practices in which one engages, and one's interest in having sexual relationships.

smart mobs Groups of people who communicate, organize, and cooperate via mobile devices.

social change Changes in the structure and organization of a society.

social media Social interaction and social mobilization facilitated by mobile devices (e.g., cell phones).

social network Individuals or organizations tied together by similar values, ideas, friendship, interests, or political activism.

sojourners Temporary residents in a foreign country.

speech community A group of people who share the same language and concerns for the vitality of the language. They usually live in the same community, but can be dispersed.

subculture Segments of a population that are distinct from mainstream culture due to ethnicity, class, religion, or behaviour.

sunna circumcision Female circumcision where only the clitoral prepuce (hood) is removed.

symbolic capital An intangible value, such as the prestige of having many children.

symbolic circumcision Circumcision rituals that do not involve the actual removal of any genitalia; for example, circumcision by words as practised in some parts of Kenya.

systemic racism Discrimination embedded in the systems of a culture that limits access to resources and opportunities for people of a certain "race."

technosociality   The fusion of technology and social behaviour (e.g., to organize protests, inform the international public).

Third Culture Kids (TCKs)   Young people who have lived significant portions of their lives in a foreign country.

transcultural / transnational identity   The fusion of two or more cultural identities, often found in global nomads.

transcultural literacy   The ability to be comfortable in a foreign environment, awareness of global citizenship, and language proficiency.

transnational communities / transnationals   Groups of people who transcend political or geographical borders to form communities, e.g., online communities.

transnational flow   The movement of people, ideas, products, etc. across international borders. Often facilitated by international communications and transportation systems.

universalism   In opposition to relativism, suggests that there are universal human rights that must be followed, regardless of culture, sex, or religion.

xenophobia   Fear or dislike of strangers, often predicated on physical appearance or religious beliefs.

LESSON PLANS AND WEBSITES

Chapter 1

1. "The Power of Place: Doing Ethnographic Studies of Local Sites," by Amanda Christy Brown and Holly Epstein Ojalvo. The Learning Network, from http://learning.blogs. nytimes.com/2010/04/15/the-power-of-place-doing-ethnographic-studies-of-local-sites/. This site provides opportunities for students to examine their assumptions and stereotypes, while learning about ethnographic fieldwork.

2. *Handbook on Ethical Issues in Anthropology*, edited by Joan Cassell and Sue-Ellen Jacobs. A special publication of the American Anthropological Association number 23, from http:// www.aaanet.org/committees/ethics/ch3.htm.
   This is an excellent source for case studies that encourage students to examine their own ethical standards. Each of the cases can be modified to fit the level of student, from high school to university.

3. "Participant Observation as a Data Collection Method," by B.B. Kawulich, *Forum: Qualitative Social Research* 6(2) Art. 43, from http://www.qualitative-research.net/index. php/fqs/article/view/466/996.
   Not only does this site present detailed information on participant observation, but it also supplies several interesting exercises and activities for teaching observation techniques and skills: Memory Exercise, Sight Without Sound, Sound Without Sight, Photographic Observations, Direct Observations, and a Participant Observation activity.

Chapter 2

1. "Anthropological Approach to Consumer Behaviour: A Marketing Educational Case of Teaching and Learning," by Robert Tian, from http://businessanthropology.blogspot. ca/2010/10/anthropological-approach-to-consumer.html.
   This site offers suggestions for consumer ethnography exercises, developing a research proposal, conducting fieldwork observations, writing a mini-report and consumer behaviour analysis. A research project based on extensive observation is also available. Enriched activity: Write a two-page advanced applied analysis of a store to submit to the retailer, making suggestions for improvement in customer satisfaction.

Chapter 3

1. AAA Science NetLinks, "Endangered Languages," from http://sciencenetlinks.com/lessons/endangered-languages/.
   This site contains several lesson plans and student activities in linguistics and endangered languages at a fairly advanced level. Some enrichment is necessary for university-level courses.

2. The American Forum for Global Education, "The Globalization of Language," from http://www.globaled.org/curriculum3.html.
   This website provides several relevant articles about endangered languages, followed by activities on endangered languages, English dominance in global affairs, and saving endangered languages. For senior high-school or university students these activities will need to be enriched.

3. Research project using resources from Simon Fraser University, from http://www.googlesyndicatedsearch.com/u/sfu?sitesearch=sfu.ca&domains=sfu.ca&q=language+revitalization.
   Numerous research projects can be created where students investigate the materials on this and other websites to learn about what is happening in language revitalization in Canada.

Chapter 4

1. "Third Culture Kid," from http://www.enotes.com/topic/Third_culture_kid.
   A detailed article on Third Culture Kids with links to additional resources. Class discussions and research projects can be developed from this information.

2. "Why Third Culture Kids Need Corporate Support," from http://www.expatica.com/fr/employment/employment_information/Third-Culture-Kids-corporate-support-_16555.html.
   An information site that explores what corporations can do to make living abroad a successful experience. This article should generate brainstorming about ways in which corporations can help TCKs adjust.

Chapter 5

1. "A Dissection of Ethnic Conflict," from http://www.pbs.org/pov/film-files/pov_nomoretears_lessonplan_lesson_plan_0.pdf. Critical analysis of ethnic conflict.
   This lesson plan should be used in conjunction with the film No More Tears Sister: An Anatomy of Hope and Betrayal. This 52-minute film recreates the struggles of human rights activist Dr. Rajani Thiranagama, who remained in her war-torn homeland of Sri Lanka to expose human rights violations. These lessons will need to be enriched for university students.

2. Lessons and activities on tolerance, from http://www.un.org/works/goingon/ireland/lessonplan_tolerance.html.
   These lesson plans focus on the conflict in Northern Ireland, rights of children, and conflict resolution.

3. World Affairs Council of Pittsburgh, from http://www.worldpittsburgh.org/resources.jsp?pageId=2161392240601289549172297.
   The lesson plans are not online but available through the webpage. Global education and transnational security issues are two of the topics.

Chapter 6

1. **"Healthy Body Image," Purdue University, from http://www.extension.purdue.edu/ extmedia/CFS/CFS-737-W.pdf.**
   A vast array of lessons for high-school students that will require some enrichment for university students.

2. **The impact of gender role stereotypes, including "Dying to be thin," and "Pondering Manhood's Price," from http://www.media-awareness.ca/english/resources/educational/ lessons/secondary/gender_portrayal/upload/The-Impact-of-Gender-Role-Stereotypes-Lesson-Kit.pdf.**
   Some enrichment of these lessons is necessary for university courses.

Chapter 7

1. **National Geographic News, "Reporter's Notebook: Female circumcision in Africa," from http://news.nationalgeographic.com/news/2002/02/0219_020219_circumcision.html.**
   Relevant information to develop a class discussion or debate.

2. **Prevention toolkit from http://www.rutgerswpf.org/sites/default/files/Prevention-Girls-Circumcision-teaching-toolkit-2009.pdf.**
   A prevention toolkit directed toward students at all grade levels, including advanced high school and first-year university.

3. **A Teacher's Guide for Nursing students. Training modules from http://www.who.int/ gender/other_health/teachersguide.pdf.**
   Provides an enormous amount of information and activities in module format on female circumcision from WHO. Caution: Western perspective only.

Chapter 8

1. **Gay Rights Lesson Plans, from http://blog.gale.com/speakingglobally/projects/ gay-rights-lesson-plans/.**
   A series of lessons on gay rights, including gays in the military, gay marriage around the world, and activism. Also includes numerous links to gay-rights issues. Lessons are suitable for senior high-school and introductory university-level students.

2. **"Teaching and Learning about Gay History and Issues," from http://learning.blogs. nytimes.com/2011/11/22/teaching-and-learning-about-gay-history-and-issues/.**
   Numerous lesson plans and resources on gay and lesbian issues, including defining a family, gay communities, gay marriage, and civil rights.

3. **"Missouri teacher planning same-sex wedding is fired," from http://www. democraticunderground.com/1002365155**
   This article should generate discussion and a class debate on gay teachers in school.

Chapter 9

1. **"Researching digital media and social change: A theory of practice approach," by John Postill, from http://johnpostill.com/.**
   Provides information on researching digital media and social change within a given organization, collective, field of practice, or neighbourhood and can be used to guide group activities and research projects. Students can choose a familiar or exotic example and come up with a brief research plan.

2. "Acceptable social networking?", from http://cybersmartcurriculum.org/cyberbullying/lessons/9–12/acceptable_social_networking/.
   High-school lessons and class activities, but the lessons are applicable to older students if enriched.

3. "Technology and social networking" lesson plans for adults, Purdue University Extension, from http://www.four-h.purdue.edu/downloads/volunteer/Tech%20and%20Social%20Network%20Lesson%20Plan.pdf.

Chapter 10

1. PBS Teachers resource, from http://www.pbs.org/teachers/socialstudies/inventory/immigration-912.html.
   A wide range of lessons on immigration that can be used in many course disciplines and that can easily be enriched for university students. Includes both interactive and offline activities.

2. Canadian Council for Geographic Education, "Going Down the Road," from http://www.ccge.org/resources/learning_centre/lesson_plans_docs/migration/NS_S_GoingDowntheRoad.pdf.
   Well-developed lesson plans for Canadian students studying the migration of human populations and settlement in Canada.

3. Migration Citizenship Education, Learning Projects, from http://migrationeducation.de/33.3.html.
   Two lessons are particularly appropriate: The United Nations Lesson Plan on Refugees and the National Geographic lesson plan on migration—why people move.

Chapter 11

1. Capacity Building for NGOs and non-profits, from http://www.widernet.org/digitallibrary/Portals/phpportals/portal.php?formatID=5&PortalPageID=1753.
   Students will find an enormous amount of information on NGOs and non-profits that may generate research projects to evaluate.

2. NGO Organizations, from http://www.labor.net.au/links/ngos.html.
   Students should choose an NGO from the comprehensive list provided on this website and research its mandate, current projects, and success rate using independent sources. Alternatively, they could read and take jot notes on five NGOs of their choosing and report to the class their activities, critically evaluating the purpose/agenda of these agencies.

3. Expedition Africa, Algonquin College, from http://lyceum.algonquincollege.com/swbp/africa/lessonPlans/index.htm.
   A lesson plan site that involves using music to raise awareness about world issues. Worksheets, resources, rubric, and complete lesson plans available, but will need enrichment for university courses.

Chapter 12

1. "Teen told she can't wear headscarf in JROTC parade," from http://www.firstamendmentcenter.org/teen-told-she-cant-wear-headscarf-in-jrotc-parade.
   An interesting news article that should generate discussion in class. Fundamental question: Should Demin Zawity have been allowed to wear her head scarf?

2. The Islam Project, from http://www.islamproject.org/education/D04_Hejab_secularism.htm.
   Lesson plans include handouts with historical information, case studies, other sources, and activities.

REFERENCES

Introduction

Ginsburg, F. (1991). What do women want? Feminist anthropology confronts clitoridectomy. *Medical Anthropology Quarterly*, 5(1): 17–19. http://dx.doi.org/10.1525/maq.1991.5.1.02a00030

Haviland, W.A., Fedorak, S., & Lee, R.B. (2009). *Cultural anthropology* (3rd Cdn. ed.). Toronto: Nelson Education.

Kottak, P.C. (2000). Teleconditioning and the postmodern classroom. In J. Spradley & D.W. McCurdy (Eds.), *Conformity and conflict: Readings in cultural anthropology* (10th ed., pp. 92–97). Boston: Allyn and Bacon.

Messer, E. (1993). Anthropology and human rights. *Annual Review of Anthropology*, 22(1): 221–249. http://dx.doi.org/10.1146/annurev.an.22.100193.001253

Overing, J. (Ed.). (1985). *Reason and morality*. New York: Tavistock Publications.

Part One: How Does Anthropology Work?

Hauch, C. (1992). Reciprocity on skid row. In J. Chodkiewicz (Ed.), *Peoples of the past and present. Readings in anthropology* (pp. 295–302). Toronto: Harcourt Brace.

Lee, R.B. (2009). Health and disease in one culture: The Ju/'hoansi. In W. Haviland, S. Fedorak, & R.B. Lee (Eds.), *Cultural anthropology*, 3rd Cdn. ed. (pp. 410–411). Toronto: Nelson Education.

Shearing, C.D., & Stenning, P.C. (1987). Say "Cheese!" The Disney order that is not so Mickey Mouse. In C.D. Shearing & P.C. Stenning (Eds.), *Private policing* (pp. 317–323). Newbury Park, CA: Sage.

Taft, M. (2009). The mock wedding folk drama in the prairie provinces. In W. Haviland, S. Fedorak, & R.B. Lee (Eds.), *Cultural anthropology*, 3rd Cdn ed. (pp. 296–400). Toronto: Thomson Nelson Learning.

Underhill, P. (1999). *Why we buy: The science of shopping*. New York: Simon & Schuster.

Chapter 1: What Are the Challenges in Ethnographic Fieldwork?

Alder, P.A., & Alder, P. (1987). *Membership roles in field research*. Newbury Park, CA: Sage.

Anderson, R. (2005). *The ghosts of Iceland*. Belmont, CA: Thomson Wadsworth.

Cassell, J., & Jacobs, S. (2006). Introduction. *Handbook on ethical issues in anthropology.* American Anthropological Association. http://www.aaanet.org/committees/ethics/toc.htm.

Clifford, J. (1997). *Routes. Travel and translation in the late twentieth century*. Cambridge, MA: Harvard University Press.

Correll, S. (1995). The ethnography of an electronic bar. The lesbian café. *Journal of Contemporary Ethnography*, 24(3): 270–298. http://dx.doi.org/10.1177/089124195024003002

DeMunck, V.C., & Sobo, E.J. (Eds.). (1998). *Using methods in the field: A practical introduction and casebook*. Walnut Creek, CA: AltaMira Press.

Erlandson, D.A., Harris, E.L., Skipper, B.L., & Allen, S.D. (1993). *Doing naturalistic inquiry: A guide to methods*. Newbury Park, CA: Sage.

Fedorak, S. (2009). *Pop culture. The culture of everyday life*. Toronto: University of Toronto Press.

Hill, J.N. (2006). The committee on ethics: Past, present, and future. *Handbook on ethical issues in anthropology*. American Anthropological Association. http://www.aaanet.org/committees/ethics/toc.htm.

Holtzman, J.D. (2000). *Nuer journeys, Nuer lives. Sudanese refugees in Minnesota*. Toronto: Allyn and Bacon.

Kawulich, B.B. (May 2005). Participant observation as a data collection method. *Forum: Qualitative Social Research*, 6(2) Art. 43. http://www.qualitative-research.net/index.php/fqs/article/view/466/996.

Knauft, B. (2005). *The Gebusi. Lives transformed in a rainforest world*. Toronto: McGraw-Hill.

Kutsche, P. (1998). *Field ethnography. A manual for doing anthropology*. Upper Saddle River, NJ: Prentice Hall.

Lewis, I.M. (1976). *Social anthropology in perspective*. Harmondsworth, UK: Penguin Books.

Li, J. (2008). Ethical challenges in participant observation: A reflection on ethnographic fieldwork. *The Qualitative Report*, 13(1): 100–115. http://www.nova.edu/ssss/QR/QR13-1/li.pdf.

Marshall, A., & Batten, S. (2004). Researching across cultures: Issues of ethics and powers. *Forum Qualitative Social Research*, 5(3): Art. 39. http://www.qualitative-research.net/index.php/fqs/article/view/572/1241.

Miller, L. (1995). Women and children first: Gender and the settling of the electronic frontier. In J. Brook & I. Boal (Eds.), *Resisting the virtual life* (pp. 49–58). San Francisco, CA: City Lights.

Nolan, R.W. (1990). Culture shock and cross-cultural adaptation: Or I was okay until I got here. *Practicing Anthropology*, 12(4): 2, 20.

Plemmons, D., & Albro, R. (2011). Items and Issues. *The Social Science Research Council*. Website. http://itemsandissues.ssrc.org/practicing-ethics-and-ethical-practice-anthropology-science-and-the-social.

Squires, S. (2002). Doing the work: Customer research in the product development and design industry. In S. Squires & B. Byrne (Eds.), *Creating breakthrough ideas: The collection of anthropologists and designers in the product development industry* (pp. 103–124). Westport, CT: Bergin and Garvey.

Tonkinson, R. (1991). *The Mardu Aborigines. Living the dream in Australia's desert* (2nd ed.). Toronto: Holt, Rinehart and Winston.

Weiner, A. (1987). *The Trobrianders of Papua New Guinea*. Toronto: Holt, Rinehart & Winston.

Whitehead, T.L. & Conaway, M.E. (Eds.). (1986). Introduction. *Self, sex, and gender in cross-cultural fieldwork*. Urbana and Chicago: University of Illinois Press.

Wittel, A. (2000). Ethnography on the move: From field to net to internet. *Forum: Qualitative Social Research*, 1(1). Art. 21. http://www.qualitative-research.net/index.php/fqs/article/view/1131/2517.

Young, W.C. (1996). *The Rashaayda Bedouin. Arab Pastoralists of Eastern Sudan*. Fort Worth, TX: Harcourt College Publishers.

Chapter 2: Of What Use Is Anthropology to the Business World? The Anthropology of Shopping

Carrier, J.G. (Ed.). (2005). Introduction. *A handbook of economic anthropology*. Northampton, MA: Edward Elgar Publishing.

Deutsch, C. (1991, Feb. 24). Coping with cultural polyglots. *New York Times*.

Ehn, B., & Löfgren, O. (2009). Ethnography in the marketplace. *Culture Unbound* 1: 31–49. http://www.cultureunbound.ep.liu.se/v1/cu09v1_thematic_section.pdf.

GBN Global Business Network (2005). *GBN: Book Club Books*. http://www.gbn.com/BookClubNewsletterDisplayServlet.srv?dt=0101.

Gladwell, M. (1996, Nov. 4). The science of shopping. *The New Yorker*. http://www.gladwell.com/pdf/shopping.pdf.

Handwerker, W.P. (2002). *Quick ethnography: A guide to rapid multi-method research*. Walnut Creek, CA: AltaMira Press.

Herselman, S. (2008). 'Dabbling in the market': Ideas on 'an anthropology of marketing.' *Anthropology Southern Africa*, *31*(1&2): 39–47.

Jordan, A.T. (2010). The importance of business anthropology: Its unique contributions. *International Journal of Business Anthropology*, *1*(1): 15–24.

Kedia, S. (2008). Recent changes and trends in the practice of applied anthropology. *NAPA Bulletin*, *29*(1): 14–28. http://dx.doi.org/10.1111/j.1556-4797.2008.00002.x

Mankekar, P. (2002). 'India shopping': Indian grocery stores and transnational configurations of belonging. *Ethnos*, *67*(1): 75–97. http://dx.doi.org/10.1080/00141840220122968

Miller, D. (1995a). Consumption as the vanguard of history. In D. Miller (Ed.), *Acknowledging consumption* (pp. 1–52). London: Routledge.

Miller, D. (1995b). Consumption studies as the transformation of anthropology. In D. Miller (Ed.), *Acknowledging consumption* (pp. 264–292). London: Routledge.

Miller, D. (1998). *A theory of shopping*. Cambridge: Polity Press.

Miller, D. (2001). *The dialectics of shopping*. Chicago: The University of Chicago Press.

NAPA (2005). *Excavating consumer habits: Big business for anthropologists*. http://practicinganthropology.org/?newsid=42.

Plattner, S. (1989a). Preface. *Economic anthropology* (pp. ix–xii). Stanford, CA: Stanford University Press.

Plattner, S. (1989b). Markets and marketplaces. In S. Plattner (Ed.), *Economic anthropology* (pp. 171–208). Stanford, CA: Stanford University Press.

Smith, N.C., Klein, J.G., & Kimmell, A.J. (2002). *The ethics of deception in consumer research*. London Business School Centre for Marketing. http://www.london.edu/facultyandresearch/research/docs/02-702b.pdf.

Suchman, L. (2003). *Anthropology is "brand": Reflections on corporate anthropology*. Centre for Science Studies, Lancaster University. http://www.lancs.ac.uk/fass/sociology/papers/suchman-anthropology-as-brand.pdf.

Sunderland, P.L., & Denny, R.M. (2007). *Doing anthropology in consumer research*. Walnut Creek, CA: Left Coast Press. www.lcoastpress.com/book_get_file.php?id=116&type=excerpt.

Underhill, P. (1999). *Why we buy: The science of shopping*. New York: Simon & Schuster.

Underhill, P. (2004). *Call of the mall*. New York: Simon & Schuster.

Wasson, C. (2000). Ethnography in the field of design. *Human Organization*, *59*(4): 377–388.

Chapter 3: What Roles Do Anthropologists and Speech Communities Play in Language Retention and Revitalization?

Abbi, A. (2009). Endangered languages, endangered knowledge: Vanishing voices of the Great Andamanese of India. *Biocultural Diversity Conservation*. http://www.terralingua.org/bcdconservation/?p=125.

Binion, S., & Shook, O. (2007). Endangered languages. Voices on the brink of extinction. *World Literature Today*, *81*(5), 12–14.

Černý, M. (2010). Language death versus language survival: A global perspective. *Beyond globalization: Exploring the limits of globalization in the regional context* (pp. 51–56). http://conference.osu.eu/globalization/publ/06-cerny.pdf.

Ethnologue (2012). Breton. http://www.ethnologue.com/show_language.asp?code=bre.

Fesl, E.M.D. (1993). *Conned!* St Lucia: Queensland University Press.

Fillmore, L.W. (2000). Loss of family languages: Should educators be concerned? *Theory in Practice*, *39*(4): 203–210. http://web.ebscohost.com/ehost/pdfviewer/pdfviewer?sid=8789b5a4-22b0-4c82-a260-d582bf455dac%40sessionmgr4&vid=5&hid=9.

Fishman, J. (1991). *Reversing language shift: Theoretical and empirical foundations of assistance to threatened languages*. Clevedon, UK: Multilingual Matters.

Fishman, J. (1996). What do you lose when you lose your language? In G. Cantoni (Ed.), *Stabilizing Indigenous Languages* (pp. 80–91). http://www.eric.ed.gov/PDFS/ED395732.pdf.

Francis, N., & Nieto Andrade, R. (1996). Stories for language revitalizations in Nahuatl and Chichimeca. *Stabilizing Indigenous Languages* (pp. 162–173). http://www.eric.ed.gov/PDFS/ED395733.pdf.

GaelicMatters.com (2011). *The Gaelic revival—past and present.* http://www.gaelicmatters.com/gaelic-revival.html.

Gallegos, C., Murray, E.M., & Evans, M. (2010). Research note: Comparing indigenous language revitalization: Te reo Māori in Aotearoa New Zealand and Mapudungun in Chile. *Asia Pacific Viewpoint, 51*(1): 91–104. http://dx.doi.org/10.1111/j.1467-8373.2009.01418.x

Goswami, R. (2003, July 31). Globalization challenges Asian languages. *Asian Times.* http://www.atimes.com/atimes/Global_Economy/EG31Dj01.html.

Gray, R. (2012, Feb. 18). Internet may save endangered languages. *The Telegraph.* http://www.telegraph.co.uk/technology/internet/9090885/Internet-may-save-endangered-languages.html.

Haspelmath, M. (1993). In memoriam: Ubykh (Tevfik Esenç). *Circassian World.* http://www.circassianworld.com/new/language/1262-tevfik-esenc-ubykh.html.

Haviland, W.A., Fedorak, S., & Lee, R.B. (2009). *Cultural anthropology* (3rd ed.). Toronto: Nelson Education.

Jacobs, S.L. (2005). Language death and revival after cultural destruction: Reflections on a little discussed aspect of genocide. *Journal of Genocide Research, 7*(3): 423–430. http://dx.doi.org/10.1080/14623520500190371

Khemlani-David, M. (1991). The Sindhis in Malaysia—Language maintenance, language loss or language death? Paper presented at the International Conference on Bilingualism and National Development. http://www.eric.ed.gov/PDFS/ED357632.pdf.

Kouritzen, S.G. (1999). *Face[t]s of the first language loss.* Mahwah, NJ: Lawrence Erlbaum Associates.

Krauss, M. (1992). The world's languages in crisis. *Language, 68*(1): 1–42.

Krauss, M. (1998). The condition of Native North American languages: The need for realistic assessment and action. *International Journal of the Sociology of Language, 132*(1): 9–21. http://dx.doi.org/10.1515/ijsl.1998.132.9

Krauss, M. (n.d.). A loss for words. *Diversity in the age of globalization.* Earthwatch Institute. http://www.wadsworth.com/anthropology_d/special_features/ext/earthwatch/alfw.html.

Laukaitis, J. (2010). The politics of language and national school reform. The Gaelic League's call for an Irish Ireland, 1893–1922. *American Educational History Journal, 37*(1): 221–235. http://web.ebscohost.com/ehost/pdfviewer/pdfviewer?sid=314fd809-3caa-4844-a12d-c254ceb7270d%40sessionmgr10&vid=5&hid=9.

Lemkin, R. (1944). *Axis rule in occupied Europe: Laws of occupation, analysis of government, proposals for redress.* Washington: Carnegie Endowment for International Peace, Division of International Law.

López-Goñi, I. (2003). Ikastola in the twentieth century: An alternative for schooling in the Basque country. *History of Education, 32*(6): 661–676. http://dx.doi.org/10.1080/0046760032000151483

McMahon, T.G. (2008). *Grand opportunity: The Gaelic revival and Irish Society, 1893–1910.* Syracuse: Syracuse University Press.

Messieh, N. (2012). National Geographic brings endangered languages into the digital age, one dictionary at a time. *TNN Media.* http://thenextweb.com/media/2012/02/19/national-geographic-brings-endangered-languages-into-the-digital-age-one-dictionary-at-a-time/.

Munro, M. (2012, Feb. 17). 'Talking dictionary' could help dying languages survives. *Vancouver Sun.* http://www.vancouversun.com/life/Talking+dictionary+could+help+dying+languages+survive/6171976/story.html.

Nahir, M. (1988). Language planning and language acquisition: The "great leap" in the Hebrew revival. In C.B. Paulston (Ed.), *International handbook of bilingualism and bilingual education* (pp. 275–296).Westport, CT: Greenwood Press.

Nettle, D., & Romaine, S. (2000). *Vanishing voices: The extinction of the world's languages.* Oxford: Oxford University Press.

Ostler, N. (2001). Endangered languages—lost worlds. *Contemporary Review, 279*(1631): 349–355. http://web.ebscohost.com/ehost/pdfviewer/pdfviewer?vid=4&hid=9&sid=314 fd809-3caa-4844-a12d-c254ceb727od%40sessionmgr10.

Ottenheimer, H.J. (2009). *Doing linguistic anthropology. The anthropology of language. An introduction to linguistic anthropology* (2nd ed.). Belmont, CA: Wadsworth, Cengage Learning.

Out of the Jungle (2006, May 1). Language nests—Nurturing First Nations languages. *Out of the jungle. Thoughts on the present and future of legal information, legal research, and legal education.* http://outofthejungle.blogspot.ca/2006/05/language-nests-nurturing-first-nation.html.

Raymond, J. (1998, Sept. 14). Say what? Preserving endangered languages. *Newsweek, 132*(11).

Reyhner, J. (1999). Some basics of language revitalization. In J. Reyhner (Ed.), *Revitalizing indigenous languages* (pp. 5–20). Flagstaff: Northern Arizona University.

Sampat, P. (2002). Our planet's languages are dying—World view. *USA Today (Society for the Advancement of Education).* http://findarticles.com/p/articles/mi_m1272/is_2682_130/ai_84184879/.

Solash, R. (2010, Feb. 19). Silent extinction: Language loss reaches crisis levels. *Radio Free Europe.* http://www.rferl.org/content/Silent_Extinction_Language_Loss_Reaches_Crisis_Levels/1963070.html.

Swarthmore News (2012). *K. David Harrison.* http://www.swarthmore.edu/x12040.xml.

van Driem, G. (2007). Endangered languages of South Asia. In M. Brenzinger (Ed.), *Handbook of endangered language* (pp. 303–341). Berlin: Mouton de Gruyter. http://www.himalayanlanguages.org/files/driem/pdfs/2007EndangeredLggsSouthAsia.pdf.

VOGA (n.d.). *Vanishing Voices of the Great Andamanese.* http://www.andamanese.net/media.html.

Yamamoto, A.Y. (1998). Retrospect and prospect on new emerging language communities. In N. Ostler (Ed.), *Endangered languages: What role for the specialist?* (pp. 113–120). Bath, UK: Foundation for Endangered Languages.

Yamamoto, A.Y., Brenzinger, M., & Villalón, M.E. (2008). A place for all languages: On language vitality and revitalization. *Museum International, 60*(3), 60–70. http://dx.doi.org/10.1111/j.1468-0033.2008.00653.x

Zuckermann, G., & Walsh, M. (2011). Stop, revive, survive: Lessons from the Hebrew revival applicable to the reclamation, maintenance and empowerment of aboriginal languages and culture. *Australian Journal of Linguistics, 31*(1): 111–127. http://dx.doi.org/10.1080/07268602.2011.532859

Chapter 4: How Do Living, Studying, and Working in a Foreign Culture Affect People?

Amazon.com Reviews for Pollock, D., & van Reken, R. (2009). *Third culture kids: The experience of growing up among worlds.* http://www.amazon.com/Third-Culture-Kids-Experience-Growing/dp/1857882954.

Appadurai, A. (1991). Global ethnoscapes: Notes on queries for a transnational anthropology. In R. Fox (Ed.), *Recapturing anthropology* (pp. 48–65). Santa Fe, NM: School of American Research Press.

Basch, L., Glick Schiller, N., & Szanton-Blanc, C. (1994). *Nations unbound: Transnational projects, postcolonial predicaments, and deterritorialized nation-states.* Langborne, PA: Gordon & Breach.

Bikos, L.H., Kocheleva, J., King, D., Chang, G.C., McKenzie, A., Roenicke, C., Campbell, V., & Eckard, K. (2009). A consensual qualitative investigation into the repatriation experiences of young adult, missionary kids. *Mental Health, Religion & Culture, 12*(7): 735–754. http://dx.doi.org/10.1080/13674670903032637

Bond, S. (2009). World of learning. Canadian post-secondary students and the study abroad experience. *The Canadian Bureau for International Education.* Ottawa, Ontario. http://www.cbie-bcei.ca/wp-content/uploads/2012/03/20100520_WorldOfLearningReport_e.pdf.

Bowman, D.H. (2012, Jan. 10). Identities blur for 'third-culture kids.' *Education Week.* Editorial Projects in Education. http://www.edweek.org/ew/articles/2001/05/09/34tck.h20.html.

Calderwood, E. (2011). Study abroad. *Harvard Review 10*: 210–218. http://web.ebscohost.com/ehost/detail?sid=88407100-0e61-4469-bfbb-cbfe787604aa%40sessionmgr11&vid=5&hid=12&bdata=JnNpdGU9ZWhvc3QtbGl2ZQ%3d%3d#db=lfh&AN=65083289.

CBC News (2009, Oct. 29). Estimated 2.8 million Canadians live abroad. *CBC News.* http://www.cbc.ca/news/canada/story/2009/10/28/canada-emigration-c.html.

Christofi, V., & Thompson, C.L. (2007). You cannot go home again: A phenomenological investigation of returning to the sojourn country after studying abroad. *Journal of Counseling and Development, 85*(1): 53–63. http://dx.doi.org/10.1002/j.1556-6678.2007.tb00444.x

Cottrell, A.B., & Useem, R.H. (1993a). TCKs experience prolonged adolescence. News/Articles Third Culture Kids: Focus of Major Study. http://www.tckworld.com/useem/art3.html.

Cottrell, A.B., & Useem, R.H. (1993b). ATCKs maintain global dimensions throughout their lives. http://www.tckworld.com/useem/art5.html.

Farrar, L. (2009). 50% of new expats leave China early. *China Daily.* http://www.chinadaily.com.cn/metro/2009-10/30/content_8873247.htm.

Fechter, A.M. (2007). *Transnational lives: Expatriates in Indonesia.* Aldershot, UK: Ashgate.

Gould, J.B. (2002). Review of *The third culture kid experiences* by David C. Pollock and Ruth E. van Reken (1999), and *Letters I never wrote* by R.E. van Reken (1986). *Journal of Loss and Trauma, 7,* 151–156.

Heyward, M. (2002). From international to intercultural: Redefining the international school for a globalized world. *Journal of Research in International Education, 1*(1): 9–32. http://jri.sagepub.com/cgi/content/abstract/1/1/9.

Hill, B.V. (1986). The educational needs of children of expatriates. *Missiology: An International Review, XIV*: 326–346.

Just Landed (2009). Expatriates worldwide. How many expats are there? *Just Landed.* Website. http://www.justlanded.com/english/Common/Footer/Expatriates/How-many-expats-are-there.

Kearney, M. (1995). The local and the global: Anthropology of globalization and transnationalism. *Annual Review of Anthropology 24*: 547–65. http://www.annualreviews.org/doi/abs/10.1146/annurev.an.24.100195.002555?journalCode=anthro.

Kebshull, B., & Pozo-Humphries, M. (n.d.). Third culture kids/Global nomads and the culturally skilled therapist. http://clinicalsocialworksociety.org/docs/continuing_education/ThirdCultureKids.pdf.

Keuss, J.F., & Willett, R. (2009). The sacredly mobile adolescent: A hermeneutic phenomenological study toward revising of the Third Culture Kid typology for effective ministry practice in a multivalent culture. *Journal of Youth Ministry, 8*(1): 7–24.

King, D. (Ed.). (1991). *Culture, globalization and the world-system: Contemporary conditions for the representation of identity.* Binghamton: State University of New York Press.

Klemens, M.J., & Bikos, L.H. (2009). Psychology well-being and sociocultural adaptation in college-aged, repatriated, missionary kids. *Mental Health, Religion & Culture, 12*(7): 721–733. http://dx.doi.org/10.1080/13674670903032629

Langford, M. (1998). Global nomads, third culture kids and international schools. In M. Hayden & J. Thompson (Eds.), *International Education Principles and Practice* (pp. 28–43).

Miller, A. (2010, Nov. 15). How many Americans study abroad each year? http://www.quora.com/How-many-Americans-study-abroad-each-year.

Miller, E.J. (1993). Culture shock: A student's perspective of study abroad and the importance of promoting study abroad programs. *A paper presented at the 10th Annual Intercultural and International Communication Conference*, Miami, Florida. https://files.nyu.edu/jrc363/public/df.pdf.

Nolan, R.W. (1990). Culture shock and cross-cultural adaptation: Or I was okay until I got here. *Practicing Anthropology 12*(4): 2, 20.

Oberg, K. (1960). Culture shock: Adjustments to new cultural environments. *Practicing Anthropology, 7*: 177–182.

Pollock, D.C., & van Reken, R.E. (2009). *Third culture kids: The experience of growing up among worlds.* London: Nicholas Brealey & Intercultural Press.

Rao, V., & Walton, M. (2004). Transnationalism and globalization. *Culture and Public Action.* http://www.cultureandpublicaction.org/conference/cc_transnationalism.htm.

Ridout, A. (2010). "The view from the threshold": Doris Lessing's Nobel Acceptance Speech. *Doris Lessing Studies, 29*(1): 4–8.

Thigpen, N. (2010). *American expatriate teachers in China.* Unpublished Master's thesis. http://digilib.gmu.edu:8080/dspace/handle/1920/5867.

Uehara, A. (1983). The nature of American student re-entry adjustment and perceptions of the sojourner experience. *International Journal of Intercultural Relations 10*: 415–438. http://studyabroad.rutgers.edu/_customtags/ct_FileRetrieve.cfm?File_ID=0006764804030A7B77017 2001A0B700009140209710D1C727301740672067D0B02727272010001.

Useem, R. H. (1993, Jan.). TCK "mother" pens history of field. News/Articles Third Culture Kids: Focus of Major Study. http://www.tckworld.com/useem/art1.html.

Vertovec, S. & Cohen, R. (Eds.). (2002). *Conceiving cosmopolitanism: Theory, context, and practice.* Oxford: Oxford University Press.

Ward, C., Bochner, S., & Furnham, A. (2001). *The psychology of culture shock* (2nd ed.). Philadelphia: Taylor & Francis.

Young, W.C. (1996). *The Rashaayda Bedouin: Arab pastoralists of Eastern Sudan.* Toronto: Harcourt Bracc College Publishers.

Chapter 5: What Are the Underlying Reasons for Ethnic Conflict, and the Consequences of These Conflicts?

Adam, G.A. (2008). Why has Darfur's indigenous population been put at risk? *Peace Review: A Journal of Social Justice 20*(20): 158–165.

AlertNet (2011, April 19). At a glance. *AlertNet. The World's humanitarian news site.* A Thomson Reuters Foundation Service. http://www.trust.org/alertnet/crisis-centre/crisis/darfur-conflict.

Ali, W. (2007, July 16). Photos: Images from Darfur crisis published for first time. *The Sudan Tribune.* www.sudantribune.com/PHOTOS-Images-from-Darfur-crises,%22874.

American Anthropological Association (2004, Dec.). Statement on the humanitarian crisis in Darfur, Sudan. Draft copy. http://www.aaanet.org/committees/cfhr/stmt_darfur.htm.

Apsel, J. (2009). The complexity of destruction in Darfur: Historical processes and regional dynamics. *Human Rights Review, 10*(2): 239–259. http://dx.doi.org/10.1007/s12142-008-0099-6

Avlon, J. (2011, Feb. 20). A 21st century statesman. *The Daily Beast. World News.* http://www.thedailybeast.com/newsweek/2011/02/20/a-21st-century-statesman.html.

Baker, R. (1983). *The psychosocial problems of refugees.* British Refugee Council and European Consultation on Refugees and Exiles. Luton: L and T Press.

BBC News. (2006, Dec. 6). Darfur conflict zones map. *BBC News.* http://news.bbc.co.uk/2/hi/africa/6213202.stm.

BBC News. (2008, Dec. 17). Thousands made slaves in Darfur. *BBC News World.* Photo. http://www.thewe.cc/contents/more/archive/darfur_sudan.html.

Ben-Ezer, G. (1990, Oct.). Anorexia nervosa or an Ethiopian coping style? *Mind and Human Interaction, 2*(2): 16–19.

Bowen, J.R. (1996). The myth of global ethnic conflict. *Journal of Democracy, 7*(4): 3–14. http://dx.doi.org/10.1353/jod.1996.0057

Bringa, T. (1995). *Being Muslim the Bosnian way.* Princeton, NJ: Princeton University Press.

Brubaker, R. (2004). *Ethnicity without groups.* Cambridge, MA: Harvard University Press.

Burr, J.M., & Collins, R.O. (2006). *Darfur: The long road to disaster.* Princeton: Markus Weiner Publishers.

Cheney, B. (2000, Oct. 28). *Ukrainian Immigration.* http://www.mbnet.mb.ca/~rfmorris/Featuring/Immigration/Ukrainian.Immigration.html.

Colson, E. (1989). Overview. *Annual Review of Anthropology, 18*(1): 1–17. http://dx.doi.org/10.1146/annurev.an.18.100189.000245

Crawford, B. (1998). The causes of cultural conflict: An institutional approach. In B. Crawford & R.D. Lipschutz (Eds.), *The myth of ethnic conflict: Politics, economics and "cultural" violence* (pp. 3–43). Berkeley: University of California.

Davis, J. (1992). The anthropology of suffering. *Journal of Refugee Studies, 5*(2): 149–161. http://dx.doi.org/10.1093/jrs/5.2.149

De Vos, G.A. (1995). Concepts of ethnic identity. In L. Romanucci-Ross & G.A. De Vos (Eds.), *Ethnic identity, creation, conflict, and accommodation* (3rd ed., pp. 15–47). Walnut Creek, CA: AltaMira Press.

Dreyer, J.T. (2003). Taiwan's evolving identity. *Paper presented at Woodrow Wilson International Institute for Scholars, Washington, DC.* http://formosafoundation.org/pdf/Taiwan's%20Identity%20(J_Dreyer).pdf.

D'Souza, F. (1981). *The refugee dilemma: International recognition and acceptance.* London Minority Rights Group No.43.

Eller, J.D. (1999). *From culture to ethnicity to conflict. An anthropological perspective on international ethnic conflict.* Ann Arbor: The University of Michigan Press.

Fenton, S. (2003). *Ethnicity.* Cambridge: Polity Press.

Harrell-Bond, B.E. (1986). *Imposing aid: Emergency assistance to refugees.* Oxford: Oxford University Press.

Harrell-Bond, B.E., & Voutira, E. (1992). Anthropology and the study of refugees. *Anthropology Today, 8*(4): 6–10. http://dx.doi.org/10.2307/2783530

Haviland, W.A., Fedorak, S.A., & Lee, R.B. (2009). *Cultural anthropology* (3rd Cdn. ed.). Toronto: Nelson Education.

Henshaw, A. (2008, Oct. 28). Trapped in Darfur refugee camp. *BBC News.* http://news.bbc.co.uk/2/hi/africa/7685248.stm.

Hinton, A.L. (2002). *Annihilating difference: The anthropology of genocide.* Berkeley: University of California Press.

Human Rights Watch (2004). *Refugees and displaced persons.* http://info.jpost.com/C003/Supplements/Refugees/3.html.

Israel, J. (Ed.). (2004). Why are we dredging up Croatia's past? The media suppressed the truth about the rebirth of Croatian fascism. *The Emperor's Clothes.* http://emperors-clothes.com/analysis/toronto.htm.

Jerusalem Post (Feb. 2003). Refugees forever—A global issue. *The Jerusalem Post.* http://www.freerepublic.com/focus/news/838625/posts.

Malkki, L. (1990). Context and consciousness: Local conditions for the production of historical and national thought among Hutu refugees in Tanzania. In R.G. Fox (Ed.), *Nationalist ideologies and the production of national cultures.* Chicago: University of Chicago Press.

Markakis, J. (1998). *Introduction. Resource conflict in the Horn of Africa.* London: Sage Publications.

Mayroz, E. (2008). Ever again? The United States, genocide suppression, and the crisis in Darfur. *Journal of Genocide Research, 10*(3): 359–388. http://dx.doi.org/10.1080/14623520802305735

Miyares, I.M., & Airries, C.A. (2007). *Contemporary ethnic geographies in America.* Lanham, MD: Rowman & Littlefield Publishers.

Mulaj, K. (2008). Forced displacement in Darfur, Sudan. *Journal Compilation.* Oxford: Blackwell Publishing.

New York Times. (2011, Dec. 6). Sudan. *The New York Times World.* http://topics.nytimes.com/top/news/international/countriesandterritories/sudan/index.html.

Omari, C.K. (1987). Ethnicity, politics and development in Tanzania. *African Study Monographs, 7*: 65–80.

O'Neill, K.L. (2004). Review of the book *Annihilating difference: The anthropology of genocide,* A.L. Hinton, (ed). (2002). *American Ethnologist 31*(3).

Parkington, J.E. (1984). Soaqua and bushmen: Hunters and robbers. In C. Schrire (Ed.), *Past and present in hunter-gatherer studies* (pp. 151–174). New York: Academic Press.

Power, S. (2004, Aug. 24). Dying in Darfur: Can the ethnic cleansing in Sudan be stopped? *The New Yorker,* 61.

Raghaven, S. (2004, July 31). Militias in Sudan are burning people alive, aid worker says. *Knight Ridder Newspapers*. http://www.freerepublic.com/focus/f-news/1182918/posts.

Ter-Gabrielian, G. (1999). Strategies in "ethnic" conflict. *The Fourth World Journal*. http://www.uni-muenster.de/Politikwissenschaft/Doppeldiplom/docs/CWIS%20-%20The%20Fourth%20World%20Journal%20-%20Strategies%20in%20Ethnic%20Confl.htm.

UN News Centre (2010, July 11). Darfur: Conflict claimed more than 200 lives in June, UN-African mission reports. *UN News Service*. http://www.un.org/apps/news/story.asp?NewsID=35290&Cr=darfur&Cr1.

U.S. Department of State (2007). *Darfur, Sudan: Confirmed damaged and destroyed villages.* Humanitarian Information Unit. http://hiu.state.gov.

Wadlow, R. (2005, Aug. 24). Darfur, Sudan: The overkill. *Toward freedom. A progressive perspective on world events since 1952.* http://towardfreedom.com/home/content/view/557/63/.

Waldron, S. (1988). Working in the dark: Why social anthropological research is essential in refugee administration. *Journal of Refugee Studies*, *1*(2): 153–165. http://dx.doi.org/10.1093/jrs/1.2.153

Welling, J.J. (2007, Spring). Non-governmental organizations, prevention, and intervention in internal conflict: Through the lens of Darfur. *Indiana Journal of Global Legal Studies*, *14*(1): 147–179. http://dx.doi.org/10.2979/GLS.2007.14.1.147

World Savvy Monitor (2008, May). The situation in Sudan and the conflict in Darfur. http://worldsavvy.org/monitor/index.php?option=com_content&view=article&id=65&Itemid=934.

World without Genocide (2011). Darfur genocide. *World without Genocide. At William Mitchell College of Law.* http://worldwithoutgenocide.org/current-conflicts/darfur-genocide.

Chapter 6: How Does Body Image Affect Self-Esteem, Well-Being, and Identity?

Altabe, M., & O'Garo, K. (2002). Hispanic body images. In T.F. Cash & T. Pruzinsky (Eds.), *Body image: A handbook of theory, research, and clinical practice* (pp. 250–256). New York: The Guilford Press.

Bonetti, D. (n.d.). Review of *Modern primitives.* http://www.researchpubs.com/books/primprod.php.

Bourdieu, P. (1977). *Outline of a theory of practice.* Cambridge: Cambridge University Press.

Brewis, A.A. (1999). The accuracy of attractive-body-size judgment. *Current Anthropology*, *40*(4): 548–552. http://dx.doi.org/10.1086/200052

Bruch, H. (1978). *The golden age: The enigma of anorexia nervosa.* New York: Vintage.

Brumberg, J.J. (1989). *Fasting girls: The surprising history of anorexia nervosa.* New York: New American Library.

Cash, T.F. & Pruzinsky, T. (Eds.). (2002). *Body image: A handbook of theory, research, and clinical practice.* New York: Guilford.

Counihan, C.M. (1999). *The anthropology of food and body: Gender, meaning, and power.* New York: Routledge.

Crook, M. (1991). *The body image trap: Understanding and rejecting body image myths.* North Vancouver, BC: International Self-Counsel Press.

Cudd, A.E. (2005). Missionary positions. *Hypatia.* http://www.infotrac.galegroup.com.

Cyberpunkreview.com (2006 June 8). *Experiences in body modification.* http://www.cyberpunkreview.com/cyberpunked-living/experiences-in-body-modification/.

Edut, O. (1998). Introduction. In O. Edut (Ed.), *Adios, Barbie: Young women write about body image and identity.* Seattle: Seal Press.

Ferguson, C.J., Munoz, M.E., Contreras, S., & Velasquez, K. (2011). Mirror, mirror on the wall: Peer competition, television influences, and body image dissatisfaction. *Journal of Social and Clinical Psychology*, *30*(5): 458–483. http://dx.doi.org/10.1521/jscp.2011.30.5.458

Gilman, S.J. (1998). Klaus Barbie, and other dolls I'd like to see. In O. Edut (Ed.), *Adios, Barbie: Young women write about body image and identity* (pp. 14–21). Seattle: Seal Press.

Gordon, R.A. (2000). *Eating disorders: Anatomy of a social epidemic* (2nd ed.). Oxford: Blackwell.

Gordon, R.A. (2001). Eating disorders East and West: A culture-bound syndrome unbound. In M. Nasser, M.A. Katzman, & R.A. Gordon (Eds.), *Eating disorders and cultures in transition* (pp. 1–15). New York: Brunner-Routledge.

Henderson, M. (2006, June 23). Ancient bling pushes back frontier of intelligence 25,000 years. *The Times* (London). http://web.ebscohost.com/ehost/detail?vid=6&hid=24&sid=5c023df6–25d8–4bfd-a3a6–547ccooad559%40sessionmgr11&bdata=JnNpdGU9ZWhvc3QtbGl2ZQ%3d%3d#db=nfh&AN=7EH1371431215.

Hesse-Biber, S. (1996). *Am I thin enough yet? The cult of thinness and the commercialization of identity*. New York: Oxford University Press.

Holmberg, C.B. (1998). *Sexualities and popular culture*. Thousand Oaks, CA: Sage Publications.

Jenks, C. (2003). *Transgression*. London: Routledge.

Kaplan-Myrth, N. (2000). Alice without a looking glass: Blind people and body image. *Anthropology & Medicine, 7*(3): 277–299. http://dx.doi.org/10.1080/713650612

Katzman, M.A., Hermans, K.M.E., Van Hoeken, D., & Hoek, H.W. (2004, Dec.). Not your "typical island woman": Anorexia nervosa is reported only in subcultures in Curaçao. *Culture, Medicine and Psychiatry, 28*(4): 463–492. http://dx.doi.org/10.1007/s11013-004-1065-7 Medline:15847051

Kawamura, K.Y. (2002). Asian American body images. In T.F. Cash & T. Pruzinsky (Eds.), *Body image: A handbook of theory, research, and clinical practice* (pp. 243–249). New York: The Guilford Press.

Kleese, C. (2007). Racializing the politics of transgression: Body modification in queer culture. *Social Semiotics 17*(3): 275–292. http://web.ebscohost.com/ehost/detail?vid=7&hid=24&sid=5c023df6–25d8–4bfd-a3a6–547ccooad559%40sessionmgr11&bdata=JnNpdGU9ZWhvc3QtbGl2ZQ%3d%3d#db=aqh&AN=25915313.

Lee, D. (1959). *Freedom and culture*. Prospect Heights, IL: Waveland Press.

Lee, S. (2001). Fat phobia in anorexia nervosa: Whose obsession is it? In M. Nasser, M.A. Katzman, & R.A. Gordon (Eds.), *Eating disorders and cultures in transition* (pp. 40–65). New York: Brunner-Routledge.

Littlewood, R. (2004). Commentary: Globalization, culture, body image, and eating disorders. *Culture, Medicine and Psychiatry, 28*(4): 597–601. http://dx.doi.org/10.1007/s11013-004-1069-3

Mackenzie, M. (1991). Reviews of the books *Fasting girls: The emergence of anorexia nervosa as a modern disease*; *Fasting girls: The surprising history of anorexia nervosa*; *!Que Gordita! A study of weight among women in a Puerto Rican community*; and *Never too thin: Why women are at war with their bodies*. *Medical Anthropology Quarterly, 5*(4): 406–410. http://dx.doi.org/10.1525/maq.1991.5.4.02a00080

Massara, E.B. (1989). *Que Gordita! A study of weight among women in a Puerto Rican community*. Immigrant Communities and Ethnic Minorities in the United States and Canada, No. 46. New York: AMS Press.

Mirante, E. (2006). The dragon mothers polish their metal coils. *Guernica. A magazine of art and politics*. http://www.guernicamag.com/features/229/the_dragon_mothers/.

Nichter, M., & Vuckovic, N. (1994). Fat talk: Body image among adolescent girls. In N. Sault (Ed.), *Many mirrors: Body image and social relations* (pp. 109–131). New Brunswick, NJ: Rutgers University Press.

Orbach, S. (2001, June 24). Give us back our bodies. *Observer*. http://observer.guardian.co.uk/comment/story/0,6903,511730,00.html.

Pike, K.M., & Borovoy, A. (2004, Dec.). The rise of eating disorders in Japan: Issues of culture and limitations of the model of "westernization." *Culture, Medicine and Psychiatry, 28*(4): 493–531. http://dx.doi.org/10.1007/s11013-004-1066-6 Medline:15847052

Ping, W. (2000). *Aching for beauty: Footbinding in China*. Minneapolis: University of Minnesota Press.

Pitts, V.L. (2000). Visibly queer: Body technologies and sexual politics. *Sociological Quarterly, 41*(3): 443–463. http://dx.doi.org/10.1111/j.1533-8525.2000.tb00087.x Medline:19569274

Pitts, V.L. (2003). *In the flesh. The cultural politics of body modification*. Basingstoke, UK: Houndsmill.

Rasmussen, S.J. (2010, Dec.). Remaking body politics: Dilemmas over female fatness as symbolic capital in two rural Tuareg communities. *Culture, Medicine and Psychiatry, 34*(4): 615–632. http://dx.doi.org/10.1007/s11013-010-9193-8 Medline:20835886

Sargent, J. (n.d.). *Judy's story.* http://www.angelfire.com/ms/anorexianervosa/.

Sault, N. (1994). Introduction: The human mirror. In N. Sault (Ed.), *Many mirrors: Body image and social relations* (pp. 1–28). New Brunswick, NJ: Rutgers University Press.

Simmons, A.M. (1998). Where fat is a mark of beauty. *Los Angeles Times.* Reprinted in E. Angeloni (Ed.), *Annual Editions Anthropology: 05/06* (2005). Dubuque, IA: McGraw-Hill/Dushkin.

The Talk. (2012, March 21). CBS.

Trampe, D., Stapel, D.A., & Siero, F.W. (2007, Jan.). On models and vases: body dissatisfaction and proneness to social comparison effects. *Journal of Personality and Social Psychology, 92*(1): 106–118. http://dx.doi.org/10.1037/0022-3514.92.1.106 Medline:17201546

van Esterik, P. (2001). Commentary. In M. Nasser, M.A. Katzman, & R.A. Gordon (Eds.), *Eating disorders and cultures in transition* (pp. 20–21). New York: Brunner-Routledge.

Viviani, F., Lavazza, A., & Gallo, P.G. (2004). Body image and growth aspects in male adolescent basketball players. *Papers on Anthropology, XIII*: 294–298.

Wykes, M., & Gunter, B. (2005). *The media and body image.* London: Sage Publications.

Young, W. (1994). The body tamed: Tying and tattooing among the Rashaayda Bedouin. In N. Sault (Ed.), *Many mirrors: Body image and social relations* (pp. 58–75). New Brunswick, NJ: Rutgers University Press.

Chapter 7: Is Female Circumcision a Violation of Human Rights or a Cherished Cultural Tradition?

Abusharaf, R.M. (2006). "We have supped so deep in horrors": Understanding colonialist emotionality and British response to female circumcision in Northern Sudan. *History and Anthropology, 17*(3): 209–228. http://dx.doi.org/10.1080/02757200600813908

Ahmadu, F. (2000). Rites and wrongs: An insider/outsider reflects on power and excision. In B. Shell-Duncan & Y. Hernlund (Eds.), *Female "circumcision" in Africa: Culture: controversy, and change* (pp. 283–312). London: Lynne Rienner Publishers.

Al Jazeera English. (2011, May 25). *People & Power* broadcast.

Althaus, F.A. (1997). Special report. Female circumcision: Rite of passage or violation of rights? *Family Planning Perspectives, 23*(3): 1–9. http://www.guttmacher.org/pubs/journals/2313097.html.

Amnesty International (1997). *Female genital mutilation in Africa: Information by country.* http://www.amnesty.org/library/index/ENGACT770071997.

Asad, T. (1996). On torture, or cruel, inhuman and degrading treatment. *Social Research, 63*(3): 1081–1109.

Assaad, M.B. (1980, Jan.). Female circumcision in Egypt: social implications, current research, and prospects for change. *Studies in Family Planning, 11*(1): 3–16. http://dx.doi.org/10.2307/1965892 Medline:7376234

Blackburn-Evans, A. (2002). Women's rites: Janice Boddy explores a shocking tradition in northern Sudan. *Edge* 3(2). http://www.research.utoronto.ca/edge/fa112002/leaders/boddy.html.

Boddy, J. (1982). Womb as oasis: The symbolic content of pharaonic circumcision in rural northern Sudan. *American Ethnologist, 9*(4): 682–698. http://dx.doi.org/10.1525/ae.1982.9.4.02a00040

Coleman, D.L. (1998). The Seattle compromise: Multicultural sensitivity and Americanization. *Duke Law Journal, 47*(4): 717–783. http://dx.doi.org/10.2307/1372912

The Economist (US). (1999, Feb. 13). 350(8106): 45.

El Dareer, A. (1982). *Woman, why do you weep? Circumcision and its consequences.* London: Zed Press.

Equality Now (1996, April 1). United States: Female Genital Mutilation and Political Asylum—The Case of Fauziya Kasinga. http://www.equalitynow.org/take_action/asylum_action91.

Erickson, A., Hayes, M., Sabatke, S., Vargo, R., & Wall, J. (2001). *Ethics in anthropology: Public presentation of anthropological material.* University of Minnesota. http://www.d.umn.edu/~lbelote/Senior_Seminar/PublicAnth-ethics_in_anthropology.htm.

Ginsburg, F. (1991). What do women want? Feminist anthropology confronts clitoridectomy. *Medical Anthropology Quarterly, 5*(1): 17–19. http://dx.doi.org/10.1525/maq.1991.5.1.02a00030

Gordon, R. (1991). Female circumcision and genital operations in Egypt and the Sudan: A dilemma for medical anthropologists. *Medical Anthropology Quarterly*, *5*(1): 3–14. http://dx.doi.org/10.1525/maq.1991.5.1.02a00010

Gruenbaum, E. (1982). The movement against clitoridectomy and infibulation in Sudan: Public health policy and the women's movement. *Medical Anthropology Newsletter*, *13*(2): 4–12. http://dx.doi.org/10.1525/maq.1982.13.2.02a00020

Gruenbaum, E. (2000). Is female "circumcision" a maladaptive cultural pattern? In B. Shell-Duncan & Y. Hernlund (Eds.), *Female circumcision in Africa: Culture, controversy, and change* (pp. 41–54). London: Lynne Rienner Publishers.

Gruenbaum, E. (2005, Sept.–Oct.). Socio-cultural dynamics of female genital cutting: Research findings, gaps, and directions. *Culture, Health & Sexuality*, *7*(5): 429–441. http://dx.doi.org/10.1080/13691050500262953 Medline:16864214

Hernlund, Y. (2000). Cutting without ritual and ritual without cutting: Female "circumcision" and the re-ritualization of initiation in the Gambia. In B. Shell-Duncan & Y. Hernlund (Eds.), *Female "circumcision" in Africa: Culture, controversy, and change* (pp. 235–252). London: Lynne Rienner Publishers.

Hills-Young, E. (1943). *Female circumcision in the Sudan: The surgical seal of chastity.* Durham University Library Special Collections Archive: SAD #631/3/36G … S437.

Howell, S. (2010). Norwegian academic anthropologists in public spaces. *Current Anthropology*, *51*(S2): S269–S277. http://dx.doi.org/10.1086/652907

Johnson, M.C. (2000). Becoming a Muslim, becoming a person: Female "circumcision," religious identity, and personhood in Guinea-Bissau. In B. Shell-Duncan & Y. Hernlund (Eds.), *Female "circumcision" in Africa: Culture, controversy, and change* (pp. 215–234). London: Lynne Rienner Publishers.

Leonard, L. (2000). Adopting female "circumcision" in southern Chad: The experience of Myab. In B. Shell-Duncan & Y. Hernlund (Eds.), *Female "circumcision" in Africa: Culture, controversy, and change* (pp. 167–192). London: Lynne Rienner Publishers.

Londoño-Sulkin, C.D. (2009). Anthropology, liberalism and female genital cutting. *Anthropology Today*, *25*(6): 17–19. http://dx.doi.org/10.1111/j.1467-8322.2009.00700.x

Low, S.M., & Merry, S.E. (2010). Engaged anthropology: Diversity and dilemmas: An introduction to supplement 2. *Current Anthropology*, *51*(S2), S203–S226. http://dx.doi.org/10.1086/653837

Lutkekaus, N.C., & Roscoe, P.B. (1995). *Gender rituals: Female initiation in Melanesia.* New York: Routledge.

Mackie, G. (2000). Female genital cutting: The beginning of the end. In B. Shell-Duncan & Y. Hernlund (Eds.), *Female "circumcision" in Africa: Culture, controversy, and change* (pp. 253–282). London: Lynne Rienner Publishers.

Martinez, S. (2005). Searching for a middle path: Rights, capabilities, and political culture in the study of female genital cutting. *Ahfad Journal*, *22*(1): 31–44.

Masland, T. (1999, July 5). The ritual of pain. In Uganda, tradition overpowers a United Nations drive against female genital mutilation. *Newsweek.*

Morsy, S.A. (1991). Safeguarding women's bodies: The white man's burden medicalized. *Medical Anthropology Quarterly*, *5*(1): 19–23. http://dx.doi.org/10.1525/maq.1991.5.1.02a00040

Moruzzi, N.C. (2005). Cutting through culture: The feminist discourse on female circumcision. *Critical Middle Eastern Studies*, *14*(2): 203–220. http://dx.doi.org/10.1080/10669920500135587

Obermeyer, C.M. (2003, Sept.). The health consequences of female circumcision: Science, advocacy, and standards of evidence. *Medical Anthropology Quarterly*, *17*(3): 394–412. http://dx.doi.org/10.1525/maq.2003.17.3.394 Medline:12974204

Orubuloye, I.O., Caldwell, P., & Caldwell, J.C. (2000). Female circumcision among the Yoruba of southwestern Nigeria: The beginning of change. In B. Shell-Duncan & Y. Hernlund (Eds.), *Female "circumcision" in Africa: Culture, controversy, and change* (pp. 73–94). London: Lynne Rienner Publishers.

Rahlenbeck, S., Mekonnen, W., & Melkamu, Y. (2010, June). Female genital cutting starts to decline among women in Oromia, Ethiopia. *Reproductive Biomedicine Online*, *20*(7): 867–872. http://dx.doi.org/10.1016/j.rbmo.2010.01.009 Medline:20400376

Sargent, C. (1991). Confronting patriarchy: The potential of advocacy in medical anthropology. *Medical Anthropology Quarterly*, 5(1): 24–25. http://dx.doi.org/10.1525/maq.1991.5.1.02a00050

Shandall, A.A. (1967). Circumcision and infibulation of females: A general consideration of the problem and a clinical study of the complications in Sudanese women. *Sudan Medical Journal*, 5(4): 178–212. Medline:12259304

Shell-Duncan, B. (2001, April). The medicalization of female "circumcision": harm reduction or promotion of a dangerous practice? *Social Science & Medicine*, 52(7): 1013–1028. http://dx.doi.org/10.1016/S0277-9536(00)00208-2 Medline:11266046

Shell-Duncan, B., & Hernlund, Y. (2000). Female 'circumcision' in Africa: Dimensions of the practice and debates. In B. Shell-Duncan & Y. Hernlund (Eds.), *Female "circumcision" in Africa: Culture, controversy, and change* (pp. 1–40). London: Lynne Rienner Publishers.

Shell-Duncan, B., Obiero, W.O., & Muruli, L.A. (2000). Women without choices: The debate over medicalization of female genital cutting and its impact on a Northern Kenyan community. In B. Shell-Duncan & Y. Hernlund (Eds.), *Female "circumcision" in Africa: Culture, controversy, and change* (pp. 109–128). London: Lynne Rienner Publishers.

Shweder, R.A. (2009). Disputing the myth of the sexual dysfunction of circumcised women. An interview with Fuambai S. Ahmadu. *Anthropology Today*, 25(6): 14–17. http://dx.doi.org/10.1111/j.1467-8322.2009.00699.x

Thomas, L. (2000). Ngaitana. I will circumcise myself: Lessons from colonial campaigns to ban excision in Meru, Kenya. In B. Shell-Duncan & Y. Hernlund (Eds.), *Female "circumcision" in Africa: Culture, controversy, and change* (pp. 129–150). London: Lynne Rienner Publishers.

Toubia, N. (Ed.) (1988). *Women of the Arab world: The coming challenge.* Papers of the Arab Women's Solidarity Association Conference. Atlantic Highlands, NJ: Zed Books.

Toubia, N., & Izette, S. (1998). *Female genital mutilation: An overview.* Geneva: World Health Organization.

Chapter 8: What Are the Socio-economic, Religious, and Political Implications of Same-sex Marriage and Changing Family Structure?

American Anthropological Association (AAA) (2004, Feb. 26). *Statement on marriage and the family.* http://www.aaanet.org/issues/policy-advocacy/Statement-on-Marriage-and-the-Family.cfm.

Awom, U., & Ukaibe, C. (2011, Nov. 1). Nigeria: Same sex marriage, a taboo. *AllAfrica.* http://allafrica.com/stories/201111010623.html.

Baird, R.M. & Rosenbaum, S.E. (Eds.). (1997). *Same-sex marriage: The moral and legal debate.* Amherst, NY: Prometheus Books.

Baskerville, S. (2006). Politics and same-sex marriage. *Society*, 44(1): 60–66. http://dx.doi.org/10.1007/BF02690469

BBC News. (2005, June 30). *Gay marriage around the globe.* http://news.bbc.co.uk/1/hi/world/americas/4081999.stm.

Bonvillain, N. (1998). *Women and men: Cultural constructs of gender* (2nd ed.). Upper Saddle River, NJ: Prentice Hall.

Burns, K. (Ed.). (2005). *Gay marriage.* Farmington Hills, MI: Thomson Gale.

Cathcart, T. (2012, Feb. 27). Gay marriage bills gains momentum, public support. *The DePaulia.* http://www.usfsp.edu/~jsokolov/2410gaymar1.htm.

CNN World (2009, Dec. 21). Mexico City legalizes same-sex marriage, adoptions. *CNN World.* http://articles.cnn.com/2009–12–21/world/mexico.gay.marriage_1_same-sex-civil-unions-union-between-two-people-legalizes?_s=PM:WORLD.

Coward, C. (2012, Jan. 23). The effect of the taboo against same-sex marriage in Nigeria. *Changing Attitude.* http://changingattitude.org.uk/archives/4983.

Demian. (2005). Marriage traditions in various times and cultures. http://www.buddybuddy.com/mar-trad.html.

Duggan, L. (2002). The new homonormativity: The sexual politics of neoliberalism. In R. Castronovo & D. Nelson (Eds.), *Materializing democracy: Toward a revitalized cultural politics* (pp. 175–194). Durham, NC: Duke University Press.

Eskridge, W.N. (1996). *The case for same-sex marriage.* http://www.simonsays.com/titles/0684824043/sameex1c.html.

Evans-Pritchard, E.E. (1974). *Man and woman among the Azande.* London: Faber and Faber.

Flaks, D.K., Ficher, I., Masterpasqua, F., & Joseph, G. (2004). Lesbians choosing motherhood: A comparative study of lesbian and heterosexual parents and their children. In A. Sullivan (Ed.), *Same-sex marriage: Pro and con* (pp. 246–249). New York: Vintage Books. Previously published in *Developmental Psychology, 31.1* (1995): 105–114, http://dx.doi.org/10.1037//0012-1649.31.1.105

Gay Bears (2002). *Alfred Kroeber.* University of California. http://sunsite.berkeley.edu/gaybears/kroeber/.

Green, A.I. (2010). Queer unions: Same-sex spouses marrying tradition and innovation. *Canadian Journal of Sociology, 35*(3): 399–436.

Gullo, K. (2012, Feb. 21). California gay marriage ban supporters ask panel to reinstate voided law. *Bloomberg.* http://www.bloomberg.com/news/2012–02–21/california-gay-marriage-ban-supporters-seek-appeal-rehearing-1-.html.

Haviland, W.A., Fedorak, S.A., & Lee, R.B. (2009). *Cultural anthropology* (3rd Cdn. ed.). Toronto: Nelson Education.

Herskovits, M.J. (2004). A note on "woman marriage" in Dahomey. In A. Sullivan (Ed.), *Same-sex marriage: Pro and con* (pp. 32–35). New York: Vintage Books.

Josephson, J. (2005). Citizenship, same-sex marriage, and feminist critiques of marriage. *Perspectives on Politics, 3*(02): 269–284. http://dx.doi.org/10.1017/S1537592705050206

Knauft, B. (2005). *The Gebusi: Lives transformed in a rainforest world.* Toronto: McGraw-Hill.

Kroeber, A. (1925). *Handbook of the Indians of California. Bulletin 78. Bureau of American Ethnology.* Washington: Smithsonian Institute.

Lahey, K., & Alderson, A. (2004). *Same-sex marriage. The personal and the political.* Toronto: Insomniac Press.

Layng, A. (2009, Jan.). Where is marriage going? *USA Today.* http://findarticles.com/p/articles/mi_m1272/is_2764_137/ai_n31329929/.

Li, C. (2010, Feb. 24). Gay rights in China: Road to respect. *China Daily.* http://www.chinadaily.com.cn/china/2010–02/24/content_9492137.htm.

McGough, J. (2004). Deviant marriage patterns in Chinese society. In A. Sullivan (Ed.), *Same-sex marriage: Pro and con* (pp. 24–28). New York: Vintage Books.

Murray, S.O. (1997). Explaining away same-sex sexualities when they obtrude on anthropologists' notice at all. *Anthropology Today, 13*(3): 2–5. http://dx.doi.org/10.2307/2783130

Oboler, R.S. (1980). Is the female husband a man? Woman/woman marriage among the Nandi of Kenya. *Ethnology, 19*(1): 69–88. http://dx.doi.org/10.2307/3773320

Peacock, J.L. (1968). *Rites of modernization. Symbolic and social aspects of Indonesian proletarian drama.* Chicago: University of Chicago Press.

Pickett, B. (2002). Homosexuality. In E.N. Zalta (Ed.), *The Stanford encyclopedia of philosophy.* http://plato.stanford.edu/entries/homosexuality.

Queers United (2008, May 18). *Open forum: Queer liberationist or gay assimilationist?* http://queersunited.blogspot.mx/2008/05/open-forum-queer-liberationist-or-gay.html.

Robinson, B.A. (2012). Same-sex marriages (SSM) & civil unions. Ontario Consultants on Religious Tolerance. http://www.religioustolerance.org/hom_mar16.htm.

Sina English (2010, July 16). Argentina legalizes gay marriage in historic vote. *Sina English.* http://english.sina.com/world/p/2010/0715/329554.html.

Smith, D. (2012, Feb. 15). Ugandan minister shuts down gay rights conference. *The Guardian.* http://www.guardian.co.uk/world/2012/feb/15/ugandan-minister-gay-rights-conference.

Stone, L.S. (May 2004). Gay marriage and anthropology. *Anthropology News.* http://www.usfsp.edu/~jsokolov/2410gaymar1.htm.

Sullivan, A. (2004). Introduction. In A. Sullivan (Ed.), *Same-sex marriage: Pro and con* (pp. xxii–xxx). New York: Vintage Books.

Walters, S.D. (2001). Take my domestic partner, please. Gays and marriage in the era of the visible. In M. Bernstein & R. Reinmann (Eds.), *Queer families, queer politics: Challenging culture and the state* (pp. 338–357). New York: Columbia University Press.

Weeks, J., Heaphy, B., & Donovan, C. (2001). *Same sex intimacies: Families of choice and other life experiments*. London: Routledge. http://dx.doi.org/10.4324/9780203167168.

Whittington, L., & Gordon, S. (2005, June 29). Canadian Commons votes to legalize same-sex marriage. *Toronto Star Ottawa Bureau.* http://marriagelaw.cua.edu/News/news2005/062905.cfm#A430CD44-D270-4302-A582E8846B68DE9D.

Wikan, U. (1978). 'The Omani Xanith—A third gender role? *Man, 13*(3): 473–75.

Williams, W.L. (1986). *The spirit and the flesh.* Boston: Beacon Press.

Wood, P., & Lewin, E. (2006). Gay and lesbian marriage. Should gays and lesbians have the right to marry? In W.A. Haviland, R.J. Gordon, & L.A. Vivanco (Eds.), *Talking about people: Readings in contemporary cultural anthropology* (pp. 134–142). Toronto: McGraw-Hill.

Chapter 9: What Is the Role of Social Media in Socio-political Revolution?

Ackerman, S. (2011, Oct. 18). Egypt's top 'Facebook revolutionary' now advising Occupy Wall Street. *Danger Room.* http://www.wired.com/dangerroom/2011/10/egypt-occupy-wall-street/.

Afify, H. (2011, Dec. 27). Egypt court ends 'virginity' tests on female detainees. *Egypt Independent.* http://www.egyptindependent.com/news/egypt-court-ends-virginity-tests-female-detainees.

The Amateur Computerist (2011, Summer). The collected works of Michael Hauben. A new website. *Netizen News, 2*(2): 2–3. http://www.ais.org/~jrh/acn/.

Anthropology in Practice (2011, Feb. 15). http://www.anthropologyinpractice.com/2011/02/.

Budka, P. (2004). Indigene Widerstandsbewegungen in Kontext von Globalisierung und Informations und Kommunikationstechnologien. Das Fallbeispiel der EZLN in Mexico. *Journal für Entwicklungspolitik, 20*: 33–44.

Budka, P. (2011, Dec. 20). From cyber to digital anthropology to an anthropology of the contemporary? *Working Paper for the SASA Media Anthropology Network.* 38th e-seminar. www.media-anthropology.net.

Budka, P., & Kremser, M. (2004). CyberAnthropology—Anthropology of cyberculture. In S. Khittel, B. Plankensteiner, & M. Six-Hohenbalken (Eds.), *Contemporary issues in socio-cultural anthropology. Perspectives and research activities from Austria* (pp. 223–226). Wien: Loecker Verlag.

Cave, D. (2011, Sept. 24). Mexico turns to social media for information and survival. *The New York Times.* http://www.nytimes.com/2011/09/25/world/americas/mexico-turns-to-twitter-and-facebook-for-information-and-survival.html.

Cohen, J. (2011, Feb. 11). Google's Wael Ghonim thanks Facebook for revolution. *All Facebook. The unofficial Facebook resource.* http://www.allfacebook.com/googles-wael-ghonim-thanks-facebook-for-revolution-2011-02.

Cosenza, V. (2011, June). World map of social networks. *Vincos blog.* http://vincos.it/world-map-of-social-networks/.

Dahdal, S. (2011, March). How social media changed Arab resistance. *Newmatilda.com.* http://newmatilda.com/2011/03/04/perfect-storm.

Davis, L. (2009, May 2). Anthropology: The art of building a successful social site. *ReadWriteWeb.* http://www.readwriteweb.com/archives/anthropology_the_art_of_building_a_successful_soci.php.

Escobar, A. (1994, June). Welcome to cyberia: Notes on the anthropology of cyberculture. *Current Anthropology, 35*(3): 211–231. http://dx.doi.org/10.1086/204266.

Etling, B., Faris, R., & Palfrey, J. (2010, Summer-Fall). *Political change in the digital age: The fragility and promise of online organizing.* The Berkman Center for Internet and Society at Harvard University. http://nrs.harvard.edu/urn-3:HUL.InstRepos:4609956.

Evangelista, B. (2011, Feb. 13). Social revolution. *San Francisco Chronicle.*

Fedorak, S. (2009). *Pop culture: The culture of everyday life*. Toronto: University of Toronto Press.

Garcia, B. (2011, May 24). Citizens, audiences part of media revolution shaping with world. *Kuwait Times*. https://www.facebook.com/note.php?note_id=156607967738139

Ginsburg, F., Abu-Lughod, L., & Larkin, B. (2003). Introduction. In F.D. Ginsburg, L. Abu-Lughod, & B. Larkin (Eds.), *Media worlds: Anthropology in new terrain* (pp. 1–37). Berkeley: University of California Press.

Gladwell, M. (2010, Oct. 4). Small change. Why the revolution will not be tweeted. *The New Yorker*. http://www.newyorker.com/reporting/2010/10/04/101004fa_fact_gladwell.

Hauben, R. (2011a, Summer). Netizens in Egypt and the republic of Tahrir Square. *The Amateur Computerist*, 20(2): 19–21. http://www.ais.org/~jrh/acn/.

Hauben, R. (2011b). The need for netizen journalism and the ever evolving netizen—news—net symbiosis. *Netizen News, 20*(2): 9–11. http://www.ais.org/~jrh/acn/.

Hirschkind, C. (2011, Feb. 9). From the blogosphere to the street: The role of social media in the Egyptian uprising. *Jadaliyya*. http://www.jadaliyya.com/pages/contributors/7521.

Hovesepian, N. (2011, Feb. 9). The Arab pro-democracy movement: Struggles to redefine citizenship. *Jadaliyya*. http://www.jadaliyya.com/pages/index/588/the-arab-pro-democracy-movement_struggles-to-redef.

Ingram, M. (2011, March 29). Malcolm Gladwell: Social media still not a big deal. *Gigaom*. http://gigaom.com/2011/03/29/malcolm-gladwell-social-media-still-not-a-big-deal/.

In Sight (2011). *Colombia groups*. http://www.insightcrime.org/criminal-groups/colombia/farc/itemlist/tag/Manuel%20Marulanda.

Juris, J.J. (2008). *Networking futures: The movements against corporate globalization*. Durham, NC: Duke University Press.

Kelty, C. (2010, Winter). Introduction: Culture in, culture out. *Anthropological Quarterly*, 83(1): 7–16. http://dx.doi.org/10.1353/anq.0.0108.

Mahmood, S. (2011, Feb. 14). The architects of the Egyptian revolution. *The Nation*. http://www.thenation.com/article/158581/architects-egyptian-revolution#.

Martin, M. (2011, June 30). Khalid Said Case postponed, police brutality persists in new Egypt. *Business Law*. http://www.ibtimes.com/articles/172344/20110630/khaled-saeed-said-egypt-postpone-delay-military-trial-police-brutality.htm.

Miller, D., & Slater, D. (2000). *The internet: An ethnographic approach*. Oxford: Berg.

NPR. (2011, Aug. 15). Internet: Road to democracy ... or elsewhere? *National Public Radio*. http://www.npr.org/2011/08/15/139640456/internet-road-to-democracy-or-elsewhere?

Peterson, M.A. (2011, May 3). Egypt's experimental moment: Contingent thoughts on media and social change. *Media and Social Change*. http://mediasocialchange.net/2011/05/03/egypts-experimental-moment-contingent-thoughts-on-media-and-social-change/.

Pink, S. (2011). Media anthropology, social change and turning theory. *Media and Social Change*. http://mediasocialchange.net/2011/05/09/media-anthropology-social-change-and-turning-theory/.

Postill, J. (2008). Localizing the internet beyond communities and networks. *New Media & Society*, 10(3): 413–431. http://dx.doi.org/10.1177/1461444808089416

Postill, J. (2009, Nov. 14). Thoughts on anthropology and social media activism. *Media anthropology blog*. http://johnpostill.com/2009/11/14/thoughts-on-anthropology-and-social-media-activism/.

Postill, J. (2011, Nov. 7). Democracy in the age of the viral reality: A media epidemiography of Spain's *indignados* movement. *Media anthropology blog*. http://johnpostill.com/2011/10/03/democracy-in-the-age-of-viral-reality-1/.

Rheingold, H. (2003). *Smart mobs: The next social revolution*. Cambridge: Perseus Publishing.

Rheingold, H. (2008). Mobile media and political collective action. In J.E. Katz (Ed.), *Handbook of mobile communication studies* (pp. 225–237). Cambridge, MA: Massachusetts Institute of Technology.

Shah, V. (2009, April 22). The psychology and anthropology of social networking. *Thought Economics*. http://thoughteconomics.blogspot.mx/2009/04/psychology-and-anthropology-of-social.html.

Shoichet, C.E. (2011, Sept. 15). Latest battlefield in Mexico's drug wars: Social media. *CNN World.* http://articles.cnn.com/2011–09–15/world/mexico.violence. internet_1_twitter-users-social-media-raul-trejo-delarbre?_s=PM:WORLD.

Spitulnik, D. (1993). Anthropology and mass media. *Annual Review of Anthropology* 22: 293–315.

Sreberny, A. (2011, March 28). A social media revolution? *Media and Social Change.* http://mediasocialchange.net/201105/12/a-social-media-revolution/.

Srinivasan, R. (2011, July 11). How the street and digital world speak to one another: From Egypt. Blog. http://rameshsrinivasan.org/2011/07/11/how-the-street-and-digital-world-speak-to-one-another-from-egypt/.

Suárez, S.L. (2011, March). Social media and regime change in Egypt. *Campaigns and Elections.* http://www.campaignsandelections.com/magazine/us-edition/175972/social-media-and-regime-change-in-egypt.thtml.

Suleiman, M. (2011, Dec. 21). Debate over authenticity of assault on Egyptian woman intensifies. *Al-Arabiya Cairo.* http://insightcrime.org/criminal-groups/colombia/farc.

Technology Review (2011, Sept.–Oct.). Key moments in the Arab Spring. *Technology Review.* http://www.technologyreview.com/files/68753/Sept11_Feature_Streetbook_p76.pdf.

The Times of India (2011, Dec. 27). 'Facebook revolution' big hit with Russians. http://timesofindia.indiatimes.com/world/rest-of-world/Facebook-revolution-big-hit-with-Russians/articleshow/11014726.cms.

Tomlin, J. (2011a, Sept. 22). Iran, Sudan, Libya, Egypt: Social media helps give women a voice. *The Guardian.* http://www.wluml.org/news/iran-sudan-libya-egypt-social-media-helps-give-women-voice.

Tomlin, J. (2011b, Sept. 22). Social media gives women a voice in Iran. *The Guardian.* http://www.guardian.co.uk/lifeandstyle/2011/sep/22/social-media-women-iran.

Tufekci, Z. (2011, Aug. 30). New media and the people-powered uprisings. *Technology Review.* MIT. http://www.technologyreview.com/view/425280/new-media-and-the-people-powered-uprisings/.

Watkins, S.C. (2011, Feb. 18). Social movements in the age of social media: Participatory politics in Egypt. *The Young and the Digital.* http://theyoungandthedigital.com/2011/02/18/social-movements-in-the-age-of-social-media-participatory-politics-in-egypt/.

Zaks, D. (2011, Aug. 15). How e-mail helped bring down the USSR. http://www.google.com/hostednews/afp/article/ALeqM5g98uUTVpjCzj2Wd7OWom-HZu6C7w?docId=CNG.f86f7de5aa4632fa5f9294df8b17a703.3e1.

Zuckerman, E. (2011, June 27). Four questions about civic media. *DML Central.* http://dmlcentral.net/blog/ethan-zuckerman/four-questions-about-civic-media.

Chapter 10: What Are the Socio-economic and Political Impacts of Human Migration?

Alsvik, K. (2009, Oct. 21–23). Integrating migrant rights and protection in migration and development policy and practice. *National Workshop on ILO instruments for promotion and protection of the rights of migrant workers.* Harare, Zimbabwe. http://www.ilo.org/public/english/protection/migrant/download/presentations/alsvik_oct2009.pdf.

Appadurai, A. (1991). Global ethnoscapes: Notes and queries for a transnational anthropology. In R. Fox (Ed.), *Recapturing anthropology.* Sante Fe, NM: School of American Research Press.

Arnold, C., & Bertone, A. (2002). Addressing the sex trade in Thailand: Some lessons learned from NGOs. Part I. *Gender Issues,* 20(1): 26–52. http://dx.doi.org/10.1007/s12147-002-0006-4

Balakrishnan, T.R., & Hou, F. (1999). Residential patterns in cities. In S.S. Halli & L. Driedger (Eds.), *Immigrant Canada: Demographic, economic, and social challenges* (pp. 116–147). Toronto: University of Toronto Press.

Bales, K. (2005). *Understanding Global Slavery.* Berkeley: University of California Press.

Butler, D. (2005, Oct. 31). Immigrants threaten Canada's peace: Poll. *The Star Phoenix* [Saskatoon] B1.

Byrne, C. (2010, Oct. 8). Ontario family facing charges in 'modern day slavery' case. *thestar.com*. http://www.thestar.com/news/ontario/article/873022--ontario-family-facing-charges-in-modern-day-slavery-case.

Canadavisa.com (2012, Jan. 4). Harper on immigration. *Canadavisa.com. Canada Immigration Lawyers.* http://www.canadavisa.com/news/entry/harper-on-immigration-040112.html.

Castles, S. (2000). International migration at the beginning of the twenty-first century: Global trends and issues. UNESCO. Oxford: Blackwell Publishers. http://www.blackwellpublishing.com/content/bpl_images/journal_samples/issj0020-8701~52~165~258/258.pdf.

Castles, S., & Miller, M.J. (2003). *The age of migration* (3rd ed.). New York: Guilford Press.

Chow, L. (1996). *Sojourners in the north*. Prince George, BC: Caitlin Press.

Chrisafis, A. (2010, Nov. 16). Immigration: France sees tensions rise five years on from Paris riots. *The Guardian.* http://www.guardian.co.uk/world/2010/nov/16/france-racism-immigration-sarkozy.

Chu, C.Y. (2011). Human trafficking and smuggling in China. *Journal of Contemporary China*, 20(68): 39–52. http://dx.doi.org/10.1080/10670564.2011.520842

CIA. World Factbook. (2009). *Trafficking in persons.* http://www.cia.gov/library/publications/the-world-factbook/index.html.

Cross, G.S. (1983). *Immigrant workers in industrial France: The making of a new laboring class*. Philadelphia: Temple University Press.

CTV News. (2011, Dec. 23). *Landmark child trafficking case catches advocates' eyes.* Ctvbc.ca. http://www.ctvbc.ctv.ca/servlet/an/local/CTVNews/20111223/bc_human_trafficking_reza_moazami_111223/20111223/.

Decreuse, B., Combes, P.-P., & Laouénan, M., & Trannoy, A. (2006). *Discrimination against African immigrants in France.* Spatial mismatch at the national level. http://www.eea-esem.com/files/papers/EEA/2010/1910/paper_laouenan.pdf.

de Francisco, A.G. (2005, Sept. 9). EU seeks better cooperation on stemming illegal immigration. *EFE World News Service.* http://www.infotrac.galegroup.com.

EFC (The Evangelical Fellowship of Canada). (2009). Human trafficking: A report on modern day slavery in Canada. http://files.efc-canada.net/si/Human%20Trafficking/HumanTraffickingReportApril2009.pdf.

Eriksen, T.E. (Ed.). (2003). *Globalisation. Studies in anthropology*. London: Pluto Press.

Fitzgerald, D. (2006). Towards a theoretical ethnography of migration. *Qualitative Sociology, 29*(1): 1–24. http://ccis.ucsd.edu/wp-content/uploads/2009/12/Fitzgerald-2006.QS_.pdf.

General Assembly resolution 55/25 of 15 Nov. 2000 in United Nations Office on Drugs and Crime (2004). Foreword. United Nations Convention against Transnational Organized Crime and the Protocols, p. iv. New York: United Nations.

Glick Schiller, N. (2009). A global perspective on migration and development. *Social Analysis*, 53(3): 14–37. http://dx.doi.org/10.3167/sa.2009.530302

Halli, S.S., & Driedger, L. (1999). The immigrant challenge 2000. In S.S. Halli & L. Driedger (Eds.), *Immigrant Canada: Demographic, economic, and social challenges* (pp. 3–7). Toronto: University of Toronto Press.

Hamilton, K., Simon, P., & Veniard, C. (2004). Country profiles. The challenge of French diversity. *Migration Information Service.* http://www.migrationinformation.org/Profiles/display.cfm?ID=266.

Innovative Research Group (2005). The world in Canada: Demographics and diversity in Canadian foreign policy. http://www.cdfai.org/PDF/The%20World%20In%20Canada%20Poll.pdf.

Kamber, M., & Lacey, M. (2005, Sept. 11). For Mali villagers, France is a workplace and lifeline. *The New York Times.* A6. http://www.infotrac.galegroup.com.

Katseli, L.T., Lucas, R.E.B., & Xemogiani, T. (2006). Effects of migration on sending countries: What do we know? *OECD Development Centre Working Paper No. 250.* OECD Publishing. http://www.eric.ed.gov/PDFS/ED504069.pdf.

Kymlicka, W. (2003). Immigration, citizenship, multiculturalism. In S. Spencer (Ed.), *The politics of migration: Managing opportunity, conflict and change* (pp. 195–208). Malden, MA: Blackwell Publishing.

Li, P.S. (1988). *The Chinese in Canada*. Toronto: Oxford University Press.

Maclean's (2005, Oct. 13). Pettigrew says more immigrants needed to help augment dwindling labour force. http://www.macleans.ca/topstories/politics/news/shownews. jsp?content=n101351A.

Moses, J. (2006). *International migration: Globalization's last frontier*. London: Zed Books.

Munck, R. (2010). Globalization, migration and work: Issues and perspectives. *Labour Capital and Society. Travail Capital et Société, 43*(1): 156–177.

Neuwirth, G. (1999). Toward a theory of immigrant integration. In S.S. Halli & L. Driedger (Eds.), *Immigrant Canada: Demographic, economic, and social challenges* (pp. 51–69). Toronto: University of Toronto Press.

Ng, W.C. (1999). *The Chinese in Vancouver, 1945–80: The pursuit of identity and power*. Vancouver: UBC Press.

Olwig, K.F. (2007). *Caribbean journeys: An ethnography of migration and home in three family networks*. Durham and London: Duke University Press Books.

Online Press Conference. (2010, Oct. 12). Human trafficking expert Benjamin Perrin exposes hidden Canada tragedy. *Online Press Conference—Campaign to End Modern Day Slavery*. http://endmodernslaveryrelease.eventbrite.com/.

Oosterman, J. (2010, June 17). Pursuing a culture of freedom: Combating modern-day slavery in Canada. *C2C Journal*. http://c2cjournal.ca/2010/06/pursuing-a-culture-of-freedom-combating-modernday-slavery-in-canada/.

Orellana, M.F., Thorne, B., Chee, A., & Lam, W.S.E. (2001). Transnational childhoods: The participation of children in transnational migration. *Social Problems, 48*(4): 572–591. http://dx.doi.org/10.1525/sp.2001.48.4.572

Perrin, B. (2010). *Invisible chains: Canada's underground world of human trafficking*. Toronto: Viking Canada.

Randall, V. (1997, 2008). Racial discrimination. The record of France. *Race, racism and the law*. Human Rights Documentation Center. http://academic.udayton.edu/race/06hrights/georegions/Europe/France01.htm.

Rosenblum, M.R., & Brick, K. (2011). *US immigration policy and Mexican/Central American migration flows: Then and now*. Migration Policy Institute. http://www.migrationpolicy.org/pubs/RMSG-regionalflows.pdf.

Schauer, E., & Wheaton, E. (2006). Sex trafficking into the United States: A literature review. *Criminal Justice Review, 31*(1): 1–24.

Simmons, A.B. (1999). Immigration policy: Imagined futures. In S.S. Halli & L. Driedger (Eds.), *Immigrant Canada: Demographic, economic, and social challenges* (pp. 21–50). Toronto: University of Toronto Press.

Smith, R.C. (2005). *Mexican New York: The transnational lives of new immigrants*. Berkeley: University of California Press.

Soria, M. (2005, Sept. 19). Immigration is an asset, not a liability. *Business Record* (Des Moines), 301. http://www.infotrac.galegroup.com.

Spencer, S. (2003). Introduction. In S. Spencer (Ed.), *The politics of migration: Managing opportunity, conflict and change* (pp. 1–24). Malden, MA: Blackwell Publishing.

Stirk, F. (2009, July 31). *Salvation Army to help deter Olympic sex traffickers*. http://www.salvationarmy.ca/2009/07/31/salvation-army-to-help-deter-olympics-sex-traffickers/.

UNODC (United Nations Office on Drugs and Crime) (2000, Dec. 12). Address at the opening of the signing conference. *UNODC*. http://unosek.org/unodc/en/about-unodc/speeches/speech_2000-12-12_1.html.

UNODC (United Nations Office on Drugs and Crime) (2008). *An introduction to human trafficking: Vulnerability, impact and action*. http://www.unodc.org/documents/human-trafficking/An_Introduction_to_Human_Trafficking_-_Background_Paper.pdf.

United Press International (2005, Sept. 24). Canada plans to increase immigration. *UPI News Track*. http://www.infotrac.galegroup.com.

Wheaton, E.M., Schauer, E.J., & Galli, T.V. (2010). Economics of human trafficking. *International Migration (Geneva, Switzerland), 48*(4): 114–141. http://dx.doi.org/10.1111/j.1468-2435.2009.00592.x Medline:20645472

Wickramasekara, P. (2008). Globalisation, international labour migration and the rights of migrant workers. *Third World Quarterly, 29*(7): 1247–1264. http://dx.doi.org/10.1080/01436590802386278

Chapter 11: What Benefits Do NGOs Provide Developing Countries, and How Can Their Presence Generate New Challenges?

Baldauf, S. (2005, April 1). A new breed of missionary; A drive for conversions, not development, is stirring violent animosity in India. *The Christian Science Monitor, 1*. http://www.infotrac.galegroup.com.

Black, M. (1996). *Children first: The story of UNICEF, past and present.* Oxford: Oxford University Press.

Bock, J.G. (2010, Dec. 6). Rising from the rubble. *America.* http://www.americamagazine.org/content/article.cfm?article_id=12597.

Boyden, J. (1997). Childhood and the policy-makers. A comparative perspective on the globalization of childhood. In A. James & A. Prout (Eds.), *Constructing and reconstructing childhood: Contemporary issues in the sociology of childhood* (pp. 190–229). London: Routledge Falmer.

Burr, R. (2006). *Vietnam's children in a changing world.* New Brunswick, NJ: Rutgers University Press.

Cudd, A.E. (2005). Missionary positions. *Hypatia 20*: 164. http://www.infotrac.galegroup.com.

Doucet, I. (2011, Jan. 13). The Nation: NGOs have failed Haiti. *NPR.* http://www.npr.org/2011/01/13/132884795/the-nation-how-ngos-have-failed-haiti.

Fraser, B. (2005, Oct. 1). Getting drugs to HIV-infected children in Cambodia. *Lancet, 366*(9492): 1153–1154. http://dx.doi.org/10.1016/S0140-6736(05)67464-8 Medline:16200691

Ishkanian, A. (2004). *Anthropological perspectives on civil society and NGO development in a post-socialist context.* Paper presented at NGO Study Group Seminar 'Ethnography of NGOs: Understanding Organization Processes,' Oxford. http://www.intrac.org/data/files/resources/291/Anthropological-Perspectives-on-Civil-Society-and-NGO-Development.pdf.

Lewis, D. (2005). *Anthropology and development: The uneasy relationship.* London: LSE Research Online. http://eprints.lse.ac.uk/253.

Lewis, D., Wood, G.E., & Gregory, R. (1996). *Trading the silver seed: Local knowledge and market moralities in aquacultural development.* London: Intermediate Technology Publications.

Lindsay, R. (2010, March 29). Haiti's excluded. *The Nation.* http://web.ebscohost.com/ehost/pdfviewer/pdfviewer?sid=d3123083-0afa-4ab6-af8b-f9745c8d9974%40sessionmgr15&vid=5&hid=19.

Lonely Planet (2011). *Map of Uganda.* http://www.lonelyplanet.com/maps/africa/uganda/.

Loomis, T. (2000). Indigenous populations and sustainable development: Building on indigenous approaches to holistic, self-determined development. *World Development, 28*(5): 893–910. http://dx.doi.org/10.1016/S0305-750X(99)00162-X

Macola, G. (2005, July). Review of *The steamer parish: The rise and fall of missionary medicine on an African frontier* by C.M. Good [Cambridge: Cambridge University Press]. *Journal of African History, 46*: 36.

Marcus, G., & Fischer, M. (1986). *Anthropology as cultural critique.* Chicago: University of Chicago Press.

Marx, G. (2005, July 31). Missionary pilot speaks the gospel in Haiti. *Chicago Tribune.* http://www.infotrac.galegroup.com.

Partners in Health (2009–2012). History. *Partners in Health.* http://www.pih.org/pages/partners-in-health-history.

People in Need Partnership (2012). *The 2010 Haiti Earthquake.* http://pinpartnership.org/landing/earthquake?gclid=CNuKjvzXgK8CFcVgTAod1zT46g.

Pupavac, V. (2000). *The infantilisation of the South and the UN Convention on the Rights of the Child.* Nottingham: Student Human Rights Law Centre.

Rohde, D. (2005, Jan. 22). Mix of quake aid and preaching stirs concern. *The New York Times.* http://www.infotrac.galegroup.com.

Sampson, S. (2002). Weak states, uncivil societies and thousands of NGOs. Western democracy export as benevolent colonialism in the Balkans. In S. Resic (Ed.), *Cultural boundaries of the Balkans.* (pp. 27–44). Lund, Sweden: Lund University Press. http://www.anthrobase.com/Txt/S/Sampson_S_01.htm.

Smith, D.J. (2010). Corruption, NGOs, and development in Nigeria. *Third World Quarterly, 31*(2): 243–258. http://dx.doi.org/10.1080/01436591003711975

Solway, J. (2009). Human rights and NGO 'wrongs': Conflict diamonds, culture wars and the 'Bushman' question. *Africa, 79*(03): 321–346. http://dx.doi.org/10.3366/E0001972009000849

Spoerri, M. (2012, Feb. 13). Outrage over Egypt's arrest of NGO workers, but US would have done the same. *The Christian Science Monitor.* http://www.csmonitor.com/Commentary/Opinion/2012/0213/Outrage-over-Egypt-s-arrest-of-NGO-workers-but-US-would-have-done-the-same.

Stephenson, C. (2005). Nongovernmental organizations (NGOs). G. Burgess & H. Burgess (Eds.), *Beyond intractability.* Conflict Information Consortium, University of Colorado, Boulder. http://www.beyondintractability.org/bi-essay/role-ngo/.

Tishkov, V. (2005). An anthropology of NGOs. *Eurozine.* http://www.eurozine.com/articles/2005-06-01-tishkov-en.html.

Tomasek, K.M. (1999). Review of *Mary Lyon and the Mount Holyoke missionaries* by A. Porterfield [Oxford University Press]. *Journal of Interdisciplinary History, 30*(1): 143–145. http://muse.jhu.edu/login?auth=0&type=summary&url=/journals/journal_of_interdisciplinary_history/v030/30.1tomasek.html.

Valentin, K., & Meinert, L. (2009). The adult North and the young South. Reflections on the civilizing mission of children's rights. *Anthropology Today, 25*(3): 23–28. http://dx.doi.org/10.1111/j.1467-8322.2009.00669.x.

Wilder, A., & Morris, T. (2008). 'Locals within locals': Cultural sensitivity in disaster aid. *Anthropology Today, 24*(3): 1–3. http://dx.doi.org/10.1111/j.1467-8322.2008.00581.x

Zanotti, L. (2010). Cacophonies of aid, failed state building and NGOs in Haiti: Setting the stage for disaster, envisioning the future. *Third World Quarterly, 31*(5): 755–771. http://dx.doi.org/10.1080/01436597.2010.503567 Medline:20821882

Chapter 12: Is the Practice of *Purdah* and Wearing *Hijab* Oppressive to Women or an Expression of Their Identity?

Ali, M.C. (n.d.). *The question of hijab: Suppression or liberation?* The Institute of Islamic Information and Education. http://www.islamfortoday.com/hijab.htm.

Amin, C.M. (2002). *The making of the modern Iranian woman: Gender, state policy, and popular culture, 1865–1946.* Gainesville: University Press of Florida.

Arnett, S.P. (2001). *Purdah: Women's History Resource Site.* King's College History Dept. http://departments.kings.edu/womens_history/purdah.html.

Barr, J., Clark, I., & Marsh, M. (n.d.). *The veil and veiling.* Women, the visual arts, and Islam. http://www.skidmore.edu/academics/arthistory/ah369/finalveil.htm.

BBC News.(2011, Dec. 12). Canada bans veils at citizenship oath ceremony. *BBC News US & Canada.* http://www.bbc.co.uk/news/world-us-canada-16152122.

Bishr, H. (n.d.). *Pro-hijab campaign in EU Parliament.* http://www.ummah.com/forum/showthread.php?43637-Pro-hijab-Campaign-in-EU-Parliament.

Bonvillain, N. (1998). *Women and men: Cultural constructs of gender.* Upper Saddle River, NJ: Prentice Hall.

Boone, J. (2010, April 30). Afghan feminists fighting from under the burqa. *The Guardian.* http://www.guardian.co.uk/world/2010/apr/30/afghanistan-women-feminists-burqa.

Brooks, G. (1994). *Nine parts of desire: The hidden world of Islamic women.* New York: Anchor Books.

Bullock, K. (2001). *You don't have to wear that in Canada.* http://www.themodernreligion.com/women/hijab-canada.htm.

Capeloto, A. (2004). *Hijab campaign: Women don scarfs in solidarity with female muslims.* http://www.freep.com/news/nw/terror2001/scarf18_20011018.htm.

Cohen, L., & Peery, L. (2006). 'Unveiling students' perceptions about women in Islam. *English Journal, 95*(3): 20–26. http://dx.doi.org/10.2307/30047039

Cunningham, E. (2010, March 27). Despite ban, Gaza men still style women's hair. *The National.* http://www.thenational.ae/news/world/middle-east/despite-ban-gaza-men-still-style-womens-hair.

Debré, J. (2003). *La laïcité à l'école: Un principe républicain à réaffirmer.* Rapport No. 1275, 2 vols. Paris: Assemblée Nationale.

de Souza, E. (2004). Introduction. In E. de Souza (Ed.), *Purdah: An anthology.* Oxford: Oxford University Press.

Fernandez, S. (2009). The crusade over the bodies of women. *Patterns of Prejudice, 43*(3–4): 269–286. http://dx.doi.org/10.1080/00313220903109185

Fernea, E.W., & Fernea, R.A. (2000). Symbolizing roles: Behind the veil. In J. Spradley & D.W. McCurdy (Eds.), *Conformity and conflict: Readings in cultural anthropology,* 10th ed. (pp. 233–240). Boston: Allyn and Bacon.

Geissinger, A. (2000). *Hijab: An issue of global concern for the Islamic movement.* http://www.crescent-online.net/2009/09/hijab-an-issue-of-global-concern-for-the-islamic-movement-1776-articles.html

Hammami, R. (1990). Women, the hijab and the intifada. *Middle East Report (New York, N.Y.), 164/165*(164/165): 24–28. http://dx.doi.org/10.2307/3012687

Hasan, M. (2010). Her dark materials. *New Statesmen, 139*(5003): 20–23. http://www.thestatesman.net/index.php?option=com_content&view=article&id=408962&catid=43.

Hoodfar, H. (1989). A background to the feminist movement in Egypt. *Bulletin of Simone de Beauvoir Institute, 9*(2): 18–23.

Hoodfar, H. (1991). Return to the veil: Personal strategy and public participation in Egypt. In N. Redcliff & M.T. Sinclair (Eds.), *Working women: International perspectives on labour and gender ideology.* (pp. 23–50). London: Routledge.

Hoodfar, H. (1993). The veil in their minds and on our heads: The persistence of colonial images of Muslim women. *Resources for Feminist Research, 22*(3/4): 5–18.

Hoodfar, H. (2003). More than clothing: Veiling is an adaptive strategy. In H. Hoodfar, S. Alvi, & S. McDonough (Eds.), *The Muslim veil in North America: Issues and debates* (pp. 3–39). Toronto: Women's Press.

Hughes, L.A. (2007, July 2). Unveiling the veil: Cultic, status, and ethnic representations of early imperial freedwoman. *Material Religion, 3*(2): 218–241. http://web.ebscohost.com/ehost/pdfviewer/pdfviewer?sid=b4863c44-cd02-4df6-b1eb-fc47be23545f%40sessionmgr112&vid=5&hid=123.

IRNA (2005). *Pro-hijab campaigners lobby in European parliament.* http://www.irna.ir/en/news/view/menu-234/0505100391115018.htm.

Islamonline.net (2005). Pro-hijab campaign in the parliament. http://www.prohijab.net/english/islam-online-article3.htm.

Keddie, N., & Baron, B. (1991). *Women in Middle Eastern history: Shifting boundaries in sex and gender.* New Haven, CT: Yale University Press.

Khan, S. (1999). *A glimpse through purdah: Asian women and the myth and reality.* Oakhill, UK: Trentham Books.

Lindholm, C., & Lindholm, C. (2000). Life behind the veil. In E. Ashton-Jones & C. Lindholm (Eds.), *The gender reader* (p. 252). Boston: Allyn and Bacon.

MacLeod, A.E. (1992). *Accommodating protest: Working women and the new veiling in Cairo.* New York: Columbia University Press.

Mahmood, S. (2003). Ethical formation and politics of individual autonomy in contemporary Egypt. *Social Research, 70*(3): 837–866.

Martin, M. (2010). In Egypt, Muslim women may lose right to wear veil. *NPR.* http://www.npr.org/templates/story/story.php?storyId=123889613.

Mernissi, F. (1991) *The veil and the male elite: A feminist interpretation of women's rights in Islam.* New York: Addison-Wesley Publishing.

Mullally, S. (2011). Civic integration, migrant women and the veil: At the limits of rights? *Modern Law Review, 74*(1): 27–56. http://dx.doi.org/10.1111/j.1468-2230.2010.00835.x

Mustafa, N. (n.d.). *Naheed Mustafa: Hijab (veil) and Muslim women*. Islamic Information and News Network. http://www.usc.edu/dept/MSA/humanrelations/womeninislam/*hijab*experience.html.

Nashat, G. (1988). *Women in the ancient Middle East. Restoring women to history*. Bloomington, IN: Organization of American History.

Paulsell, S. (2011, July 12). Veiled voices. Faith Matters. *Christian Century, 128*(14): 33. http://www.christiancentury.org/article/2011-06/veiled-voices.

Read, J.G., & Bartkowski, J.P. (2000). To veil or not to veil? A case study of identity negotiations among Muslim women in Austin, Texas. *Gender & Society, 14*(3): 395–417. http://dx.doi.org/10.1177/089124300014003003

Risinger, M. (2012, Jan. 6). Redefining the burqa: A reflection from Afghanistan. *Gender across borders: A global voice for gender justice*. http://www.genderacrossborders.com/2012/01/06/redefining-the-burqa-a-reflection-from-afghanistan/.

Saldanha, A. (2010, Sept. 9). Palestine: For Gaza students, no graduation without hijab. *Global Voices*. http://globalvoicesonline.org/2010/09/09/palestine-for-gaza-students-no-graduation-without-hijab/.

Scott, J.W. (2005). Symptomatic politics. The banning of Islamic head scarves in French public schools. *French Politics, Culture & Society, 23*(3): 106–127. http://dx.doi.org/10.3167/153763705780793531

Shilandari, F. (2010, Sept.). Iranian women: Veil and identity. *A Forum on Human Rights and Democracy in Iran*. http://www.gozaar.org/english/articles-en/Iranian-Woman-Veil-and-Identity.html.

Shirazi, F. (2001). *The veil unveiled: The hijab in modern culture*. Gainesville: University Press of Florida.

Talvi, S.J.A. (2002). *The veil: Resistance or repression?* Book review essay. http://www.alternet.org/story/14826/the_veil%3A_resistance_or_repression/?page=4.

van Santen, J.C.M. (2010). "My 'veil' does not go with my jeans": Veiling, fundamentalism, education and women's agency in northern Cameroon. *Africa, 80*(02): 275–300. http://dx.doi.org/10.3366/afr.2010.0205

Women in World History Curriculum (2011). Historical perspectives in Islamic dress. *Women in the Muslim world. Personalities and perspectives from the past*. http://www.womeninworldhistory.com/essay-01.html.

Young, W.C. (1996). *The Rashaayda Bedouin. Arab pastoralists of Eastern Sudan*. Toronto: Harcourt Brace College Publishers.

Zahedi, S. (n.d.). *Hijab* harassment. *Islam for Today*. http://www.islamfortoday.com/*hijab*canada5.htm.

Conclusion

Knauft, B. (2005). *The Gebusi: Lives transformed in a rainforest world*. Toronto: McGraw-Hill.

Lee, R.B. (2003). *The Dobe Ju/'hoansi* (3rd ed.). Toronto: Thomson Nelson Learning.

Mandelbaum, D.G. (1979). *The Plains Cree: An ethnographic, historical, and comparative study*. Canadian Plains Studies, No 9. Canadian Plains Research Center, University of Regina.

SOURCES

Figures

Figure 1.1: Dr. Bruce Knauft in the Midst of Armed Gebusi Men. Copyright © Eileen Knauft and reprinted by permission of Bruce Knauft.

Figure 2.1: "Fantasyland" at the West Edmonton Mall. Reprinted by permission of Dr. Debra Bear.

Figure 4.1: A Graduating Class from Cairo American College at the Pyramids. Reprinted by permission of Robert Fedorak.

Figure 5.1: A Darfur Camp. Copyright © Lynsey Addario / VII.

Figure 5.2: Darfuri Refuges in Bahai, Chad. Reprinted by permission of Peter Biro.

Figure 6.1: Media Portrayal of Young, Beautiful, "Perfect" Women. Courtesy of iStockphoto.com.

Figure 6.2: Collection of Barbie Dolls. Reprinted by permission of Janna Cadieux.

Figure 6.3: Tuareg Woman. The Tuaregs of Northern Nigeria. Reprinted by permission of Citizenside / Marie-Ghaicha.

Figure 6.4: Modern Primitives Emulate Tribal Body Modification Rituals. Reprinted by permission of Fakir Musafar.

Figure 8.1: Two Women Celebrate Their Marriage. Courtesy of iStockphoto.com.

Figure 9.1: Najla Hariri Defies Ban on Women Driving in Saudi Arabia. Reprinted by permission of Najla Hariri.

Figure 9.2: Egyptian Man Using Cell Phone to Tweet News from Tahrir Square in Cairo. Reprinted by permission of Heba Farouk.

Figure 11.1: Haitian Tent Camp. Reprinted by permission of Lisa Epatko and PBS NewsHour © 2012 MacNeil / Lehrer Productions.

Figures 12.1a and 12.1b: Women Wearing the *Hijab*. Courtesy of iStockphoto.com.

Maps

Map 1.1: Location of Gebusi in Papua New Guinea. Copyright © 2005 McGraw-Hill Companies.

Map 3.1: Gaeltacht Region of Ireland. Copyright © Angr. Licensed under the terms of the GNU Free Documentation licence.

Map 3.4: Basque-Speaking Territories. Reprinted by permission of Spanish Fiestas.

Map 5.1: Conflict Zones in Darfur. Adapted from BBC News, 6 December 2006, http://news.bbc.co.uk/2/hi/africa/6213202.stm. Reprinted by permission of the BBC.

Map 7.1: Countries Practising Female Circumcision. Adapted from Map: Countries Practicing FGM. Reproduced with permission from the publisher from *The Day Kadi Lost a Part of Her Life* by Isabel Ramos Rioja and Kim Manresa. Spinifex Press: 1998.

Map 10.2: Mekong River Basin. Adapted from Vincenzo Consenza. Licensed under the terms of the CC BY-SA.

Map 11.1: Uganda. Courtesy of CIA World Factbook.

Table

Table 7.1: Countries Where Female Circumcision Is Documented. Reprinted by permission of the World Health Organization Press and Copyright © Amnesty International Publications, ACT 77/007/1997, www.amnesty.org.

Every effort has been made to contact copyright holders; in the event of an omission or error, please notify the publisher.

INDEX